Emanuel Celler

Emanuel Celler

Immigration and Civil Rights Champion

Wayne Dawkins

University Press of Mississippi / Jackson

The University Press of Mississippi is the scholarly publishing agency of
the Mississippi Institutions of Higher Learning: Alcorn State University,
Delta State University, Jackson State University, Mississippi State University,
Mississippi University for Women, Mississippi Valley State University,
University of Mississippi, and University of Southern Mississippi.

www.upress.state.ms.us

The University Press of Mississippi is a member
of the Association of University Presses.

First printing 2020
∞

Library of Congress Cataloging-in-Publication Data

Names: Dawkins, Wayne, author.
Title: Emanuel Celler: immigration and civil rights champion / Wayne Dawkins.
Description: Jackson: University Press of Mississippi, 2020. | Includes
bibliographical references and index.
Identifiers: LCCN 2020017652 (print) | LCCN 2020017653 (ebook) | ISBN
9781496805355 (hardback) | ISBN 9781496829870 (trade paperback) | ISBN
9781496829887 (epub) | ISBN 9781496829894 (epub) | ISBN 9781496829900
(pdf) | ISBN 9781496829863 (pdf)
Subjects: LCSH: Celler, Emanuel, 1888–1981. | Jewish legislators—United
States—Biography. | Legislators—United States—Biography. |
Politicians—United States—Biography. | Civil rights—United States. |
Emigration and immigration law—United States.
Classification: LCC E748.C4 D39 2020 (print) | LCC E748.C4 (ebook) | DDC
328.73/092 [B]—dc23
LC record available at https://lccn.loc.gov/2020017652
LC ebook record available at https://lccn.loc.gov/2020017653

British Library Cataloging-in-Publication Data available

To Claudia, Carmen, and Camille

Contents

Preface

Emanuel Celler was floor manager for four constitutional amendments, and he is the godfather of civil rights legislation, a major player in the 1957, 1960, and landmark 1964 Civil Rights Acts. Most of all he was cosponsor of late twentieth-century immigration reform, now a hot-button twenty-first-century topic. "I accomplished a few things," US representative Emanuel Celler told *Washington Post* reporter Richard Lyons in 1972. The congressman accomplished much more than "a few things." During fifty years of public service Celler had a hand in the enactment of at least four hundred laws.

The history of twentieth-century America can be divided into two eras: pre-1965 immigration reform and post-1965 immigration reform. In the first two-thirds of the century, America was perceived as a European-stocked nation dominated by Anglo-Saxon Protestants. Because of 1960s voting rights and immigration reform laws, a majority-white Democratic-red South changed into a white Republican-red South. The changes opened up the Democratic Party in the North, and in the South, southern blacks emerged in the blue Democratic Party.

Those two decisions—immigration and voting rights—created the America we have now. We know about President Lyndon B. Johnson's 1960s-era accomplishments. But few know the less grandiose, yet crucial, accomplishments of a forgotten man, Emanuel Celler. One duty of the historian is to reintroduce and reappraise the forgotten elements of the past.

By 1953, Emanuel Celler had served less than four years as chairman of the House Judiciary Committee. A liberal Democrat, he had experienced plenty as an elected official: the Roaring Twenties, the Great Depression of the 1930s, President Franklin D. Roosevelt's New Deal, and World War II. Celler unequivocally supported the postwar establishment of a state of Israel—an issue close to Celler's heart both because of his personal background and because of the ethnic composition of his Brooklyn district. In 1953 Celler published *You Never Leave Brooklyn*, an autobiography that covered his first thirty years as a congressman. Celler's primary accomplishments in the House by that time included modest immigration reforms and a mixed record of placing regulatory controls on corporate monopoly power.

Although Celler, who was sixty-five at the time of *You Never Leave Brooklyn*, had much to say in his autobiography, his best legislative work still lay ahead of him. A dozen years later Celler cowrote revolutionary immigration reform that in the final three decades of the twentieth century altered the racial and ethnic demographics of America. Celler legislated tenaciously and boldly when discriminatory ethnic- and race-based immigration policy became a foreign policy liability.

A dozen years before four decades of Euro-specific immigration policies began in the 1920s, one out of seven Americans was foreign born. By 1970, such social engineering widened the ratio to one out of twenty Americans being foreign born. After 2010 and four decades of immigration reform, the gap narrowed again and returned to one of every seven Americans being foreign born. Eighty-one percent of immigrants now come to the United States from Latin America and Asia. That's the reverse of fifty years earlier when 85 percent of all foreign-born immigrants were from Europe and Canada.

In addition, Celler was a behind-the-scenes change agent in a handful of 1950s and 1960s civil rights milestones. President Lyndon B. Johnson and before him aides to presidents Dwight Eisenhower and John F. Kennedy urged Celler to hold prompt hearings regarding civil rights and voting rights bills. Furthermore, the Judiciary Committee chairman was the lead writer and floor manager of these bills.

After four decades of portrayals as a white, European-heritage America, the United States of post-1960s immigration reform is an undeniably multiracial and multicultural representative of every continent on earth. Until the policies were changed, it would have been unimaginable to witness the elections of South Asian–descent governors of Louisiana and South Carolina, US senators of Cuban descent from Florida, Texas, and New Jersey, a biracial president who is the son of a Kenyan college student who married a white Kansan in Hawaii, a non-mainland US state.

Celler also took pride in being the lead House author of the Twenty-Fourth Amendment to the US Constitution that abolished poll taxes, a tool that southern segregationists had used for generations to disenfranchise black voters. Celler was also lead writer of two other constitutional amendments, the Twenty-Third that granted voting rights to residents of the District of Columbia, and coauthor with Senator Birch Bayh, D-Indiana, of the Twenty-Fifth Amendment that established an orderly succession if the president were unable to function. For all these reasons, this is a good time for a biography of Celler (1888–1981), an important, unsung American leader.

I "found" the congressman while conducting research nearly a decade ago for a 2012 biography of voting rights champion and journalist Andrew W. Cooper, another little-known hero from Brooklyn. Celler's district was among five gerrymandered districts that were redrawn after Cooper's 1966 voting rights lawsuit, which resulted in Shirley Chisholm, America's first black congresswoman, winning one of the redrawn congressional seats. Cooper became an irascible political journalist whose words raised the profile of Brooklyn at the end of the twentieth century.

Bernard Lemelin, Canadian writer/scholar, in 1994 pointed out that Celler was often there around the margins of written accounts about immigration yet overlooked for his major accomplishments. In the twenty-first century, Celler's work on the Twenty-Fifth Amendment looms large with an unstable, autocratic, and possibly criminal president in office. Only months after Celler was out of office, the amendment was used for the first time in 1973 to determine the line of succession when disgraced Vice President Spiro Agnew vacated the office. Speaker of the House Gerald Ford ascended to vice president. President Richard Nixon resigned a year later and Ford assumed the Oval office. His replacement was Nelson A. Rockefeller, governor of New York, and he served from 1974 to 1977.

Celler was a workhorse legislator, routinely thinking ahead. In the 1930s, Celler drafted a bill to establish the "Star-Spangled Banner" as the US national anthem. A Maryland congressman representing the district where the patriotic song was penned earned credit for the eventual 1931 law, yet Celler's initiative facilitated the outcome. Celler, who was constantly reminded of the ethnic diversity of his "alien" Brooklyn district, pressed and pressed the executive branch and State Department in 1939, the year World War II began, for the United States to reestablish diplomatic relations with the Vatican, which the two nations had not had since 1867. Celler was unable to bring change during World War II, yet he planted the seeds. Only in 1984, three years after Celler's death, were US-Vatican relations restored.

Furthermore, his exemplary record of defending and supporting disenfranchised and oppressed African American citizens earned Celler the status of godfather of civil rights legislation. Celler was a consistent and dogged champion for civil and human rights when these issues seemed to be hopelessly stuck in neutral. Celler battled southern segregationists unmoved by antilynching bills to end domestic terrorism against southern blacks. Yet Celler persisted and lobbied for black civil rights in the 1940s and 1950s. In 1957, he had a breakthrough in proposing a civil rights bill that became law and succeeded again in 1960. Critics, including some in the civil rights community, poo-pooed the laws as weak and ineffective. Even so it turned out both pieces of civil rights legislation were the foundation that made the 1964 Civil Rights Act possible. The Voting Rights Act followed a year later because of the force of history.

Emanuel Celler's primary legacy is immigration reform that embraced people from every corner of the globe yearning to be free Americans.

Emanuel Celler

1

Early Life, 1888–1906

Two years before Emanuel Celler was born, clergyman, editor, and author Josiah Strong wrote *Our Country: Its Possible Future and Its Present Crisis* that inspired many American's opinions of their country's place in the world. Strong's thesis was that global Anglo-Saxon power was based in America and it was God's will for white Protestants to rule America—and as needed, to flex its muscles anywhere it pleased. Moneymaking power was a striking feature of Anglo-Saxon Americans, wrote Strong. So was another exceptional characteristic of English-speaking whites, an "instinct or genius for colonizing. His unequaled energy, his indomitable perseverance, and his personal independence, made him a pioneer."[1]

The notion that there was such a thing as a white race was new; the concept emerged about the time post–Civil War Reconstruction ended in 1877 and the notion was conventional wisdom by the time of American involvement in World War I, forty years later in 1917.[2] Being American and Caucasian at the dawn of the twentieth century, according to Strong, meant that at home and globally "any remaining unsettled land will be colonized and made English."[3] Theology and morality merged into a (white) Protestant ethic of disciplined achievement, yet capitalistic sorcery contradicted the high-minded ideals, explained historian Jackson Lears. Success was a slippery business and Gilded Age titans too often operated as insincere confidence men.[4]

The attitudes of Strong and like-minded peers contradicted American isolationist instincts that traced back to George Washington, Thomas Jefferson, and John Adams. A century after the American Revolution, America had become a booming industrial power. New inventions and new ideas emerged every day. Expansion seemed inevitable.

When Emanuel Celler was born, Booker T. Washington was in his seventh year of running Tuskegee Institute in Alabama. Washington keenly took note of the hundreds of thousands of European immigrants streaming into America, additional people who could dilute the potential of the formerly enslaved black population and render those freed men and women useless. Washington preached compliant industriousness. He counseled Negroes to pursue practical educations and learn trades, but he did not suggest competing with whites for political and economic power.

Washington's attempt to bargain with the Gilded Age South was futile. In that region there was something profoundly different about racism in the nineteenth century—it was more self-conscious, more systematic, more determined to assert scientific legitimacy. The whole concept of race, never more the flimsiest of cultural constructions, acquired unprecedented biological authority during the decades between Reconstruction and World War I.[5]

In 1883, the US Supreme Court ruled that the 1875 Civil Rights Act was unconstitutional. Although the Civil War–era Fourteenth Amendment said that ex-slaves and free northern blacks were citizens, the high court's ruling undermined the law. Post-slavery blacks effectively became serfs in a feudal society, which was evident in the South, and occasionally, in the North, Midwest, and far West. With European immigration surging, by 1890, black people represented 11.6 percent of nearly 75 million American inhabitants. Their share was significantly down from the previous decade when they comprised 13.1 percent of a nation of about 50 million people.[6]

———————

In 1848, the year revolutions erupted in Germany and Austria, fifteen-year-old Ernest Mueller fled Hanover, Bavaria, Germany for the United States in pursuit of political freedom, liberty, and economic opportunity. Peasants and bourgeoisie rebelled against entrenched monarchs across Europe. The lower and middle classes made many gains, but the elites cracked down violently. Many Europeans left for America, away from the bloody chaos. Mueller was one of those escapees.[7] He took the months-long journey on a crowded, grimy passenger ship with hundreds of other immigrants. With the destination, New York Harbor, in sight, the ship began to sink. A young woman on board panicked and jumped overboard. Young Mueller instinctively jumped in and rescued the stranger.[8]

In a matter of months, the teenage boy and girl, strangers in a strange land, married after a brief but intense courtship. Ernest Mueller was Catholic. The teenage girl he married was Jewish. Ernest Mueller converted to Judaism in order to marry. The couple lived in Brooklyn, the former five Dutch towns of the 1600s that by the mid-1800s was a city of 139,000 people that resembled a network of quaint villages.

Across the water was New York City—Manhattan Island—accessible only by boats. The Mueller family's neighbors in Brooklyn included colonial-rooted Anglos and Dutch, free Africans, and arriving Irish, German, and other European immigrants.[9]

Ernest Mueller made his living as a tassel maker. He and his wife raised a family during an era of booming Irish immigration into America. The potato blight in the old country destroyed several years of crops and starved thousands of Irish citizens. The Irish had another reason to flee. Many of them were tired of British rule that denied the rural Catholic Irish self-governance, property ownership, and other rights.[10]

The Muellers produced nine children in the marriage, six girls and three boys. All of the girls married men of the Jewish faith. Josephine, the fourth-from-eldest daughter, married Henry H. Celler.[11] Emanuel Celler was born May 6, 1888, in a frame house on Sumner Avenue off Floyd Street. He was the third of four children. His siblings were Mortimer, born in 1880; Jessie, born in 1882; and Lillian, born in 1889.[12]

The Brooklyn neighborhood where they lived was the southernmost end of Williamsburg, the former town that began to bleed into Bedford Corner, part of a neighborhood that would be renamed Bedford-Stuyvesant in the next century. Emanuel was born six weeks after a blizzard crippled the East Coast and virtually shut down New York City for two days. The storm began as pre-spring rain, then temperatures dropped from twenty degrees to a low of one degree below zero and snow accumulated. Winds whipped as high as eighty miles per hour. People ran out of provisions. Bread and milk trucks halted deliveries. Hundreds of people died—two hundred in New York City, four hundred in Maine and as far south as Maryland's Chesapeake Bay—from lack of sustenance, or from exertion in the thigh-deep snow. Damages from fires during that freeze were estimated at $25 million.[13] One of those who succumbed was Republican Party stalwart Roscoe Conkling, the former US senator from New York and a Radical Republican during a dozen years of post–Civil War Reconstruction.[14]

Among ordinary people, milkman Xavier Zwinge of Livingston, New Jersey, ignored the snowfall and departed on his rounds. But after wading through the snow Zwinge abandoned his route. He parked the horse outside of a tavern that had a red-hot stove, beverages, and neighbors.

Hours passed and the horse, tired of waiting in the cold, trotted home and placidly munched oats in the barn. Mrs. Zwinge saw the horse but no husband. She screamed and assumed Xavier Zwinge died. A local newspaperman published a tale of the milkman's last ride. The next morning, Xavier Zwinge staggered the three miles home. He opened the door and faced red-eyed relatives and long-faced neighbors. His wife looked at him and fainted. "My God, Xavier! You're dead! It says so in the newspaper." "I don't give a damn what it says in that sheet," roared the milkman. "The hell I'm dead. I'm drunk, that's what I am!" He then passed out.[15]

When Emanuel was an infant, Grover Cleveland was president of the United States. Cleveland served most of his term without a vice president because Thomas A. Hendricks died a year after the 1884 election and was not replaced. In November 1888, the incumbent lost to Republican Benjamin Harrison of Indiana. Cleveland, a former New York governor, won the popular vote by 96,000 ballots of nearly 11 million cast. However, Harrison beat him handily in the electoral college, 233–168.[16]

A political dirty trick may have denied Cleveland reelection. When the British ambassador was asked who would win the presidency, he said "Cleveland," and believed the query was from a naturalized American and former Briton. However, the question was written in a letter from a member of the California Republican Party. The correspondence was circulated in the press, intended to inflame Irish American voters. The tactic succeeded.[17]

Emanuel was born into an America that was a mainland consisting of forty-two coast-to-coast states. A few western territories, including Oklahoma and Arizona, were not yet part of the union. Hawaii was a collection of islands settled by American planters. Soon, with the help of Washington, those settlers toppled the queen and colonized the lands.

———— · ————

Emanuel was born five years after the Brooklyn Bridge connected his city with New York. Two years before his birth, the Statue of Liberty was placed in New York Harbor. The gift from France depicted a giant woman emerging from chains, wearing a crown, and holding a torch, welcoming the "huddled masses" to America.

The new bridge transformed Brooklyn. More families streamed across the bridge from Manhattan to settle in homes in the village-style borough—still a separate city. Before the great bridge, Kings County grew quickly in the

1800s. In 1820, this westernmost piece of Long Island was a town of 7,000, unlike the 130,000 people packed in the lower third of Manhattan Island.

Thirty-five years later in 1855, Brooklyn consolidated the towns of Williamsburg and Bushwick into a city of 205,000 inhabitants. Brooklyn had become America's third-largest city, a mix of industry and country life—shipyards; warehouses; glass, furnace-casting, and stone-cutting factories, breweries, and tanneries.[18]

By 1860, 37 percent—104,000—of Brooklyn inhabitants were foreign born. Among them, 54 percent were Irish and 25 percent were German. The black population of 4,920 continued to shrink and would dwindle to 1 percent of the city by 1870.[19]

Emanuel's Brooklyn, the northwest section, was without a doubt urban, although it was not unusual to see pigs roam the street, or goats and cows in neighbors' backyards. Dairymen stopped passersby and attempted to sell raw milk. South of where the Cellers lived in the village-like neighborhoods of Flatbush, Flatlands, and Gravesend, farms were still common and very productive. Through the 1880s, Kings County was the nation's second-highest producer of vegetables and fruit; its neighbor on the eastern border, Queens County, was number one.[20] Horse-drawn carts hauled cabbages, celery, beans, and peas to eager consumers—including Manhattanites who no longer lived near farms.

Yet between two tumultuous decades, 1890–1910, the years Emanuel attended elementary and high school, then as an adolescent finished college, the hyper-industrialization of Brooklyn wiped out the farms.[21]

Emanuel lived on a street named after abolitionist Charles Sumner, a US senator from Massachusetts. Sumner's antislavery convictions were so strong that an opponent to the Republican senator in 1856 beat him to a bloody pulp with a cane on the chamber floor. US representative Preston Brooks of South Carolina had taken great offense to Sumner's antislavery speech that mocked fellow Carolinian, US senator Andrew Butler.[22] Sumner's passion for equality and justice would live on in the mid-twentieth century through the thoughts and actions of Brooklyn-born Emanuel Celler.

————— · —————

Tammany Hall ran New York City political life in the late 1800s. Tammany was synonymous with William Marcy "Boss" Tweed, but he was prosecuted and forced out. By 1878 he was in jail and in disgrace.[23] Tammany became cleaner, yet it was still a political machine to which many immigrant families owed their jobs. That machine often functioned as the center of social life. It sponsored boat rides and picnics that doubled as opportunities to network and secure jobs. Emanuel's father, Henry, was a Democratic district leader.

In 1896 when Emanuel was eight years old, he walked about a half mile east with his father to Arion Hall in Bushwick.[24] They went there to hear William Jennings Bryan, a Democratic Party advocate for farmers and working-class laborers. Henry Celler hoisted Emanuel on his shoulders so the boy could see and hear the fiery speaker from the heartland. That July, Bryan proclaimed in an impassioned speech that US currency should not be based solely on a gold standard simply because Europeans and the Gilded Age robber barons wanted it. "You shall not press down upon the brow of labor this crown of thorns," he said. "You shall not crucify mankind upon a cross of gold."[25]

The Celler family was respectably middle class. The parents had the means to afford a maid-of-all-work. They favored music, so their home included violins and a piano. There were also books in the house, although those seemed to rank after the passion for musical instruments. Impressionable Emanuel liked what he called "dress up night," the third Mondays of opera season, when there was a flush of excitement on Mom's face, and Dad seemed two inches taller. "La Traviata," "Il Trovatore," and "Aida," Mom's favorites, became Emanuel's too.[26]

———— • ————

When Emanuel walked a few blocks away from his house at Sumner and Floyd, he could hear and smell his neighbors' poverty. He quickly realized that many neighbors were the working poor. Not far from his frame house were the Brooklyn dockyards where laborers toiled. When Emanuel reached early adolescence, he became keenly conscious of his ambition. What would it take to experience places beyond the Brooklyn streets? Emanuel read anything he could get, and self-identified as the scholar of the family. He grew impatient with the structured and unquestioning pace of family life.

There were "things" to be done, parents and elders would say, but they were routines that would not challenge the established order. *Why was it acceptable to see suffering poor people?* the teenager wondered, when he caught glimpses of Fifth Avenue's gilded elegance. Emanuel read intensely, in search of answers.[27]

Introspectively, he perceived himself as a snob. Emanuel also took note that his parents encouraged his pursuit of a life of the mind. His mother, Josephine—small, round, blue-eyed, and prematurely gray—was instinctively shy, yet the shyness disappeared when she talked with him, her "Manny." Siblings

Mortimer, Jessie, and Lillian could never draw the same warmth from their mother as son Emanuel. Josephine showed equal devotion to her husband, but for son Manny, she vicariously transferred her ambitions. Manny would grow up to be erudite and famous.[28]

While Josephine was shy, husband and father Henry was hearty and affable. He was a joiner of clubs: the Democrats, the Masons, and the Odd Fellows. He owned a business—a 25,000-gallon whiskey tank was in the basement of the family home—and was apparently comfortable engaging customers and business associates.

Henry too singled out Emanuel for special treatment. Music was an integral part of the household, yet often when the patriarch was addressing his pride, Henry spoke directly to Emanuel. When the clubs invited Henry to talk politics, he addressed his son, who was sitting in the audience.

The first floor of the Sumner Avenue house served as the store. Emanuel worked for his father, who showed him the rectifying process for liquors, bottling, and distribution. One of Emanuel's tasks was to paste Echo Springs labels on the liquor bottles.[29]

The teenager worked, studied, and played with equal intensity, he acknowledged in his 1953 autobiography. He didn't say what and how he played, but it's probable that he played stickball games on the streets. Other games could have been marbles or "skully," with thumb and index finger, plucking corked bottle tops into chalk-drawn boxes on the sidewalk. By 1900, mass-produced cars were still a few years away, so horse-drawn carriages and carts remained common. Trolleys traversed the main streets.

That explained the name for the hometown baseball team: In the 1890s, twenty years before the Brooklyn Dodgers moved to iconic Ebbets Field in Flatbush, the team played at Eastern Park between Pitkin and Sutter avenues in the East New York neighborhood. The baseball Dodgers name was inspired by fans who artfully dodged whizzing trolley cars on two sides in order to get to the ballpark.[30]

Emanuel had a happy childhood. Ambition, restlessness, and eagerness did not interfere with joy. He was self-aware. What did his siblings think of him, the coddled, favored son who apparently was being groomed for success? Celler said he did not witness rivalry, jealousy, or loathing. If his sisters or brother harbored such feelings, they hid them remarkably well.[31] As for temperament, Emanuel tried to emulate his gregarious father, but the boy felt inauthentic. He did not have many friends. Emanuel's true self favored his shy mother, but the boy hid and disguised his shy nature. This personality conflict became evident during Emanuel Celler's adult life. The public Celler appeared combative and argumentative, yet not cruel or vindictive.

The private, intimate Celler was genial and playful.[32] Emanuel did harbor one major complaint. Although he loved music, he did not like playing the violin, but both parents insisted. He complied, but his love was the piano, which Celler would indulge with great joy as an adult.[33]

The boy's hometown was geographically reshaped at the end of the nineteenth century. In 1898, when Emanuel was ten, the city of Brooklyn agreed to merge with New York County (Manhattan), plus Queens, the Bronx, and Richmond County (Staten Island), and reemerge as New York City. That transformed the five united counties into the second most populous city in the world after London. In July 1902 when Emanuel was fourteen, Willis H. Carrier invented air conditioning in Brooklyn. The Cornell-trained mechanical engineer solved a humidity problem for a local printer. Oppressive indoor conditions curled the color pages. With the product problem solved, Carrier's indoor cooling spread to the human condition.[34]

In 1902, Emanuel enrolled at Boys' High School, on Marcy Avenue at Madison Street, about a mile southwest of his Sumner Avenue home. Boys' High was a college preparatory public school that emphasized math and science.

Varsity athletics were low priority there (at that time, as Boys' High later became a New York City power in basketball, at least), yet Emanuel played a lot of basketball and volleyball, activities that would soon prove valuable. Its students—boys who were poor, near-poor, and not-so-poor, all reputedly earnest—were matches for the ambitious Emanuel.

In August, a month before Emanuel started high school, Oliver Wendell Holmes became an associate justice of the US Supreme Court. During deliberations Holmes eloquently and effectively—during a Gilded Age of robber barons—supported the principle that "public interest" took priority over profits. Also that month, President Theodore Roosevelt visited New England and Midwest states and spoke out against the irresponsibility of trusts and monopolies. Crowds received Roosevelt enthusiastically because much of the public had agitated for relief from unregulated big business.[35]

As Emanuel attended classes, Ida Tarbell's exposé, "History of the Standard Oil Company" rolled out in installments in *McClure's* magazine. Other carefully researched and reported muckraking stories emerged, including *The Shame of the Cities* by Lincoln Steffens and *The Jungle* by Upton Sinclair. The writers tackled poverty, monopoly, and corruption, all issues that interested—and disturbed—the precocious teenager.

During the summers of 1902–1905, after high school, Emanuel worked full-time at his father's home-based whiskey rectifying business. Through "rectifying" the owner refined his product, often with repeated distillation that gave the whiskey a distinct taste. Henry Celler felt confident and expanded his business.

———————•———————

In 1905, seventeen-year-old Emanuel met Stella Baar, a girl of slight build with a head of dark, curly hair, gray-blue eyes, and a delicate, fragile face.[36] Both teenagers were members of Reform synagogues and they became acquainted at parties.[37] Stella—born in Vienna, Austria—was a student at Girls' High School on Nostrand Avenue, a handful of blocks south of Boys' High. Smitten, Emanuel met Stella every day at her school and walked her to her home on McDonough Street while carrying her books. Emanuel read poetry to her. The teenagers became so inseparable, potential suitors assumed Stella was "Manny's girl" and maintained a respectable distance.

Josephine and Henry Celler were concerned that he was so attached to one girl, yet they made no overt attempts to separate the teenagers. Stella's mother, however, never stopped trying to separate her daughter from Emanuel. The boy, the girl's mother believed, was jeopardizing her prospects of meeting someone better.[38] However, at Boys' High, classmates perceived Emanuel as a rich, "real American." Their proof was that his father was a successful businessman. Henry Celler could afford a maid and he rented out two rooms of the Summer Avenue house for extra income. His son was a grandchild of immigrants, Emanuel's parents were first-generation native born. Many of Emanuel's schoolmates were immigrant boys. They were attending a college prep public high school and were eager to break away from their parents' lives as laborers and petty tradesmen. The boys aspired to be professionals, lawyers, actors, doctors, teachers, and writers.[39]

Emanuel graduated from Boys' High in the summer of 1906. He applied and was accepted to Columbia University in uptown Manhattan. A week after the June high school graduation, Celler, eighteen, walked into a post office to mail a letter and noticed that the board of education had posted a list of job opportunities. He saw an opening for a playground director. He applied and got the job. Celler was assigned to the basement of P.S. 84 at Belmont and Christopher avenues in Brownsville. From 9 a.m. to 3 p.m., he taught age eight- to sixteen-year-old boys. Celler walked into a summer job with no routine, no compulsory attendance, and little if any discipline. Older boys bullied younger boys and fistfights broke out and had to quashed.

Celler was not much older than the sixteen-year-old man-children. Yet the boys accorded him authority because what he had, they wanted: Celler was American, and most of the boys were newly arrived immigrants.[40] Celler taught the boys American games and American slang and helped them shake off old-country ways. "Hi feller," an eight-year-old called out from across the basement. The other boys shouted and applauded; one of them was talking "American."[41]

Old World elders had to adjust to their new generation's and nation's leisurely ways. Once, when Celler and his boys were playing baseball, a child threw a wild pitch that shattered the window of a small tailor shop across the street from P.S. 84. Celler dreaded the task, but he knew he had to walk to the shop and brave the wrath of the tailor.

The small, shriveled merchant stood before Celler and waved his arms wildly and screamed, "Those good-for-nothings! What are they doing playing ball anyway? They should be in cheder [Hebrew school], learning the Torah. Is this what America teaches them—breaking people's windows?"

The rant continued. In time Celler calmed the tailor and then begged him to come to the school and watch the children play. The recreation counselor explained that in America playing was one of the natural birthrights of all children, rich or poor. The old and young man talked about an hour. The next day Celler returned to the shop with a jacket and asked that it be mended. "Will you come and see the children?" he asked. The man walked with Celler across the street.

Silently, the tailor watched the children play then he left. Fifteen minutes later the merchant returned and shyly offered Celler a package. It was a shiny, new baseball. Celler suspected that the incident reminded the old man of his youth, one that had known no play and no fun.

Americans housed in the percolating urban laboratories of Brooklyn and New York City learned about the evolving nature of work, leisure, and what it meant to be American. For the Europeans—Irish, Italians, and Jews of Germany and Balkan states—pouring into East Coast port cities, becoming American meant assimilating, shedding old-country ways and adapting the language (including dialects), culture, and the work and play habits of the industrial new society. American opinion considered their country an Anglo-Saxon nation. It was in the arriving Europeans' interest to Anglicize—alter their names, accents, and appearance—and their whiteness could blend, or melt, as a British Jew would soon write.[42]

Some would not easily melt. Colonial America had included a substantial African population—in some of its mid-Atlantic states such as Maryland and Virginia the black population was 40 percent—but by the 1890s and early 1900s blacks represented 10 percent of the total population and their numbers were declining. Possibly, the flood of European immigrants would dilute and then erase the American Negroes, most of them concentrated in the agrarian South. In 1895, when Negro leader Booker T. Washington urged his people to pull themselves up by their bootstraps, the self-help message urged whites to employ native blacks who were loyal and generally obedient.

When President Theodore Roosevelt in October 1901 invited Washington to the White House for dinner and conversation, white southerners protested and lashed out violently against blacks.[43] Despite accommodating overtures, most white Americans despised Negroes.

Even as Jim Crow policies were tightening its grip of black southerners, at that time in some parts of the South, black men voted, held office, organized unions, denounced injustice, demanded public services, cut deals, and took bribes. For example, in the sugar country of Louisiana where black residents constituted a majority, white officials arrested fourteen black so-called ringleaders linked to a Knights of Labor organizing effort. The men had to be disciplined, said the justice of the peace, because "the great arm of the great wheel of agriculture is the nigger. Next is the mule."[44] When black workers walked out to protest cut wages in fall 1887, planters encouraged the governor to send in the state militia with a Gatling gun. The strikers were detained, and vigilantes killed more than fifty people.

At about the same time in Virginia, that commonwealth evolved to have the largest number of black landowners in the former Confederacy. A readjustment movement that grew into a biracial machine of the black farmers and poor hill-country whites managed to elect a black man to the US Senate and fund public services, notably public education, much to the consternation of a white elite Democratic Party ruling class. On a Saturday before a November election, Democrats evoked visions of uppity Negroes trying to "force ladies from the pavement." A street altercation resulted in the deaths of four blacks, roving bands of whites patroling the streets and the Democrats narrowly winning the election.[45]

Soon white middle- and upper-class citizens became disgusted with wholesale corruption and frequent political violence. Some began to openly suggest that the only way to make white supremacy legitimate was to make it legal and disenfranchise black people with laws rather than guns. Mississippi led the disenfranchisement movement. Warned one leader, "The old men of the present generation can't afford to die and leave the election to their children and grandchildren, with shotguns in their hands, a lie in their mouths and perjury on their lips in order to defeat the negroes." Newspaper editorialists concurred, wrote historian Jackson Lears in 2009: "There must be devised some legal defensible substitute for the abhorrent methods on which white supremacy lies."[46]

State after state followed Mississippi, which rewrote its state constitution to include literacy tests, poll taxes, and other barriers to thwart black voters.[47] Blacks were systematically segregated and excluded from participation in public life as white immigrants blended into the American fabric by fits and starts in the North, West, and Midwest.[48]

The American Dream was created at the expense of nonwhites. Texas, California, and Arizona (the latter was not a state but a territory) had been Mexican lands before the United States conquered them. People of native Latino heritage lived on the lands. The Anglo rulers suppressed their Spanish culture. The so-called Indians—the first Americans—either were annihilated or pushed onto reservations and then forcibly moved again when even marginal lands became desirable to white settlers.

In a mainland United States then settled from coast to coast, poverty, reform-minded journalists, and social workers took pains to expose monopoly corporate greed and the exploitation of workers. In the early 1900s, one in every five American workers walked off their jobs to go on strike.[49]

Emanuel Celler, a young, middle-class second-generation American of Jewish and German heritage, paid attention to the squalor and meanness in his Brooklyn community. He was ambitious and prepared to be successful, even as he was guided by a sense of service and compassion. Celler read about current events voraciously and battled in his mind to make sense of the ideas he consumed. A third family elder was about to profoundly influence his future.

2

Columbia University,
Young Lawyer, 1906–1921

In 1906, a few months before Emanuel Celler began his freshman year at Columbia University, Henry Celler's overextended whiskey business failed. He may have been too trusting and too lax with business partners. Also, Henry Celler's bad choices—and timing—occurred months before a financial panic of 1907 roiled America. In an era of weak federal banking and securities regulation, trust companies recklessly speculated with investors' money. In an effort to monopolize the copper market, New York firms drove stocks so high they crashed the market. Depression-like conditions haunted much of the United States that year.[1]

The comfortable, respectable middle-class financial support Henry Celler built for his family—a station the neighbors had regarded as "rich"—collapsed. Henry Celler, the former business owner, had to support his family as an employee of another man's business. He obtained a job as a wine salesman with a regular route and customers, more often than not Brooklyn's Italian immigrants.

Emanuel Celler earned some money for college costs during the summer at his recreation center job. Granduncle Samuel Grabfelder, a successful whiskey distiller from Louisville, Kentucky, agreed to finance Celler's college education. "Uncle Sam" was a millionaire who was born in Bavaria in 1844 and came to America in 1857 at age thirteen. Ten years later, Grabfelder opened his business in Louisville. He was well read and loved music and art, the latter of which he acquired, and he envied the graces of those with formal schooling. With riches, Grabfelder became a philanthropist.[2] He gave generously—$40,000 in 1900—to the National Jewish Hospital for Consumptives in Denver and served on the institution's board.[3]

Grabfelder attached conditions to his grandnephew's support.[4] "What do you really want to be?" asked the great-uncle. "A lawyer," answered Celler. "Then, be one and I will help you," said Grabfelder. "I am not giving the money to you. It will be a loan. This is how you will pay me back: Someday, when someone stands before you in need of help, you will help him and I will help you. In this way only will I consider the loan repaid."[5] Celler's promise in 1906 set the tone for the professional career he started about a decade later.

———— · ————

About the time Celler was to start classes at Columbia, his father died at the age of fifty-five. His son now faced multiple challenges and stresses. He had to become the head of the household. Celler attended Columbia classes in and around 116th Street and Broadway in Manhattan during the mornings. That meant at least a one-hour trek each way to school. He would board the westbound Myrtle Avenue elevated train at Summer Avenue and cross the Brooklyn Bridge, then in lower Manhattan transfer at Park Row Terminal to an uptown subway.[6] Automobiles were new and rare; fewer than 100,000 vehicles existed in all of America.[7]

Celler took over his late father's wine route. Immediately after classes he returned to Brooklyn and sold product all afternoon until 7 p.m. At quitting time, Celler quickly ate dinner. His mother, Josephine, was sickly. A nurse was at the house to wait on her, but the mother set conditions: Celler was to stay at her bedside from 7 to 10 p.m. Celler in his scant free time, dove into his studies and read until about 2 a.m. Then he took a handful of hours' sleep and the day would resume again—caring for his three siblings, attending college classes uptown, selling wine in Brooklyn through the afternoon, sitting with his mother at night, and then studying.

In midwinter 1907, Josephine Mueller Celler, forty-eight, died. Months short of his nineteenth birthday, Emanuel Celler had lost both parents and became fully responsible for his three siblings.[8] Girlfriend Stella Baar spent time with Celler when he returned from the wine route. She accompanied him twice a week to a classroom and sat as he took Italian lessons. Celler wanted to be better equipped to talk with his customers.[9] He was frustrated that he did not have enough time at Columbia. He kept up with his reading and assignments, but he wished there was time to soak in the collegiality of campus life. Still, his work and household responsibilities took priority. After his freshman year, during the summer, Celler looked for additional work. On a post office bulletin board was a listing for a teacher of Venetian ironwork.

Celler reacted by going to a public library and checking out books explaining the craft. After an hour of reading, he learned the skill was work done with aluminum strips, solder, wire, and pliers to coil the aluminum into fanciful figures. Celler persuaded the board of education to hire him and was again assigned to P.S. 84 in Brownsville. Celler learned Venetian arts along with the boys he taught and shared their joy and wonder in fashioning candelabras, vases, plates, ash trays, and picture frames.[10]

Before the end of Celler's freshman year, the United States adjusted its immigration policies. In California, especially the San Francisco Bay area, Anglos fomented hysteria against Japanese newcomers who arrived as married couples and seasonally worked the land. Many of the newcomers returned to Japan, but others remained in the states. Just before Celler was born and through 1906, 300,000 Japanese emigrated to California and Hawaii.[11] Unlike Chinese immigrants who arrived in the American West after the 1850s and overwhelmingly were men, the Japanese government encouraged its citizens to immigrate only as couples. Review boards in their native country certified that the immigrants were healthy and literate and would credibly maintain and represent Japan's national honor.[12]

President Roosevelt pondered proposing the naturalization of Japanese immigrants. But those thoughts evaporated because of a diplomatic debacle that led to pragmatic choices. The mayor and the political boss of San Francisco both were under investigation for corruption. As a diversion, both men railed against an alleged Japanese problem in the community. Japanese children—all eighty-seven of them—were removed from the public schools and isolated in an "Oriental school" because those children purportedly crowded out whites. The Japanese government issued a diplomatic protest. Roosevelt summoned Mayor Eugene Smitz and the school board to the White House.[13] The visitors agreed to withdraw the anti-Japanese school plan. Roosevelt in turn sought authority from Congress to limit Japanese immigration that did not come directly from Japan but from Hawaii, Mexico, and Canada. Again, the Japanese government protested. After further talks, both nations in 1907 reached what was called a "gentleman's agreement": whereby the Roosevelt administration would enact no new embarrassing immigration restrictions and the Japanese would bar male laborers from migrating to the continental United States.[14]

At the start of Celler's junior year—October 1908—Henry Ford began mass producing Model T cars. Also that fall, William Howard Taft was elected president over William Jennings Bryan and minor candidates.[15] The Republican winner was a longtime judge. Taft continued Roosevelt's conservation and trust-busting policies, yet the twenty-seventh president received little credit. Roosevelt's shadow loomed large over Taft—quite a feat because at three hundred pounds Taft was the most physically imposing US president, before or since. After leaving the White House, Roosevelt embarked on a year-long expedition to Africa and returned to a hero's welcome in America.

In May, Celler earned an AB (bachelor of arts) degree from Columbia. In September, he returned to 116th and Broadway to attend Columbia Law School. The notion of professional schools to train lawyers was a new American concept. Well into the late 1800s, the so-called "right way" to prepare lawyers for the bar was through office apprenticeships; this was supposed to be in tune with American ideal of the self-made man. However, Columbia and kindred institutions tenaciously worked at proving the value of academic preparation and certification.[16]

Columbia Law School opened in 1858 on Lafayette Place, then from 1873 to 1883 was housed on Great Jones Street. In October 1909—when Celler was in the fall semester of his senior year—the cornerstone of the new law school building was placed at Amsterdam Avenue and 116th Street. Kent Hall was dedicated October 31, 1910. The five-story building contained lecture rooms that could seat 50 to 250 students.[17] Celler was among 117 students in the law school class of 1912. His classmates overwhelmingly were from New York City or the Northeast. A few dozen students were from faraway places such as Portland, Oregon; Des Moines, Iowa; Oklahoma City; Pomona, California; Lake Charles, Louisiana; Georgetown, Texas; and Dayton, Washington. Average annual tuition was $150 and book expenses were $38.[18]

Celler began law school the same year Columbia appointed a new dean, Harlan Fiske Stone. He succeeded George W. Kirchwey, who remained on the teaching faculty. Stone was born in New Hampshire in October 1872 and enrolled at Amherst College in 1890. He initially prepared to study medicine but soon gravitated to law, art, and literature. At five feet, ten inches and 195 pounds, he played center for the football team.

Stone was among nine students elected Phi Beta Kappa at Amherst. Upon graduation he became a school principal and in 1895 he enrolled at Columbia Law School. After graduation Stone practiced law at Clark, Sullivan, and Cromwell in Manhattan. He became first a lecturer, then an adjunct professor at Columbia Law before returning to practice. After an absence of a few years, Stone returned as dean. He inherited a faculty of eleven professors, six of them in endowed chairs. The new dean added four more faculty members.

Stone's teaching style was not pretentious or showy. He did not have the encyclopedic mind of Francis Burdick or the detailed knowledge of the past like Nathan Abbott. Stone was not a master pedagogue like Charles T. Terry, neither was he witty and amusing like former dean Kirchwey. Yet his classes were never tedious or boring. Stone's razor-like mind, his quick replies, and his penetrating questions energized his students.[19]

Stone rarely lectured. Occasionally he would pause to summarize a section of the course. By and large, Stone's method was Socratic. It was up to the students to distinguish the cases; he never did it for them.[20] Celler admired Stone's self-contained poise that allowed him to proceed logically from one thought to the next. As he drove points home, Stone demonstrated precision and passion.

Celler tried to imitate the dean. When he felt moved to gesticulate or pound the table, Celler stopped in mid-sentence and tried to resume with the calm demeanor of Dean Stone. A challenge on Stone's watch was the decision to admit women to the School of Law. When Celler was a student, his professional school was the only one on campus that prohibited women.[21] Celler did not know this while in school, but within a decade, he and Stone would work closely in the legislative and judicial corridors of Washington, DC: the teacher becoming a Supreme Court justice and his student becoming a congressman who chaired the Judiciary Committee.

In March 1911, Celler's spring semester, the Triangle Shirtwaist fire occurred in lower Manhattan. Shirtwaists—tapered women's blouses with puffy sleeves—were fashionable at the time. Russian immigrant co-owners Max Blank and Isaac Harris had a lucrative business and employed five hundred female laborers on the eighth to tenth floors of the triangle-shaped Asch Building at Washington Place and Greene Street. They paid pittances to their workers—many of them immigrants thirteen to fourteen years old. In 1909 the workers struck for higher wages. Competing manufacturers met some of the workers' demands, but the Triangle company co-owners resisted. At 4:30 p.m. Saturday, March 25, minutes before quitting time, someone noticed that a fire had started in a scrap bin on the eighth floor. Attempts to douse the flames with buckets of water failed. The fire quickly spread to flammable items—cotton and paper—on the crowded work floor. Rescuers turned on water hoses, but they did not work.

There were delays in evacuating the workers from all three work floors because some doors were bolted. The inferno grew and the disaster resulted in 146 deaths.[22] All but fifteen of the dead were women, and all except ten of the fatalities were immigrants. Triangle Shirtwaist symbolized the exploitative, hazardous working conditions at many Industrial Age businesses, outrages that consumed Celler when he was a precocious teenager and haunted him as a young adult. In the end the Triangle co-owners were indicted, but acquitted at trial. Workplace safety and compensation laws were enacted by the state legislature.[23]

In May, Celler graduated with an LLB (bachelor of laws) degree.[24] A month out of law school, Celler, twenty-four, experienced with the rest of the country a bruising three-way campaign for US president. There was Republican incumbent William Howard Taft, anointed in 1908 by former two-term president Theodore Roosevelt. Friends and foes linked Taft to the political establishment and the industrialists. Taft's Democratic Party challenger was Woodrow Wilson, a native Virginian who was elected governor of New Jersey in 1910 and before that was president of Princeton University. Where Taft represented the status quo, Wilson campaigned as a progressive reformer. He pressed for stronger corporate regulation, a public service commission in the Garden State, tax reform, and conservation.

Celler campaigned for Wilson. His work meant door-to-door lobbying, and speaking from the tail end of a truck after a drum and fife ensemble played or fireworks and bright lights from Roman candles helped attract crowds.[25] "I am not a conservative," Wilson once said. "I am a radical."[26] Wilson's reformist style mirrored Roosevelt's second term. The difference was the president was largely stymied by the fat-cat Congress. Wilson, however, got reforms passed in his state, and similar rising tides occurred in Wisconsin and California.[27]

Although he was a native southerner, Bourbon Democrats did not trust Wilson, and northern status-quo Democrats resented Wilson's zeal for reining in political patronage and freewheeling corporations. The road to the presidency was bumpy too for GOP incumbent Taft. In February, Roosevelt came out of retirement from electoral politics to challenge his onetime friend. During the spring primary season (primaries were a new concept then), Roosevelt tallied a string of victories including a defeat of Taft in his home state Ohio.

At the summer convention in Chicago, Roosevelt overwhelmingly attracted the most delegates, yet the party bosses manipulated the rules and anointed Taft the Republican candidate. Roosevelt in turn launched a third-party candidacy under the National Progressive Party, better known as the "Bull Moose" Party because fifty-three-year-old candidate T.R. said he felt as fit as its namesake. The tight three-way race resulted in a number of November surprises.

Wilson was elected America's twenty-eighth president and ended the Democrats' sixteen-year lockout from the White House. He won nearly 43 percent of 14.8 million votes cast. Roosevelt, the former president who ran as a third-party outsider, finished second with 28 percent of the votes. Taft, the well-financed incumbent, finished third with 23 percent.[28] The split between

Republicans Roosevelt and Taft opened the door for a Wilson win. Theodore Roosevelt lost the election but many of his ideas won the future. Within a decade, American women would gain the right to vote. By welcoming women as leaders in the National Progressive Party, Roosevelt assisted women's long struggle to share the franchise. Wilson, meanwhile, won the election and like Roosevelt he had a progressive vision that served the masses, women, children, and workers. On Wilson's watch, federal income tax was launched and US citizens elected their senators; those elected officials were no longer the unapologetic lobbyists for rich industrialists.

Wilson's—and Roosevelt's—progressive visions were in synch with the promise Emanuel Celler made in 1906 to Samuel Grabfelder. Granduncle Samuel promised to finance Celler's education at elite Columbia University. The student completed his coursework and after six years earned bachelor's and law school degrees. Celler was to repay the loan by serving others, the underdogs of society. His first clients were immigrants in his Brooklyn neighborhood. Helping them and other disenfranchised people became Celler's career habit.

The same year he graduated from Columbia School of Law—1912—Emanuel Celler was admitted to the New York bar. At age twenty-four he began to practice law at Meyer Krashauer, 51 Chambers Street in lower Manhattan.[29] Celler's first clients were his wine route customers. He did not abandon the wine delivery route he had inherited from his father because of his new professional commitments.

In his first case, Celler represented an immigrant client in federal court. His wife, Stella, recalled that the client's alleged offense was voting without being a citizen; the Polish immigrant had believed he was one. In court, the US attorney and an assistant sat at the opposite table from Celler and his client. "We ought to have another lawyer," said Celler's client. "Why?" the counselor asked. "You can hardly afford to pay for one lawyer, much less two."

The immigrant explained: "Well, because when the U.S. Attorney stands up before the judge, the other lawyer at the desk thinks. When you stand up before the judge, nobody thinks." Meanwhile, a relative of the Polish man asked, "Who's the lawyer?" When another man pointed toward the youthful five-foot, two-inch Celler, that relative exclaimed, "What, that kid!"[30] Stella was so nervous she scratched her leg obsessively and ended up with a large hole in her stocking. She did not hear the judge say "case dismissed." Indeed, Celler won his first case—alleged voter fraud—and was paid $25.

In 1914, 1.2 million immigrants—overwhelmingly from Europe—arrived in America.[31] For a dozen years before then, European powers built battleships, grew standing armies, and forged alliances in anticipation of war. On June 28, 1914, a Serbian gunman shot the archduke of Austro-Hungary and his wife in Sarajevo. The unpopular monarch represented a small nation state. Still, the murderous act triggered a world conflict.

———————•———————

Two days after the assassination that started World War I, Emanuel Celler married Stella Baar during a Reform Jewish ceremony performed by Rabbi Nathan Krass, the future rabbi of Temple Emanu-el on Manhattan's Fifth Avenue. Sixty guests witnessed the wedding.[32] The couple moved into a one-bedroom, four-room apartment in a four-story house on Caton Avenue near East 17th Street in Flatbush. That avenue had been the boundary that separated the city from farmland when Celler was a boy. Their monthly rent was $35 and the Cellers believed that no section of Brooklyn was more gracious than theirs.[33]

Sometime in 1916, Emanuel Celler let go of the wine route he had managed since college and focused solely on practicing law. He flourished to the extent that he soon would organize two banks and serve as a director of two other banks.[34]

On March 17, 1917, Jane B., Stella and Emanuel Celler's first child, was born. Both parents cared for the child at their Caton Avenue apartment. The couple belonged to Temple Beth Elohim, a liberal congregation at Garfield Place.[35]

Celler, grandson of German immigrants and husband of an Austrian immigrant, said little to nothing about his life during World War I in his autobiography or his oral history. During the war Celler did serve as a government appeal agent on the draft board according to his congressional biography.

In the postwar era, America turned isolationist. The country was less welcoming than before to European immigrants. After peak arrivals in 1914, a combined 1 million immigrants arrived in America for the next three years. In 1918, immigration thinned to 110,000, slowed because of the great war in Europe and disrupted migration patterns. By 1921, the numbers rebounded to 800,000. Still, what once had been an open door was about to slam shut.[36]

Historian Jackson Lears explained during an era of Anglo-American Protestant Revival, the purveyors' attitudes promoted a reassertion of self-control against threats posed to it by immigrant masses and mass-marketed temptations that included consumer products and moving pictures. The chief temptation was alcohol, dispensed in saloons that in the East were hotbeds of immigrant corruption and in the West were franchises operated by the major breweries.[37]

Xenophobic dimensions of Protestant revitalization became apparent. Prohibition was an appealing instrument of social control for respectable Anglo Saxons, North and South. Offended or frightened by the unseemly pleasures of the sporting crowd, Protestant moral reformers embraced Prohibition as a means of allaying racially inflected fears of social disorder (footloose free blacks, liquored-up Irishmen, beer-swilling Germans, and wine-guzzling Italians)—and keeping the unwashed classes sober, self-disciplined, and on time for work.[38]

America was about to enter a silent civil war. The nation's elites associated alcoholic beverages—often wine for the Italians, whiskey for the Irish, and beer for the Germans—with immigrants. Temperance societies moved forcefully to banish all alcoholic drinks. American women, especially, argued convincingly that alcohol destroyed families.

During the war, a bill moved through Congress for support of an eighteenth amendment to the Constitution that prohibited the manufacture, sale, or consumption of alcohol. By January 1919, thirteen months after the proposal, enough states ratified the bill to make Prohibition the law. Most of the affirmative states were in the American interior, away from the East Coast states with high concentrations of immigrants who drank sparingly, socially, or in excess. At the start of Prohibition, liquor consumption fell and arrests for drunkenness dropped. But time determined whether a ban on drinking was a practical, safe, and enforceable law.[39]

Anti-immigrant attitudes surfaced in other ways. January 1920 marked the season of the "Red Menace," warrantless raids on dozens of union halls and private residences that rounded up thousands of people. Those raids targeted Russians—some, but not all, communists. US attorney general A. Mitchell Palmer's sweeps amounted to psychological warfare with no war in sight.[40]

Then in April the robbery and fatal shooting near Boston of two male couriers with $15,000 in payroll funds resulted in the arrests of Italian immigrants Nicola Sacco and Bartolomeo Vanzetti. Witnesses said two of the five assailants "looked very Italian." Sacco and Vanzetti, both swarthy, fit the descriptions. The suspects reputedly had anarchistic leanings. Judge Webster Thayer reportedly called the immigrants "dagos" and "sons of bitches." The police investigation, based on both men's assumed guilt, was also flawed. High-standing American leaders deplored the trial conducted in the "red scare" atmosphere. Nevertheless, a jury convicted Sacco and Vanzetti of murder in 1921. They were imprisoned for six years and were executed in August 1927.[41] Legislative hostilities toward immigrants escalated soon after.

———— • ————

Celler's second child, Judith S. Celler, was born in 1921. Cerebral palsy incapacitated the infant. Doctors diagnosed baby Judith as a spastic paraplegic who could not move her legs or arms, but her brain function was normal,

Emanuel Celler wrote in his autobiography: "Nothing of the mind was affected, and her intelligence shone out of her eyes, set in a face that was as lovely as Jane's."[42] The parents resolved to do the best they could to care for their daughter and to ensure that Judith would eat, play, and talk with the entire family. Teachers and professors were brought to Judith. In a May 1962 letter to a high-ranking White House official, Celler wrote that Judith, thirty-five at that time, had the education equivalent of a master of arts and she was a devotee of opera and the arts. Celler's letter was intended to arrange a visit by Judith to the Kennedy White House. Previously, Judith had visited during the Coolidge, Roosevelt, and Truman administrations, Celler wrote.[43]

Shortly after Judith's birth, the Cellers moved north from their Caton Avenue apartment at the southern edge of Prospect Park to 303 McDonough Street off Lewis Avenue in Stuyvesant Heights. They lived in that brownstone for twenty-six years. Emanuel Celler's personal life and career blossomed during the Progressive and World War I eras. Shortly after the end of that "war to end all wars," Emanuel Celler launched his long career in politics.

In 1921, during the early months of the administration of President Warren Harding, Congress passed the Johnson Quota Act, which limited European immigration to 3 percent of the number of respective nationality groups that were in the United States in 1910.[44] In 1922, Congress followed up with the Cable Act that partially repealed the Expatriation Act of 1907. At that time, American women who married foreign nationals could lose their citizenship.

The revised act said American women who married Asians would lose their citizenship.[45] This law reflected the anti-immigrant, antiblack, isolationist "return to normalcy" that had been a cornerstone of Harding's campaign.

3

Elected to Congress, 1922–1923

By 1922, Emanuel Celler and many immigrants lived inside the Tenth Congressional District of Brooklyn. Republicans had controlled the seat for at least eight previous years. Lester D. Volk was the 1922 officeholder. In March 1920, he won a special election to replace Reuben Haskell, another Republican who resigned in order to become a Kings County judge. Haskell had served in Congress since 1914. Volk was reelected to the full two-year term in November 1920.[1] He was a physician and a former legislator in the New York State Assembly. Volk (1884–1962) was a first lieutenant in the US Army Medical Corps during World War I. As an energetic member of American Jewish War Veterans, he organized and led 82,000 veterans who marched in the 1920 New York Bonus Parade. Volk's feat earned him successive days of front-page coverage in the *New York Times*. That exposure apparently aided his election to Congress. Volk was among thirteen American Legion members elected to Congress.[2]

Volk self-identified as a staunch Republican, yet he behaved like a maverick. A decade earlier, voters had elected him to the state legislature as a National Progressive candidate because he supported Theodore Roosevelt's "Bull Moose" Party that split away from the GOP and unintentionally facilitated the 1912 election of Democrat Woodrow Wilson. During his single two-year term in the state legislature, Volk was appointed to a special commission to investigate police corruption in New York City. He declined to seek reelection in order to pursue what he described as medical, legal, and journalistic endeavors in Brooklyn.[3]

Volk criticized sloppy Prohibition enforcement. He described the Christmas night shooting death of Monk Eastman by Jeremiah "Jerry" Bohan, a Prohibition agency employee, as "a public scandal." Eastman was a reputed gangster who had reformed then served with distinction in World War I. New York governor Al Smith pardoned Eastman for his civilian indiscretions. However, during the predawn hours of December 26, 1921, Eastman and Bohan were drinking in a Manhattan saloon. The men got into an argument over how much to tip the server.

The argument—initiated by Eastman—continued outside and Bohan shot Eastman, then fled in a taxicab. The newspapers reported that Bohan—a former liquor dealer—was a Bureau of Prohibition agent, but in fact he was an administrative employee of the bureau.[4] Volk lambasted the operation of the bureau and called for an investigation.[5]

New Yorkers were among the most resistant Americans to the Eighteenth Amendment. Many of these residents challenged the federal government commitment to enforcing the law. New York City and state were the ultimate battlegrounds between pro-alcohol "wets" vs. "drys," the anti-alcohol forces and temperance societies. Two hundred agents policed the entire Empire State from the Canadian border north, and to the south the one-hundred-plus-mile Long Island coastline. Thousands of underground speakeasies opened as soon as drinking establishments shut down in compliance with the Eighteenth Amendment and the Volstead Act. One Virginia pastor called New York "Satan's seat" because so much booze purportedly fueled debauchery, mayhem, and routine defiance of federal law.[6]

———————————

As the midterm congressional elections approached, President Warren Harding was poised to take a beating. The political climate had changed from 1920 when Harding, the Republican, won the White House by 7 million votes. Harding was undistinguished yet likable, unlike Woodrow Wilson, who was intellectual and earnest but not very charismatic. Harding did not possess Wilson's moral compass. The president's direction either enabled corrupt behavior by his associates or provoked voter backlashes. Numerous historians have argued that Harding was not personally corrupt, but he cavorted too much with "the Ohio gang," his dishonest cronies inside the White House. Harding was aware of their shortcomings, but they were the people with whom he drank whiskey, smoked, and swapped jokes late into the night. These were not role models of temperance during Prohibition. "Trays with bottles containing every imaginable brand of whiskey" was what Alice Roosevelt Longworth, the former president's daughter and Washington social doyenne, encountered during one of the late-night card games.[7]

The ringleader of "the Ohio gang" was Harry Daugherty, Harding's appointee for attorney general. Daugherty interpreted Prohibition as a profit center, not a constitutional amendment to be enforced. He survived two indictments and congressional impeachment for allegedly defrauding the US government in disposing of alien property confiscated from German nationals.[8]

Brooklyn Democratic Party operatives Hymie Shorenstein and Aaron L. Jacoby approached Celler and encouraged him to challenge Volk in the November 1922 midterm election. They offered Celler the nomination because no other Democratic aspirant wanted it. To many insiders at that time, the Tenth District looked like a safe Republican seat.[9] Yet Volk was not anchored to the post. He had served only one full two-year term, plus the final few months of his GOP predecessor's term. Stella Celler did not want her husband to accept the challenge. They had two small girls, one of them severely physically disabled and in need of special attention. Furthermore, Emanuel Celler was busy with his law practice.[10] But at thirty-four, Celler took a calculated risk and ran for the seat.

In his 1953 autobiography, Celler portrayed himself as a major underdog. He may have embellished his chances with melodrama. The Tenth District was not an automatic Republican seat. Democratic Party representatives held the district for a dozen years before Reuben Haskell won the seat in 1914. One of those Democrats, William Sulzer, resigned to become governor of New York.[11] The *Brooklyn Eagle* newspaper projected that Harding and the Republicans were positioned for beatings at the polls. "GOP victories in west will not help Mr. Harding," read a November 2 front-page account. Two days later the *Eagle* announced, "Republican rallies in East New York apathetic." Part of the account read, "The campaign now at most apathetic in history; no real issues—no leaders."[12]

The newspaper's top political reporter was Henry W. Suydam, a former US State Department official who resigned to join the *Eagle* as a correspondent.[13] In the Sunday, November 22 *Brooklyn Eagle*, Suydam projected that seven New York City districts—including the Tenth that Celler coveted—were competitive and worrisome to the GOP, and that the only safe congressional district was the Sixth in Brooklyn.

Celler the novice was a spirited campaigner. At Sumner Hall, located at Fulton Street and Sumner Avenue, he addressed a predominantly African American audience and accused incumbent Lester Volk of "dragging the slime of politics as he plays it across the path of education." Celler produced a blotter he said Volk had distributed among schoolchildren living in the Tenth Congressional District. The blotter "carried an inscription purporting to be a lesson in civics by means of which Congressman Volk's name is made to appear prominently in connection with the names of the chief executives of the state and nation. . . . No man has the right to bring politics into the schoolroom. Furthermore, he has grossly misused the government franking privilege—Congressional mailings to constituents intended as 'official business'—by sending out recently a circular letter asking his constituents if they want seeds . . . Merely a trick to get his name before voters and it will cost you $15,000."[14]

The next day, Celler traveled to the Hall of Records at Fulton Street and Court Square to address the Society of Old Brooklynites, elders who included many Civil War Union veterans. The candidate referenced the 1861 draft riots: "That was a time when Brooklyn proved its levelheadedness and steadiness," Celler said. "Not only were there no draft riots in Brooklyn, but Brooklyn came to the aid of New York City, helping to quell riots there."[15]

Volk was a Prohibition foe because he did not believe the federal government had the resources to enforce the laws.[16] Challenger Celler, meanwhile, was not an enthusiast of Prohibition. His longtime family businesses after all, involved selling whiskey, bourbon, and wine. He criticized what he called "the evils of Prohibition," inept and at other times corrupt federal so-called enforcement that bred graft and violent crime alongside consumers' determination to drink wine, beer, and hard liquor. Celler surmised that Prohibition was futile. Volk and Celler were the leading competitors—but not the only ones—for the Tenth District seat. Three single-issue candidates also ran. One of them went after Celler, accusing him of drinking. "This man drinks," alleged the Temperance candidate. "He drinks and he has a way with women." The adversary's cheap shot was baseless and gained no traction. During the torch-lit rally, a man in the crowd yelled back, "That's wonderful. We won't have to break him in."[17] Celler recalled that it was not uncommon for an opponent to stand on one side of the street while he was on the other trying to out-shout the adversary.[18]

In his 1953 autobiography, Celler said he upset Volk by a margin of 3,111 votes. The election resulted in Celler coming in on top, 20,210 votes or 45.6 percent of the total; Volk, 17,099 votes (38.6 percent); Jerome T. De Hunt, Farmer-Labor candidate, 6,522 votes (14.7 percent); Bernard Cook, Prohibition candidate, 262 votes; and James P. Cannon, Workers candidate, 196 votes.[19] In addition to the newspaper, the *Brooklyn Eagle* provided the 1922 election night returns via a new medium, radio. On Wednesday, November 8, a three-line banner headline read, "GOP keeps slim grip on Congress, holds state senate by one vote; Harding silent on national defeat." The surprise of the midterm drubbing was US senator William Calder's defeat. The New Yorker was a Harding pal with eighteen years in the Senate. The Republicans lost thirteen New York House of Representatives seats in addition to the US senator.[20]

Celler arrived at Capitol Hill at a time of vicious anti-Semitism and a rising anti-immigrant movement. In September 1922 as Celler campaigned for office, Congress passed the Cable Act. This meant American women who married male foreign nationals would not lose their US citizenship. But, female foreign nationals who married American men did not automatically become American citizens.[21] In February 1923, a month after he took office, the US Supreme Court deemed East Indians ineligible for citizenship because federal law allowed only free whites to become naturalized citizens. In the case of *U.S. v. Bhagat Singh Thind*, the high court conceded that East Indians were Caucasians and that anthropologists considered the Asians to be of the same race as white Americans. Nevertheless, the majority opinion delivered by Associate Justice Alexander George Sutherland said that "the average man knows perfectly well that there are unmistakable and profound differences." The *Thind* decision resulted in successful efforts to denaturalize some people who had previously become citizens. Thind, a Sikh, World War I veteran, and University of California at Berkeley graduate, had been granted citizenship in Oregon. His case represented a particular threat in California, where a 1913 law prohibited aliens who were ineligible for citizenship from owning or leasing land.[22]

Celler's Jewish and Catholic parents came to America in the mid-1800s from Germany. A bigger wave of European Jews arrived in America during the last decades of the 1800s and the first decade of the new century. Most of those immigrants were keenly aware that it benefited them to discard their old-country ways and "Americanize." Some called their reengineering "purification." Scholar John Cuddihy explained that the Jewish immigrants who escaped the Russian pogroms arrived in the Anglo-American world of *goyim*, or "beyond the pale." After some years in America, urban Jews committed to a process of modernization, civilization, and assimilation.[23]

In Celler's home city of New York, Jewish immigrants-turned-citizens zealously practiced this cultural feat. Public education was their vehicle for advancement. New York required all children to attend school until at least age fourteen. A 1910 survey reported that more Jewish children continued studies past age sixteen than any other ethnic group. By 1916, Jewish students had become ubiquitous at the city's college campuses. They represented 44 percent of enrollment at Hunter College and 73 percent at City College. By 1920, Jews began flooding America's oldest college, Harvard University in Cambridge, Massachusetts, and the newcomers comprised one-fifth of the student body.

By 1923, the increasing presence of Jewish students in the Ivy League provoked a backlash. Harvard had traditionally enrolled children of Anglo-American elites who could settle for "gentleman's Cs." They and their parents wondered why the children of Jewish immigrants could study, compete, and achieve so relentlessly. Their A-efforts squeezed out the Anglo students who had previously felt entitled to attend.[24] Harvard president Abbott Lawrence Lowell said there was little anti-Semitic feeling among faculty. But because hostile feelings were growing across the country, the university chose to limit its Jewish American admission: "To receive just as many boys who come, or whose parents have come, to this country without the background as we can effectively educate; including in education the imparting, not only of book knowledge, but of ideas and traditions of our people. Experience seems to place that proportion at about 15 percent."[25]

Commentators took note. "As the Jewish population increases, animosity grows with it," said Abraham Cahan, author and editor of the *Jewish Daily Forward*, a Yiddish newspaper. "Nations love only themselves, not strangers. If we get too close to the Americans with our language and customs, they will be annoyed." In Middle America, Detroit car maker Henry Ford led an anti-Semitic campaign against "international Jews," alleging that their loyalties were not to America but to their own greedy interests. Jewish financiers, Ford claimed, were not building anything, while Jewish labor leaders organized unions in order to interrupt work.[26] Many Americans despised economically poor Eastern European Jews who came to America and after a generation became assets to their adopted country. The Anglo elite that included Harvard's president, Abbott Lawrence Lowell, observed Horace Kallen in 1923, "do not want Jews to be assimilated into undergraduate society. What troubles them is the completeness with which the Jews want to and have been assimilated." Second-generation Jews often faced discrimination when they sought white-collar employment. Classified advertisements sometimes specified interest in hiring "Christians only." Quality hospitals turned away Jewish doctors for internships.[27] That may partially explain why Celler's uncle Sam Grabfelder established hospitals in Denver and other cities. Anti-Jewish antagonism spread as that ethnic group escaped the lower Manhattan ghetto and narrowed the differences between themselves and Gentiles. In New York, Jews moved to the outer boroughs of Brooklyn and the Bronx, or uptown to Harlem, which originally was imagined as a suburb. Jews also fanned out to middle-class communities elsewhere in America where they often faced restrictive housing covenants.[28]

Celler was in office for seven months when President Warren G. Harding died on August 2, 1923. During the summer Harding had toured the West and Alaska, probably to get away from scandals linked to his "Ohio gang" cronies. Harding, fifty-seven, contracted pneumonia and appeared to recover, then died from an embolism.[29] Vice President Calvin Coolidge of Vermont succeeded Harding. Six months later on February 3, 1924, the twenty-eighth president, Woodrow Wilson, died.[30] The progressive Democrat had battled oligarchs and monopoly sympathizers in Congress and presided over America during World War I.

Post–World War I, President Wilson was in Paris, engaged in arduous negotiations for a lasting peace with European powers. The Treaty of Versailles, wrote Wilson biographer John Milton Cooper, "left sore winners and unrepentant losers." Congress did not support the treaty with enthusiasm. Sensing that, Wilson pressed on unilaterally. Because of the physical and emotional exertion involved, Wilson, sixty-two at the time, became gravely ill from a stroke in October 1919. He was barely able to function (although his close associates suppressed that reality). Wilson's wife functioned as surrogate president for a year.[31]

Wilson's stroke caused the worst crisis of presidential disability in American history. At that time, the Constitution was silent on orderly presidential succession if the elected president died or was physically incapable of serving. Decades later, Celler cowrote a constitutional amendment—the Twenty-Fifth—that established orderly presidential succession during a health crisis in the executive branch.

After the war, Wilson, sixty-seven, advocated a League of Nations even as Congress roundly rejected the idea. Wilson suffered a massive stroke while he was pressing for the League. There was evidence that he was not physically able to govern, so his wife did the work behind closed doors.

America was an Anglo-Saxon-ruled nation for the first two-thirds of its history. But from the 1880s to early twentieth century, most of its 40 million white immigrant arrivals—Jews, Italians, and Irish—came from places other than England and Germany. During that period, the Anglo ruling class embraced social Darwinism and eugenics, the idea of racial purity as a worthy societal goal. For example, Edward A. Ross, professor and author of *The Old World in*

the New, promoted in 1914 the myth of Nordic supremacy and the need to preserve Anglo-Saxon Americanism against "pollution" through immigration.[32]

Anti-Semitism dominated nativists' anti-immigration crusades. Congress
passed a new immigration law in 1921. Historian John Higham wrote that the
new law targeted a large influx of Jews—119,000 from Central and Eastern
Europe during 1920–21—whom lawmakers and government officials deemed
"abnormally twisted, unassimilable, filthy, un-American and often dangerous in their habits." Burton J. Hendrick, author of the 1923 book, *The Jews
in America*, concurred. The 1921 immigration law was "chiefly intended—it
is just as well to be frank about the matter—to restrict the entrance of Jews
from Eastern Europe."[33]

As some decision makers succeeded in keeping immigrants out, others
led assaults on the American-born children of immigrants. Henry Ford, mass
producer of automobiles, emerged as an American folk hero, even as a "paper
pogrom," his hysterical brand of anti-Semitism waged against Jews, represented his sinister side. Ford's instrument was his Detroit-area newspaper,
the *Dearborn Independent*, that volleyed charges of a Jewish conspiracy—by
bankers—to rule the world. Ford also targeted Bernard Baruch, an American
Jew who served as President Wilson's chief of the War Industries Board.
Ford's newspaper series, "The Scope of Jewish Dictatorship in the United
States," tagged Baruch as "the most powerful man in the world." It pejoratively
labeled him a "Jewish copper king," although the leading public servant had
no such mineral holdings.[34]

Elsewhere, Jewish American professionals who attempted to participate in
mainstream society were rigidly excluded from companies and businesses.
This exclusionary phenomenon occurred just as American society evolved
into a social structure that was increasingly urban and corporate. Sociolo-
gist E. Digby Baltzell wrote that social status became less a matter of family
standing in a community and more a matter of a person's affiliations in associations that carried prestige on a national scale.[35] Excluded Jewish American
professionals organized into associations within their ethnic group—that
is, the American Jewish Committee—and then endured Anglo ruling-class
criticism that they engaged in "insular behavior."

Other immigrants became targets of anti-immigrant backlash, even as the
working-class and working-poor Italians and Irish of the early 1920s did not
compete for the middle-class and elite education competitions in numbers
comparable to Jews.

Emanuel Celler lived in and served a section of Brooklyn teeming with
the immigrants and their American-born children, despised by the Anglo-
American rulers. A few Jewish American political pros encouraged Celler

to run for Congress, and the thirty-four-year-old lawyer followed their advice and succeeded.

As he prepared to split time between Washington, DC, and New York to represent constituents from the Tenth Congressional District of New York, the freshman congressman faced a blistering anti-immigration assault that would reshape the United States for the next half century.

4

Passion, Emotion, Fear, and Hate, 1924–1927

When newly elected Emanuel Celler arrived in Washington in March 1923, he was assigned to the congressional committees on accounts, claims, and civil service. He studied monopoly power, the issue that had consumed him since his schoolboy days.[1] Another Washington freshman from New York was Samuel Dickstein, a Democrat who represented predominantly Jewish, Irish, and Italian American lower Manhattan.[2] The demographics of their districts made these men natural allies. In a matter of months, the two would join forces for their first major legislative battle.

Like Celler, US senator David A. Reed, a Republican from Pennsylvania, was a congressional newcomer. He was appointed in 1922 to fill a seat vacated by the death of William E. Crow. Meanwhile, Representative Albert Johnson was a Republican who had represented the Northwest state of Washington since 1913. The experienced Republican congressman and the freshman GOP senator were co-architects of the 1924 Immigration Act that favored specific white people, based on so-called national origins.[3]

In 1921, Congressman Johnson took a preliminary step toward enacting this new policy. His Johnson Quota Act became law. It limited immigration to 350,000 people in 1921–1922 and imposed quotas of 3 percent of each nationality living in the United States in 1910. Immigrants from Canada, Mexico, and Caribbean Western Hemisphere countries were exempt. That act, author Deirdre Moloney wrote in 2012, was pivotal in establishing a restrictive national origins-based US immigration policy and framed debates over which newcomers should be allowed to live in the United States, and which of those were eligible for citizenship. The rationale for immigration control was also developed, wrote Moloney, whether that control was based on racial identity, gender, workforce imperatives, religious views, political and social beliefs, or activism.[4] Economic and political considerations factored into the passage of the 1921 Emergency Quota Act. In May 1922, Congress extended Johnson's quota law until 1924.[5]

That year, the Johnson-Reed immigration bill reduced the former quota percentage from 3 to 2 percent and changed the basis of the quota from the year 1910 to 1890. The largest quota was assigned to Great Britain, Germany, and Ireland, with Scandinavian and other Northern European countries receiving smaller, but still, significant quotas.[6] A ban on immigration among Asians, particularly Chinese, from the so-called Asia-Pacific Triangle—a precedent since 1882—continued. Photographic identification as a means of immigration control was introduced in order to screen the Chinese. Ironically the ban on Chinese laborers increased the value of Mexican immigrants (who at that time were counted as "white" in the Census) in the Southwest.[7] Immigration from Africa to the United States was out of the question.

In large part, a determination to exclude the Jews inspired the 1924 immigration legislation.[8] Many, but not all, came from Eastern European countries—including Poland and Russia—that Anglo-Americans now deemed undesirable. At the same time, settled Jewish Americans were punished for assimilating and then competing with Anglo-Americans for places in elite universities and white-collar professions. Polite American society rejected Italians, particularly the swarthy souls from Sicily, as violent, politically radical, and exotic.[9]

The Immigration Act of 1924 reflected a mixture of passion and emotion, fear and hate, tempered by idealism and vision: Americans had become afraid of foreigners. The nativists distrusted and hated them.[10] The temper of Congress echoed the temper of the country, Celler wrote in his autobiography.[11] Most Americans in the 1920s contended that allowing so much immigration in earlier decades was highly undesirable, that the United States was a white or Anglo-Saxon nation, and that the socioeconomic and cultural contributions of other immigrant and nonwhite groups were either invalid or insignificant.

Eugenics and "scientific" measuring of American demographics and ethnic and racial heritage profoundly influenced the creation of the Johnson-Reed Act.[12] Madison Grant was the author of the Nordic superior race theory. His 1916 book *The Passing of the Great Race* influenced Albert Johnson and other leaders.

Over the years Grant lobbied the Immigration Restriction League, applied his thesis as propaganda for the American Defense Society, the work of the Eugenics Research Association and the American Eugenics Society (formerly known as ECUSA), the sessions of the International Eugenics Congress, and the manipulation of data in *A Study of American Intelligence*. All that had ensured that scientific racism was part of the atmosphere in which Americans moved in 1924.[13]

A congressional committee invited Grant to testify about immigration restrictions. But arthritis confined the fifty-eight-year-old to his bed. In a testament to the power of malevolent ideas, Grant's physical presence was not really required on Capitol Hill in 1924. He had already done his part.[14]

While economic and political considerations had factored heavily in the passage of the 1921 Emergency Quota Act, the debate in 1924 was, as cultural anthropologist Franz Boas admitted, primarily about "the idea of the racial superiority of the 'Nordic.'" Madison Grant owned the patent to that idea.

Hearings on the Johnson bill concluded. The House Immigration Committee by an overwhelming majority reported the measure favorably on March 24, 1924, by a vote of 15–2. The two Jewish members, Samuel Dickstein and Adolph J. Sabath, cast dissenting votes. They charged in their minority report that the bill was "a palpable injustice" based on an anthropological theory that was, in fact, "pure fiction."[15] The attacks on Grant carried over into the floor debate, where Dickstein and Sabath were joined by a small group of young, urban Jewish representatives, Celler, Meyer Jacobstein, and Nathan Perlman; also Catholics, William Patrick Connery Jr., James Gallivan, Charles Anthony Mooney, John Joseph O'Connor, Patrick O'Sullivan, and Peter Francis Tague, and Fiorello La Guardia, who was of dual heritage.[16]

Grant was the chief ideologist of the immigration restriction forces. His opponent was Franz Boas, a German-born anthropologist and professor at Columbia University. Boas was a cultural relativist who debunked theories that Western civilization was superior to others based on racial criteria. He was author of the 1911 book, *The Mind of Primitive Man*, a series of lectures on culture and race. Boas took an active role in advising the anti-immigration restrictions bloc.[17]

"My first bitter shock came with the first really big debate on the floor of the House in which I participated," Celler wrote in his autobiography. "The debate was long, passionate and bitter. I believe that not in the three decades I have been in Congress," Celler recalled in 1953, "have I heard such venom spilled on the floor of the House."[18]

One representative rose to say, "We have admitted the dregs of Europe until America has been Orientalized, Europeanized, Africanized, and mongrelized so that insidious degree that our genius, stability, greatness and promise of advancement and achievements are actually menaced."

Another congressman rose to proclaim with great vehemence, "The hour has come. It may be even now too late for the white race in America, the English-speaking people, the laborer of high ideals, to assert his superiority in the work of civilization and to save America from the menace of a further immigration of undesirable aliens. I wish it were possible to close our gates against any quota from southern Europe or from the Orientals, the Mongolian countries and the yellow races of men."

Members of the New York congressional delegation—Celler, Dickstein, Fiorello LaGuardia, Meyer Jacobstein—and some other House members rose to vigorously challenge the angry majority.[19] The waves of hate grew higher and bolder, said Celler. "Will the gentleman yield?" the Brooklyn congressman pleaded again and again. The hatemongers ignored him. When Celler got up to speak, he felt verbally outgunned, yet he used every rhetorical device at his command. He displayed color-coded charts in an attempt to show America's strength in terms of ethnically diverse population, and how the periods of greatest immigration coincided with America's greatest economic development. "Let us at least be truthful," said Celler. "In fact, deception is futile. It is as clear as the sun that the majority of the Immigration Committee and most proponents of this measure like the gentleman from Kansas [Jasper N. Tincher], who blurted out his true feelings while taking on the bill, do not want 'wops,' 'dagoes,' 'Hebrews,' 'hunkies,' 'bulls,' and others known by similar epithets.[20] Just so, in 1840, 1850 and 1860 you did not want the 'beery Germans' and 'dirty Irish.' The Germans and Irish were mongrels, self-seekers, disreputable, and would not assimilate. We know now how good a citizenry they have become."[21] The immigrant Slavs, Poles, and Italians who Celler knew were courageous people who had left the security of the past and journeyed to America with hope for themselves and their children and worked to make America richer by creating new industries and new jobs. For example, the Kwolek family emigrated to America from Poland in the early 1900s. Celler did not know this family; however, a 2014 obituary proved the point the congressman made ninety years ago: Their daughter Stephanie, born in western Pennsylvania in 1923, grew up to become the DuPont Company chemist who invented Kevlar, the revolutionary fiber that fortified bulletproof vests.[22] These despised immigrants and their American-born offspring brought their diverse cultures that made the American bloodstream flow with greater vigor in the arts, sciences, and craft skills. These immigrants were not the "bolshevists" vilified by most members of Congress.[23]

Celler ally Jacobstein of Rochester, New York, challenged the discriminatory, eugenicist theories of the immigration reform advocates. "Nothing is
more un-American," said this son of Polish Jewish immigrants. "Nothing
could be more dangerous. In a land the Constitution of which says that all
men are created equal, than to write into our law a theory which puts one race
above another, which stamps one group of people as superior and another
inferior. The fact that it is camouflaged in a maze of statistics will not protect
this nation from the evil consequences of such an unscientific, un-American
and wicked philosophy."[24]

Emanuel Celler was among the few opponents of the bill, and the freshman representative delivered his first major speech on the floor of the House
against the measure.[25] In his 1953 autobiography, Celler explained why the
immigrant community he grew up in and later served shaped his views on
immigration, civil rights, and American-style equal opportunity:

> There were men older than I in Congress, men of more experience, of more
> learning. Yet the talk of the strength of America, her self-sufficiency, the prof-
> its and the prices did not fit into the picture I knew. I knew the women in the
> Brooklyn tenements who scrubbed their floors again and again in the helpless
> fight against squalor. I knew the timid, perplexed son of the immigrant—part
> of him in the old world, part of him in the new—serious and hungry, filling
> the free schools and the free colleges of New York. I knew the Negro, kept
> down in poverty and degradation.
>
> The folklore of Poland, of Lithuania, or Russia, or Italy became part of my
> folklore because I heard it so often. I knew their richness and their laughter
> and their disappointing heartbreak of the struggle in America to adjust. I
> knew also, their pride, the unfulfilled dream of independence that had first
> brought them here.[26]

Emanuel Celler emerged as Grant's chief critic during the floor debate.
Physically frail Grant was not present, so opponents confronted his ideas in
absentia. Celler, who consulted with Boas, despaired that, "We have grown
accustomed to hear a great deal of loose thinking, senseless jargon and a
pompous jumble concerning Nordic superiority." Celler boldly named the
focus of his contempt: "The fallacy of Nordic supremacy was made popular
by one, Madison Grant, who wrote a book called *The Passing of the Great
Race*. This book had a great vogue, and correspondingly it has created a
great mischief. The opinions expressed in his book are most dangerous. The
opinions are rendered more dangerous because they come from a man who
has contributed a great deal that was good to the subject of zoology."[27]

Celler charged that *The Passing of the Great Race* was "about as fine an example of dogmatic piffle as have ever been written," and he denounced the "Nordic myth" as being "outrageously absurd." He lamented that Albert Johnson and the House immigration committee had fallen under Grant's conjurations, and suggested that the committee should have heard from a serious scientist like Franz Boas, "But, no; the committee only wanted those who believed in 'Nordic' superiority; men who deal in buncombe, like Grant and [Lothrop] Stoddard [author of *The Rising Tide of Color against White World Supremacy*]." Celler then attempted to offset Grant's influence by reading to the House excerpts from Boas's *Mind of Primitive Man*.[28] Despite such spirited, sarcastic dissent from Celler and his colleagues, the anti-immigration bill passed the House 323–71 on April 12, and then the Senate by 62–6 on April 18 under the leadership of cosponsor US representative David Reed, R-Pennsylvania. Less than a month later, the Johnson-Reed bill sailed through the House 308–69 and, on the same day, by 69–9 in the Senate. President Coolidge signed the bill into law May 26.

Before signing, the president declined to meet with Northeast immigrant leaders who pleaded for a veto. Forty-one years after US-born poet Emma Lazarus (1849–1887) invited Europe to send its huddled masses to America, America withdrew its invitation to most of them.[29]

The Johnson-Reed immigration restriction law established racial and ethnic criteria for entering the United States. It privileged specific nationalities, scorned others, and based each nationality quota upon "the whole white population of the United States, with due regards to the national origin of that population."[30] Also for the first time, would-be immigrants were required to obtain visas issued by US State Department consulates in their home countries—and to document their identities with photographs.

Within four years, the United States shifted from a system of open immigration that placed the burden of proof for exclusion on federal government inspections at Ellis Island in New York Harbor. Aliens had to prove their desirability to the consular officer in their home country before being granted a visa that allowed them to enter the United States.[31] Non-US North Americans—Canadians, Mexicans, and Caribbean people—were exempt from the new restrictions.

———————•———————

When President Coolidge signed the Johnson-Reed Immigration Restriction Act in spring 1924, he was a caretaker president, filling what was left of the late Warren Harding's term. In the following November's presidential election, Coolidge won the popular vote by 54 to 29 percent and handily won the electoral college 382 to 136. His main challenger was Democrat John W. Davis of West Virginia. Third-party Progressive candidate Robert La Follette of Wisconsin took a respectable 17 percent of American's popular votes, plus 13 electoral college votes.[32] Coolidge's agenda was reducing income taxes, restoring relations with Mexico, and paring down the burgeoning power of the presidency. The Yankee from Vermont (who lived in Massachusetts while president and previously was governor) was unassuming, wry, and taciturn. His demeanor endeared him to many voters.[33]

On Coolidge's watch the Ku Klux Klan hit its apex, after reemerging during the Wilson years and then expanding during the Harding years. Twenty-first-century scholars such as Nancy MacLean caution that the Klan of the 1920s numbered as many as 5 million members and it would be unwise to dismiss these white men as deranged outcasts of popular imagination. Klan members were drawn from the broad middle of America's class structure and mobilized support through campaigns waged on the prosaic theme of upholding community moral standards.[34]

A year after the Johnson-Reed Act became law, the anti-Catholic, anti-Semitic, and anti-immigrant American majority attitude emboldened a march of thousands of hooded Ku Klux Klan members in Washington, DC, on August 8, 1925. The Klan had been nearly dormant by 1915 but William Joseph Simmons, a Georgia man, inspired by the popular movie *Birth of a Nation*, revived the withering society.

Estimated national membership in the secret society ranged from 3 to 8 million whites. Middle-class doctors, lawyers, and ministers donned Klan robes. The second incarnation of the Klan expanded hatred beyond black Americans to non-Protestants, foreigners, and urbanites. These hooded domestic terrorists spread their affiliates from the southern states into Indiana, Ohio, Pennsylvania, and elsewhere.[35]

Despite the isolationist and xenophobic American temper, on January 27, 1926, the US Senate adopted a resolution that permitted the United States to join the World Court of International Justice. The body was to gain jurisdiction over all international problems brought before it by member nations. The Senate resolution contained a handful of exceptions and for the next decade the United States took part in international conferences and deliberations but did not become a permanent member of the World Court or League of Nations.[36]

In 1927, Emanuel Celler traveled to Paris as a delegate to the Interparliamentary Union Conference, a conclave of members of parliaments, or in America's case, members of Congress. Celler glimpsed the concept of one-world cooperation. Two years after his overseas trip he introduced a bill calling for a United States Peace College that could train young Americans for diplomatic posts.[37] "In 1927, for the first time, I traveled through Europe, bringing with me, quite naturally, the American standard of material well being," Celler wrote in his autobiography. "I observed what every American traveler, naïve and otherwise, took pride in remarking—the differences between European and American tools of living. Making that observation and letting it go at that was not enough. There must be a reason for this difference, for this concentrated wealth in the hands of a few and the grim daily struggle for bread for the majority of the people.

"I remember talking to Tomas Masaryk when I was in Czechoslovakia. We talked in his high, wide study lined with books. There were books everywhere. As I walked in, I caught glimpse of the other rooms and every room was over laden with books. His study was the room of a man searching in the books of history, political science, economics and in poetry for the answers for his people, so that political and social democracy could mark the progress of the new Republic of Czechoslovakia. He was a man consumed by hunger. If that economic pattern, he told me, of the much for the few and the little for the many could be broken, then that could be the beginning of a new era of hope."[38]

When Celler returned to Washington, he once again studied the growth of monopoly power in America. In 1926, during his second term, Celler introduced House Resolution 73 that called for the investigation of American Telephone and Telegraph Company, a rare government-approved and -regulated monopoly.[39] The year after that, in 1927–28, Celler introduced a bill to prevent obstruction and burdens upon interstate trade and commerce in copyrighted motion picture films in the young, rapidly expanding Hollywood.[40] At that time, Hollywood achieved a technological breakthrough with the first feature-length talking film: *The Jazz Singer*. It starred Lithuanian-born immigrant Asa Yoelson, who Americanized his persona and became Al Jolson.[41] With burnt cork Jolson blackened his face—as minstrel entertainers had for decades—to caricature Negroes' enticing yet forbidden music, blues and jazz, while at the same time masking his true ethnicity from the hostile Anglo-American ruling class. Thirty years after his election to Congress, Emanuel Celler, sixty-five, wrote that he believed he was a timid legislator during his first decade in Congress.[42]

In 1970 at age eighty-two, Celler revised that self-evaluation. He told interviewer Lawrence Rubin that he'd been a gadfly at the start of his legislative career: "I would attack attitudes sponsored by the majority, like, for example, immigration. When I first entered Congress, the prevailing spirit was strict immigration, based on racial lines, and I opposed that."[43]

Celler was true to his ethnic immigrant constituents in New York—and to his principles. Although their elders expected freshmen members of Congress to be seen and not heard, Celler refused to sit quietly and accept a fear- and hate-inspired anti-immigration law that could pass unchallenged. He emerged as the lead inquisitor of the urban caucus that opposed the Johnson-Reed Act.

Celler and company lost that major battle. The congressman did not give up the fight. He dug in for what would become a four-decade struggle to get the law overturned.

5

Celler Asserts Self, Chips at Immigration, 1930s

Emanuel Celler played a key legislative role in establishing the "Star-Spangled Banner" as America's national anthem. Lawyer Francis Scott Key wrote the poem in 1814 while detained on a British warship during the bombardment of Fort McHenry in Baltimore during the War of 1812. After the bombing subsided, the forty-two-by-thirty-foot US flag was still flying. Key recommended that his poem be sung to the tune of a popular British drinking song "To Anacreon in Heaven."[1]

Fifty years later during the Civil War, Key's lyrics emerged as one of America's favorite patriotic songs. By the early 1900s, "The Star-Spangled Banner" had become an official song of the US military, but not the national anthem. When Robert L. Ripley of *Ripley's Believe It or Not* reported that fact in a November 3, 1929, syndicated cartoon, that newspaper feature shocked 5 million Americans into writing letters to Congress demanding that Key's verse become official.[2]

On January 31, 1930, Representative Leonidas C. Dyer, R-Missouri, convened a subcommittee of the Committee on the Judiciary. Celler was among its twenty-three members. Representative John Charles Linthicum, whose Baltimore congressional district included Fort McHenry, and other witnesses presented testimony urging that the bill be approved to establish a national anthem. The bill included a House Resolution, written by Celler: "A bill to make The Star-Spangled Banner the national anthem of the United States of America, be it enacted by the Senate and House of Representatives of the United States of America in Congress assembled, That the poem written by Francis Scott Key entitled 'The Star-Spangled Banner,' with music by John Stafford Smith, be, and the same is hereby, declared to be the national anthem of the United States of America and under its care and protection."[3]

The House approved the bill on April 21, and the Senate followed suit nearly a year later on March 3, 1931. That day President Hoover signed the legislation and made it law.[4]

Emanuel Celler in 1928 formed the Brooklyn National Bank and was its chairman of the board. Brooklyn National was an independent banking institution with a $2 ½ million capital surplus.[5] At that time Celler was intensely interested in serving the interests of consumers and small business merchants who felt oppressed by monopoly corporate power.

That year, twenty-five hundred formerly independent manufacturing and mining companies disappeared as a result of mergers and acquisitions. Nonbank companies owned 48 percent of US assets. Back in 1909, Louis Brandeis warned that two hundred nonbank companies owned 33 percent of the country's assets.[6] Brooklyn National Bank became a site that printed money. Over a four-year period, it issued $1.5 million in six denominations.[7] Celler's interest in banking complemented his congressional service on the committees on Accounts, Claims and Civil Service during the 1920s.[8]

Celler also monitored foreign loans by US bankers as the country entered its next decade. Celler questioned the appropriateness of American banks loaning $60 million to Romania while overlooking that country's oppressive treatment of its ethnic minorities. Secretary of State Frank B. Kellogg in April 1928 objected to the wording of Celler's resolution and also said the federal government had never attempted to dictate the way another government should formulate its policies toward minorities.[9]

At that time in 1928 the Empire State's leading politician was Irish Catholic governor Alfred E. "Al" Smith. Voters elected the progressive reformer known as the "happy warrior" governor of New York in 1918, then swept him out of office during the Republican surge of 1920. They then returned him to office in 1922, and he stayed there for most of the Roaring Twenties. At the June 1928 Democratic National Convention in Houston, delegates nominated Smith to run for president of the United States.[10] The candidate's religion and ethnicity would dog his presidential campaign. When asked in a 1927 open letter from attorney Charles C. Marshall where his loyalties would lie if there were a conflict between the United States and the Vatican, Smith answered in the *Atlantic Monthly*, "I recognize no power in the institution of my Church to interfere with the operations of the Constitution of the United States or the enforcement of the law of the land."[11]

Where Marshall was skeptical, leading Al Smith critic Bishop James Cannon Jr. was incendiary. A Virginia political boss and a Methodist, Cannon attacked the governor from the South and flooded the region with tracts and pamphlets that falsely accused Prohibition-foe Smith of aspiring to be "the cocktail president." Cannon denounced the leaders of Catholicism as "the Mothers of ignorance, superstition, intolerance and sin," and dismissed Smith's ardent supporters as the "kind of dirty people that you find today on the sidewalks of New York."[12]

On Election Day, November 6, 1928, California Republican Herbert Hoover crushed Al Smith 444–87 in the electoral college.[13] The popular vote was closer. Of 36.4 million votes cast, Hoover won 59 to 41 percent. In New York State, Al Smith's successor as governor was Franklin Delano Roosevelt, a distant relative of Teddy Roosevelt. In a few years FDR would break a twelve-year Republican Party lock on the White House.

President Hoover became commander-in-chief as revolutionary developments in transportation defined the late Roaring Twenties. Charles Lindbergh in 1927 piloted the first trans-Atlantic airplane flight. One year after Lindberg's solo trip from New York to France, Amelia Earhart flew a trans-Atlantic journey from America with several passengers.[14] Commercial airline flight soon joined ship and rail as modes of passenger travel. At the end of the decade the first electric passenger train—invented by Thomas Edison—rolled on tracks in New Jersey. Mass-produced automobiles had been an established American staple for two decades. Henry Ford sold 15 million Model T cars by 1927 and competitors General Motors and Chrysler offered alternatives. When Emanuel Celler was a college student in 1908 there were a mere 500,000 vehicles in circulation. By the end of 1929, exported automobiles exceeded cotton as a leading US commodity. Half of northern American families owned vehicles. Automobile ownership cut across class and racial barriers. Cars liberated farmers from their land. Affordable, accessible automobiles were credited with expanding the American middle class.[15] Hoover's memorable presidential campaign slogan was "A chicken in every pot and a car in every garage."

The end of the 1920s acknowledged that Prohibition was a decade-old policy mess. Federal enforcement was weak, undermanned, and at times lethally inept. While people distilled "white lightning" and moonshine in backwoods counties, "rum runner" boats pierced gossamer-thin three-mile territorial Atlantic and Caribbean offshore barriers and delivered barrels of liquor. More booze rolled from the north over the Canadian border. In April 1929, a US Coast Guard cutter sank the ship *I'm Alone*, two hundred miles offshore in the Gulf of Mexico on suspicion that the vessel was an illicit rum runner. The ship turned out to be of Canadian registry, which resulted in a vigorous protest from that country's government.[16]

About one hundred days into Hoover's presidency, signs of a financial collapse began to surface. Farmers were becoming desperate for financial relief. By June, Congress passed an Agriculture Marketing Act and established a Federal Farm Board that included a fund to aid farmers' cooperatives and sell surplus produce at stable prices.[17]

Industrially, steel and automobile production declined, yet stock market prices continued to climb. By September, prices climaxed at a three-year bull market high.[18] By October 23 there were signs of panic at the New York Stock Exchange because of steadily declining market prices. By mid-November $30 billion in value of listed stocks were wiped off the New York Stock Exchange. Some traders who watched their paper fortunes vanish killed themselves. Working-class people endured depressed wages, unemployment, and a Great Depression. By January 1930, unemployment doubled compared to 1928 and reached 4 million people, or 8.7 percent of the eligible adult working population.[19]

America was conflicted. The overall mood was isolationist and xenophobic, yet its officials were participating in international organizations and activities. During the final weeks of the Coolidge presidency, the United States was represented at the International Conference on Economic Statistics of the League of Nations, the Pan-American Conference on Conciliation and Arbitration, and the International Civil Aeronautics Conference—the latter two events hosted in Washington.[20]

Celler and like-minded colleagues chipped at the wall in search of openings and small concessions in the existing American immigration law. It irked US representative Samuel Dickstein, D-New York, that the generous German quota of approximately 50,000 visa slots per year was never filled during the 1930s. The restrictive policies of the National Origins Act strained US relations with some European countries.[21] In 1931, Celler was the successful author of a bill that extended non-quota status to parents over age fifty-five and husbands of US citizens who had been married between June 1, 1928, and July 1, 1931. Hoover signed the bill into law in July 1932.[22]

The other Hoover in Washington, J. Edgar Hoover, director of the FBI, was coping with early 1930s Depression-era lawlessness. The economic collapse meant numbing inactivity for many people but reckless criminal behavior by others. Although many Americans did not openly blame immigrants for the crime wave, a la Sacco and Vanzetti in the 1920s, the presence of some hyphenated Americans at communist and socialist political activities at times labeled immigrants as undesirables. Prohibition on alcohol also fueled lawlessness. J. Edgar Hoover hired a famous Washington newsman—Henry Suydam of the *Brooklyn Eagle*—to teach him about public relations and image making. Within a year Hoover had learned these media tactics so well he was able to dismiss Suydam and promote the bureau himself.[23]

Celler's contribution to law enforcement in 1931 and 1932 was his work to strengthen the Federal Trade Commission, originally known as the Bureau of Corporations, established in February 1903. "Protecting America's Consumers" was the agency's motto.[24]

———————•———————

The Great Depression deepened during the Hoover presidency. Financial misery rolled from Wall Street to Main Street. Unemployment approached 4 million Americans in January 1930, 4.5 million in October, and nearly 5 million by January 1931.[25] Congress may have aggravated the Depression when it passed the Smoot-Hawley Tariff bill that raised prices on imported items and threatened international trade. Smoot-Hawley was consistent with America's isolationist mood. Hoover signed the tariff act into law in June 1930. More than one thousand prominent economists who in a petition declared the act was a bad idea could not dissuade the president.[26]

Celler said the financial panic loosened his inhibitions against being different: "What I had known, what I had seen, in Brownsville, in Pitcarn Avenue, Brooklyn, in the Bushwick section of that borough, in the Park Places of Brooklyn, the markets of Brooklyn, had now become the generalized, commonplace experience of the whole nation."[27] Difficult economic times emboldened Celler to speak passionately about issues he cared about: inequitable immigration laws, civil rights and judicial reform, and economic freedom, specifically antitrusts. "These all have," said Celler decades later, "a common theme—the equality of opportunity for all people without regard to race, color, religion or national origin. Equality of opportunity, I realized, means independence in the fullest sense."[28]

Hoover succeeded in securing moratoriums on debts, and Congress in December 1930 appropriated $116 million in public works projects in order to stanch unemployment. By spring, the 102-story Empire State Building was dedicated. It would remain the world's tallest building for four decades.[29]

The Depression nevertheless tightened its grip. By fall 1931, more than eight hundred banks closed as Americans withdrew cash from banks and hoarded gold. Among the bank failures was the Bank of the United States, which was New York–based and privately held. In December 1930, of its 450,000 depositors, 400,000 were impoverished Jewish immigrants who lost all their savings, on average of $400 each.

In New York State, Governor Roosevelt responded to Depression challenges with programs, such as unemployment insurance, old-age pensions, and child labor laws.[30] At the Democratic Party convention at the end of June, delegates deadlocked between candidates FDR, John Nance Garner of Texas, and failed 1928 nominee Al Smith. Roosevelt won the nomination after the fourth ballot when Garner surrendered his delegates and in return accepted the vice-presidential nomination. Earlier that month the GOP convention endorsed President Hoover for reelection.[31]

In the summer months before the fall election Hoover with Congress tried to ease the economic pain. The president signed a $3 billion Relief and Reconstruction Act that channeled money toward state and local agencies for public works and relief. Congress adopted the Federal Home Loan Bank Act that authorized a dozen regional banks to provide discounted loans that would lower mortgages and stimulate home construction.

Still under the watch of a man largely credited with saving post–World War I Europe from starving, economic conditions worsened for working- and middle-class America. By 1932 the unemployment rate zoomed to 23.6 percent compared to 8.7 percent in 1930. Since the '29 crash, stock prices had plummeted 85 percent, automobile production operated at 20 percent of capacity, and steel at 12 percent capacity. An advertisement that sought 750 men to dig a canal in Birmingham, Alabama, attracted 12,000 applicants.[32]

—————— · ——————

On Election Day, November 8, Roosevelt beat Hoover 59 to 41 percent out of 38.6 million votes cast. The electoral college vote was an FDR rout, 472–59.[33] Roosevelt the aristocrat exuded confidence and the voters signaled they wanted a bold change.

"In March of 1933 we witnessed a revolution in manner, in mores, in the definition of government," said Celler of Roosevelt assuming the presidency. "What before had been black or white sprang alive with color."[34]

Among the revolutionary changes was the arrival of Frances Perkins, the first woman Cabinet secretary (Labor) in US history. She was the New York State industrial commissioner in Roosevelt's administration. By the end of the New Deal, Perkins's ambitious progressive agenda—minimum wage, maximum hours, child labor ban, public works, federal relief—became law at the federal level.[35] Not-so-revolutionary changes improved Americans' morale. Just days into the job, FDR sent a three-sentence message to Congress encouraging the legislators to amend Prohibition's Volstead Act and allow consumption of beer. The Senate cooperated, and the president signed the bill.[36]

The year 1933 marked a decade of congressional service in which Celler shed the self-doubt of his early years in Washington. He had come to care passionately about independence for India, after in 1933, Mahatma Gandhi was imprisoned for acts of civil disobedience toward the British colony. Gandhi engaged in weeks-long hunger strikes and granted interviews to international journalists that advocated Indian freedom and self-determination. That example and rhetoric influenced Celler, "who sought integrity for every living entity," the congressman wrote in his autobiography: "The large words, Justice, Peace, Plenty, Freedom—words which have many meanings as those who speak them wish to give—meant to him the eyes and souls and the bellies of every living human being."[37]

One incremental change in India's region, Asia, was the 1934 Tydings-McDuffie Act that provided a framework for the US territory the Philippines to become independent by 1946. The act's advocates were strange bedfellows, white nativists who were racially hostile to Filipinos working on the US mainland, and Filipino nationals fed up with their abusive colonizers and eager for self-determination on their island. Tydings-McDuffie stripped Filipinos of their status as US nationals and severely restricted their immigration to this country by establishing an annual quota of fifty.[38] Celler's copious papers did not suggest any engagement in the Philippines issue.

The congressman from Brooklyn also expressed concerns about the condition of Negro citizens. When A. Philip Randolph, leader of the all-black Brotherhood of Sleeping Car Porters union, wanted Congress to undertake a study of racial issues, he brought the proposal to Celler for introduction. Also, Celler promised to introduce a bill to award a congressional medal for bravery to Matthew Henson, the African American who accompanied Admiral Robert E. Peary to find a passage to the North Pole. Celler promised to introduce a second bill in order for Henson to retire from his job as messenger at the Custom House in New York and receive an annual pension (equivalent to $40,209 in 2016 dollars). Celler cited Peary's praise of Henson as proof of his devotion and heroism on Peary's expeditions. Celler's advocacy raised awareness and Henson (1866–1955), who lived most of his life in obscurity, was recognized later in his lifetime.

At age seventy-one, Henson in 1937 became the first African American voted into the Explorers Club of New York. In 1945 he received the Navy Medal, and in 1954 Henson received public recognition by President Eisenhower at the White House, about a year before Henson's death at age eighty-eight.[39]

An average of fifty African Americans per year were reported as having been lynched, mostly in the South.[40] "The lynching of three Negroes, one of them a woman, by a mob in Aiken, S.C., calls for condign punishment and revives the desire for an anti-lynching law," wrote Celler in a letter to the *New York Times*. "Among other things it is suggested that all self-respecting Americans refuse to stop at Aiken as a winter resort. Aiken people have forfeited all rights to patronage and should be treated as pariahs by the rest of the country until the wrong is expiated."[41] In 1936, a flag flew from NAACP headquarters in New York that read "A man was lynched today."

Jazz singer Billie Holiday's 1939 song "Strange Fruit" was a ballad about lynching.[42] Unlike the very early 1900s when lynchings were public spectacles celebrated with photo postcards and cruel mockery of Negro victims ("Please do not wake" read a sign placed in front of a black man hanging in a town square in Georgia) during the 1930s, an antilynching movement gained momentum.[43]

Black-owned publications reporting on lynching fueled that protest movement. When mainstream press such as *Time* and *Life* magazines dived in, they portrayed the phenomenon as socially unacceptable behavior. Hollywood weighed in too with movies such as *Fury* (1936), about a wrongly accused prisoner who barely survived a lynch mob attack.[44] The spotlight of publicity placed southern elites on the defensive—not least because their valued Negro labor was fleeing domestic terrorism. Northern liberal whites, including elected representatives such as Celler, decried the immorality of lynching. Celler acted legislatively to end the practice—he wrote a few of the two hundred bills submitted in the 1900s—but his was a minority voice among scores of pro-lynching white southerners. Three bills made it to a vote of the Congress. All were defeated.[45]

Lynching was a primary reason blacks moved northward. Starting in World War I, black migration within the US mainland became a steady stream from the agrarian South to three regions: from the Mississippi Delta and Alabama to Midwest cities Chicago, Detroit, and Milwaukee; from the Carolinas and Virginia to New York, Boston, Philadelphia, and Washington, DC; and from Louisiana and Texas to Oakland and Los Angeles. From 1915 to 1970, six million blacks fled the South and culturally changed the American landscape.[46]

The Depression did not deter black movement. Like refugees, families and individuals fled violent oppression and searched for work instead of sharecropping. The 1930 census indicated a Negro population of 9.7 percent, the lowest share ever recorded in US history. Restrictive overseas immigration ended the percentage decline of African American population. Even when the federal government reformed immigration policies thirty years later, the black population trended upward each decade, beginning in 1940.[47]

Democracy was turning inside out around the world. In December 1933, Congress and President Roosevelt repealed Prohibition, the former Eighteenth Amendment, by adopting the Twenty-First Amendment to the Constitution and ended a failed fourteen-year attempt to squelch alcohol consumption.[48] At that time Americans continued to wrestle the relentless Great Depression. Unemployment in 1934 stood at 21.7 percent. Meanwhile, economic pain spread around the globe.

That should have signaled a life-or-death challenge to America, although many of its citizens were not aware of it at the time. In Germany, Adolf Hitler of the National Socialist German Workers Party (aka Nazi) in March 1933 was named chancellor by President Paul von Hindenburg. Hitler's rise to power began in 1919, from the ashes of Germany's humiliating World War I defeat. His minority Nazi party grew, then dominated, because of miscalculations by bigger political parties, and backroom deals that went awry. A Hitler political rival, who agreed to support his chancellorship if named second in command, wrongly thought he could check Hitler's fascist instincts that flared throughout the 1920s.[49]

By March 1933, the same time FDR took office and attempted to reassure an economically battered America, Hitler and his brain trust were well on their way to erasing the democratic levers of institutions and assuming dictatorial power. Nazi violence against political rivals expanded to target Jewish citizens.[50] European Jews became more than prospective immigrants who wanted to reunite with relatives in America. They fled as refugees from a monster committed to terrorizing and killing them. That challenge compelled Emanuel Celler to take action.

6

World War II, FDR, and Jewish Refugees

In 1936, twenty-five years after their paths had crossed at Columbia Law School, Emanuel Celler's professor, Harlan Fiske Stone, became an associate justice of the US Supreme Court. That year, Stone wrote a memorable, dissenting opinion in the case of *U.S. v. Butler, et al.* Justices Louis Brandeis and Benjamin Cardozo joined Stone in the dissent that accused the judicial majority of applying a "tortured construction of the Constitution" in ruling that state and local governments could not levy taxes regarding the Agricultural Adjustment Act, a New Deal program. "I do not question the motives of my brethren," Stone wrote to a former campus colleague who cheered his opinion, "I do question a method of thinking, which is perhaps the greatest stumbling block to the right administration of judicial review of legislation."[1] On June 12, 1941, Stone became chief justice of the high court. That same year, Congressman Celler became a partner in the New York law firm of Weisman, Celler, Quinn, Allan, and Spett.

President Roosevelt was in the final months of this first term. The stubborn Great Depression had made him a polarizing figure, beloved by poor- and working-class Americans who appreciated his progressive social programs and optimistic rhetoric but despised by capitalists and conservatives who believed Roosevelt was arrogant, autocratic, and prone to centralizing the government and even private enterprise. The president countered that the opposition GOP leadership amounted to Four Horsemen: Destruction, Delay, Deceit, and Despair.

FDR's predecessor Herbert Hoover was a one-term president largely because of the devastating Depression. Did the same fate await Roosevelt? By June, the Republicans nominated Kansas governor Alf Landon to take on FDR. The GOP platform strongly opposed the New Deal and even picked up conservative Democratic supporters. The Democrats, at their political convention, nominated FDR by acclamation and cautiously supported the New Deal platform. By fall, *Literary Digest* reported that its survey predicted a Landon landslide. In a November 3 rout, voters overwhelmingly reelected FDR by 62 to 37 percent, based on 44.5 million votes cast. In the electoral college, Landon was crushed 523–8 and won only Maine and Vermont.[2]

Pressure was on the Roosevelt administration and Congress to slay the Great Depression. At the same time, war drums overseas haunted the leaders. Benito Mussolini of Italy invaded Ethiopia in October 1935. In July, civil war in Spain resulted in General Francisco Franco emerging as the strongman. In Asia, Japan embarked on the 1937 rape of Nanking, China.

American isolationists resisted any urge to intervene in the fascist eruptions across the Atlantic or the atrocities on Far Pacific shores. Celler fought back. On July 31, 1935, Celler spoke at a protest meeting in New York organized by people concerned about fascist, anti-Semitic attacks on European Jews, especially in the new Nazi Germany. FDR administration officials believed Celler harshly accused the president of inaction against growing fascism. The next day, August 1, Celler addressed a letter to "Franklin." In it, he assured the president that his remarks in New York did not attack the administration's foreign policy. "I knew that you were doing everything in your power upon lofty humanitarian grounds," wrote Celler, "not only to protect the interests of American citizens in Germany of Jewish and Catholic origin, but that you deeply sympathized with the aims and aspirations of all those who believe in religious liberty." Celler signed off as "Manny." Roosevelt in a written reply called the incident "water under the bridge."[3]

Subtle diplomatic moves notwithstanding, FDR demonstrated little motivation toward involving Americans in overseas aggression. That passivity emboldened Adolf Hitler, the most dangerous player in Europe. By August— Hitler, declared fuhrer of a one-party Nazi state—hosted the Olympic Games. Hitler expected a show of white, Aryan athletic supremacy by the host nation. Jewish athletes from Germany were barred from competing. In America, athletic organization leaders heatedly debated the merits of boycotting the Olympics in order to deny Hitler a propaganda platform. The Americans decided to go. Germans removed anti-Jewish signage just before the squads from other nations competing arrived for the Berlin games.

The final results contradicted Hitler's grand expectations. Although German gymnast Konrad Frey won six medals—three of them gold— the brightest star of the XI modern Olympic Games was American Negro Jesse Owens. He won four gold medals in track and field events and left the fuhrer visibly distressed. Immigrant American children were medal winners, too, including Samuel Balter, a Jew, who won gold for the new Olympic sport, basketball.

Marty Glickman and Sam Stoller were benched for the 4-x-100-meter relay race. Glickman, who later became a sports journalist, said the decision by the coach and Olympic chairman Avery Brundage was motivated by anti-Semitism and also by a desire to spare Hitler the likelihood of watching two American Jews on the winning podium.[4] Six Hungarian Jews also won gold.

Aware that trouble was brewing, FDR delivered his October 1937 "Quarantine" speech three months after Japan invaded China. "War is a contagion," said FDR, "whether it be declared or undeclared. It can engulf states and peoples remote from the original scene of the hostilities. We are determined to keep out of war, yet we cannot insure ourselves against the disastrous effects of war and the dangers of involvement. We are adopting such measures as will minimize our risk of involvement, but we cannot have complete protection in a world of disorder in which confidence and security have broken down."

America, said Roosevelt, was spending 12 percent of its budget on the military. Ten percent of the world spent up to 50 percent on militarization in order to attack 90 percent of the peace-loving nations. The Roosevelt administration tried tamping down aggression in other ways. Secretary of State Cordell Hull negotiated trade agreements that lowered tariffs, after the hostile Harley-Smoot Act of 1930.[5] Also, neutrality agreements negotiated in 1935 and 1937 attempted to avert military entanglements with the Europeans. "America hates war," said FDR in closing. "America hopes for peace. Therefore, America actively engages in the search for peace."

FDR's warning did not move the isolationists.[6] By November, Hitler revealed his war plans at the Hossbach Conference. In March 1938, Germany announced a union with Austria and by August the Nazi army had mobilized.[7] Despite Hitler's aggression, British prime minister Neville Chamberlain appeased the fuhrer at Munich in September 1938. In two weeks, Nazi soldiers occupied Sudetenland, Czechoslovakian territory largely inhabited by German speakers. That occupation forced the Czech government to resign in March 1939.

In March 1938, Celler introduced a bill that would have exempted victims of religious and political persecution from the quota system. About the same time, colleague Samuel Dickstein, then chairman of the House Immigration Committee, introduced a similar bill that would have allocated unused quota slots to refugees.[8]

By March 1939 there was a total Nazi occupation of Czechoslovakia. That same month the Spanish Civil War ended. In August, Germany signed a nonaggression pact with the Soviet Union. The Stalin-led Russian Soviets were a marginal US ally.

In July 1939, Celler sent a strongly worded letter to Secretary of State Hull urging the United States to resume diplomatic relations with the Vatican. Celler criticized Congress's 1867 decision to abruptly cut off relations with the pope's court. Seven decades later, Pope Pius VII's efforts to compel peace in Europe offered hope for the beginning of a new phase of relaxed tensions. Celler called the pope's efforts "a clarion call to the civilized peoples of the world that religious and personal liberties are inherent in our Democracy."[9] Sumner Welles, undersecretary of state, followed up on Celler's letter. On August 2, he wrote to Roosevelt, "I think it is unquestionable that the Vatican has many sources of information, particularly with regard to what is actually going on in Germany, Italy and Spain, which we do not possess, and it seems that the question of whether it would be desirable for our government to obtain access to this information was of considerable importance." Full, formal US-Vatican diplomatic relations did not resume at that time of world war. Nevertheless, Celler's letter set in motion a process that restored relations forty-five years later.[10]

* * *

On September 1, Germany invaded Poland. In retaliation, Britain, France, and New Zealand declared war on Germany. World War II was under way.[11] Four days after the Polish invasion, the United States declared that it was neutral, but in a few days Canada declared war on Germany and a battle of the Atlantic began.

At the start of 1940, German submarines, known as U-boats, attacked British and allied (including American) ships. That January and February, 440,000 tons were sunk or destroyed. During a three-month stretch in summer and fall, as many as twenty-eight U-boats were sinking ships in the Atlantic at will.[12] The Nazi German army pushed westward. During May 26 to June 4, British and French soldiers retreated to Dunkirk on the French coastline. The British Royal Navy launched Operation Dynamo and 338,000 troops were evacuated across the twenty-one-mile channel to England. Eighty Royal Air Force pilots died while flying air cover to protect the ships from Nazi bombing.[13] That June, Germany invaded, and quickly occupied France.[14] With France overrun and England reeling, FDR threw Britain a lifeline. In September, America traded fifty old naval destroyers in exchange for the rights to construct naval and air bases on British colonies in the Western Hemisphere. The Lend-Lease agreement was Roosevelt's most overt signal to Americans that they were involuntarily engaged in the world war.[15]

Celler was willingly engaged as author of *The Draft and You*, a reader-friendly 120-page book published by New York–based Viking Press on September 26, available three weeks after the Lend-Lease agreement. The large format 8-by-11-inch book included forewords by US senator Edward R. Burke of Nebraska and US representative James W. Wadsworth of New York. "Enactment of the military training bill in its present form was required by the emergency need for manning the national defense machine," wrote Burke. "As soon as the proper reserves have been created, certain changes in the act should be made in order that it may function with a minimum of interference with the individual's planning of his life."

Wadsworth's eight-line co-foreword praised the author: "Congressman Celler has done a useful thing in preparing this work on selective service, including a brief history of our unfortunate experiences with the volunteer system (Celler was a draft board appeal official during World War I). His work is particularly valuable at this time in that it corrects a vast amount of misinformation concerning the selective draft. Innocently or otherwise, this misinformation has been spread far and wide over the country and, in my judgment, accounts to a large degree for opposition to the measure. Mr. Celler dispels the fog, throws light upon the subject and establishes the truth."

Celler's preface explained that the book was a primer of 433 pages of Selective Service Act essential forms and indices. The regulations, he cautioned, were in a state of flux and periodic changes would depend upon experience and developing exigencies.

Here was what was at stake: For the first time in American history the nation needed a trained and prepared fighting force ready for imminent war. Hitler, Celler reminded readers, did not declare war on Belgium, The Netherlands, Norway, or Demark; the fuhrer and his armies swept in and conquered. "All that's standing between Hitler and our armed forces," Celler wrote, "is the Atlantic Ocean and the British Navy. Once the British Navy is gone (perish the thought!) the Atlantic becomes a pond."[16]

The Draft Act was a precautionary measure in order to avoid the mistakes of World War I, when raw recruits were thrown into battle at the start of

US involvement in 1917 and became cannon fodder. The 1940 plan called for 800,000 men ages 21–35 to register for the draft each year, be trained, and serve for a year. After a year of service these men would be replaced by 800,000 more conscripts. The Selective Service and Training Act was in force for five years, through 1945. For the first time, the draft was a democratic process. "The rich and powerful will have no greater rights than the poor and indigent," wrote Celler. Deep in the book the author chronicled the history of recruiting dating back to Moses and Aaron of the Old Testament and ancient Greece and Rome. As for the American experience, Celler noted that during the Civil War, the Union did not deploy a draft until two years into the fighting when volunteer calls collapsed, and the rebelling Confederate South nearly had a stranglehold on the North. The draft allowed rich men to escape serving; they could hire substitutes or purchase exemptions for $300. (New York City in 1863 experienced lethal draft riots. Irish immigrants were tapped to fight as substitutes. In turn a number of them killed black neighbors in anger over a rich man's war that was a poor man's fight.)[17]

Celler thanked four military officers for assistance in writing and planning *The Draft and You*. The congressman also praised his son-in-law, Sydney B. Wertheimer, an assistant US attorney, who "collaborated most diligently to hasten the fashioning of the work, so that it might be published opportunely, soon after the passage by Congress of the Draft Act."[18]

During 1939, Palestine was a British colony populated by Arabs and Jews. British colonial secretary Malcolm MacDonald drafted a white paper that proposed partitioning Palestine and creating a homeland for Jews. Celler, monitoring the developments, said the proposed new nation could be home for the "driven Jew," as in violently driven out of Germany, Poland, and other countries as world war spread.

Celler spoke out against Britain's immigration quota. It called for moving 75,000 essentially European Jews at a rate of 15,000 people each year to the new Jewish homeland between 1940 through 1944. Celler believed the human pipeline trickled when it needed to gush. The total number, said the congressman, "was woefully insufficient because of the attitudes of Russia and Poland and the other of these benighted states—Germany, especially Germany, with Hitler."[19]

That year a presumed unnamed Orthodox rabbi visited Celler's Brooklyn office. Cloaked in a long black coat and hat, the rabbi bitterly complained that the world would have shown greater interest if 6 million cattle were slaughtered in Europe rather than 6 million Jews.[20]

As Jews were being killed or interned in concentration camps, escape doors elsewhere closed shut. Canada blocked refugees, said Celler, and Australia

enacted restrictive immigration laws. Several ghastly incidents made Palestine as Jewish homeland look like a mirage. Jewish refugee ships *SS Struma*
and *SS Patria* were stopped in the harbor of Haifa. Jewish operatives, wrote
Zionist scholar Ami Isseroff, attached bombs to the ship propellers only to
disable the ships but the operation went awry. The explosion occurred before
passengers could safely disembark and the *Patria* sank in sixteen minutes.
Among 1,800 refugees, 267 died and 167 people were injured.[21] The other Jewish refugees on the *SS Struma* were sent to the island of Mauritius, essentially
a Devil's Island, said Celler, because those refugees could not enter Palestine.[22]

On June 24–28 at the Republican National Convention in Philadelphia,
instinctively rather than logically, the GOP rejected its isolationist leaders
and instead chose Wendell L. Willkie as its presidential candidate and challenger to FDR. Willkie was raised on an Indiana farm and became a corporate
lawyer in New York. He had never run for public office or held a government post. Willkie was a registered Democrat months before he switched
parties. Yet he was an outspoken critic of FDR's domestic policies and an
internationalist. Willkie's supporters said he was courageous, independent,
and a man of integrity.[23]

At the Democratic National Convention in Chicago July 15–19, FDR was
nominated to run for an unprecedented third term. He changed vice presidents by dropping John Nance Garner of Texas and adding Cabinet member
Henry A. Wallace, his former secretary of agriculture. That season the president appointed two prominent Republicans to his Cabinet: Henry L. Stimson
as secretary of war, and Frank Knox as secretary of the navy. That signaled to
the world that America was politically united.[24] On Election Day, November
5, Willkie got close to FDR in the popular vote but the incumbent won 55
percent to 45 percent out of 49.5 million votes cast. The results in the electoral
college were lopsided—FDR cruised ahead with 449 votes compared to 82
for Willkie.[25] FDR's campaign opponent was not an obstructionist; on foreign
policy Willkie agreed that American intervention in the war was inevitable.

When the new year began January 8, 1941, FDR presented a $17.5 billion
federal budget in which 62 percent—$10.8 billion—went toward defense.[26]
Three years before, the United States was spending 12 percent of its budget
on the military. That was before the Nazis overran Poland, occupied France,
and concentrated on conquering Britain.

Celler was a loyal interventionist. In December 1940, he had a personal
battle to fight. Doctors diagnosed Celler with an epidural abscess that led to

osteomyelitis of the vertebra. The source of the illness was as unlikely as it was innocuous: his barber had plucked an ingrown hair on his cheek. After a succession of operations, Celler remained hospitalized for five months and returned home to Brooklyn in May, around the time of his fifty-second birthday.[27] Within ten days almost unendurable pain returned him to the hospital. Celler drifted in and out of consciousness.

His wife, Stella, informed Celler that in his delirium, he expected every nurse to be a foreign correspondent. Celler asked questions about the Congress, Germany, and Great Britain. He insisted that the nurse on duty at 3 a.m. call Press Secretary Steve Early at the White House. Another time, Celler instructed a nurse, "Take this letter down," and he "uttered a long, rambling, incoherent, effusive outpour to President Roosevelt." When done, Celler ordered the nurse to "Now read it back." That nurse fled in fear. Nurses whispered among themselves about the tyrant of a congressman on their floor. "How can I know," one nurse asked Stella, "whether President Roosevelt is going to change the Secretary of State?"[28] The congressman learned that the doctors, almost unanimously, determined that he had an incurable condition. In June, surgeon Dr. William Linder of Brooklyn was called in to operate. Linder's operation—Celler's fifth—cured the infected disc in his spine.[29]

Celler left the hospital in August 1941. He caught up on his reading and resumed thinking about the fast-moving overseas war news. Domestically, the intervention debate raged on. That month, a poll indicated that 74 percent of Americans opposed entering World War II as the ally of Britain. FDR scolded isolationist members of Congress as "Little men of little faith who play petty politics in a world crisis."[30]

As Americans fretted about Europeans attempting to pull them in, warfare in Asia affected US citizens too. America's government decided to sell scrap metal exclusively to England. That policy angered Pacific aggressor Japan. Then in July, FDR announced that all Japanese assets in the United States were frozen as retaliation for Japan's occupation of French Indochina.[31]

US-Japan trade halted, placing both countries on a collision course for war. In November Japan's ambassador to the United States asked for a lifting of trade restrictions, and for US noninterference in Japan's activities in China and the Pacific. FDR warned isolationist skeptics in Congress that an eruption was about to occur.

In late fall, a massive Japanese naval fleet set sail for Hawaii with the mission to wipe out much of America's naval fleet anchored at the base of Pearl Harbor. On Sunday morning, December 7, Japanese fighter planes launched from aircraft carriers far out in the Pacific dropped bombs on the battleships and destroyers. Meanwhile, submarines counterpunched with torpedoes. The attack planes also bombed and raked the Pearl Harbor airfield with gunfire, preventing US pilots and their planes from getting into the air to retaliate. The devastating not-so-surprise attack destroyed nineteen ships (six of them battleships) and 150 planes and resulted in 2,403 deaths and 1,178 injuries. With most of the US Pacific fleet out of commission, Japan expected to throw the knockout punch that would result in an American surrender. Instead, FDR and Congress declared war on Japan. On December 11, Germany and Italy declared war on the United States. After years of avoiding war, America was yanked into Atlantic and Pacific conflicts.

A week after the Pearl Harbor attack, Celler taunted to their faces former isolationists clamoring for war, declaring they should "apologize to President Roosevelt."[32]

On January 14, 1942, FDR announced in a proclamation that all alien residents must register with the federal government. On February 20, the president issued an executive order authorizing the War Department to designate "military areas" and to exclude anyone from them considered a potential danger. The tone was neutral, yet executive order No. 9066 targeted 110,000 Japanese Americans who lived along the Pacific Coast. A few thousand alien German and Italian inhabitants were locked up, but millions of German American and Italian American citizens were able to continue to live their lives without constraints.

That was not the case for Robert Kashiwagi, who was interned: "As far as I'm concerned, I was born here, and according to the Constitution that I studied in school, I had the Bill of Rights that should have backed me up. And until the very minute I got onto the evacuation train, I said, 'It can't be.' I said, 'How can they do that to an American citizen?'"[33]

Wholesale Japanese American internment was supposed to also include those living on the US colony Hawaii. But those islanders were spared. Wealthy landowners said they needed the laborers to tend to their sugar and pineapple plantations. On the mainland, FBI director J. Edgar Hoover opposed the internment; Japanese American citizens, he said, did not pose security risks. In California, the roundup of the Japanese was an undisguised land grab. The Asians had arrived in America at the turn of the century and quickly made the desert bloom with citrus fruit. Resentful whites wanted the industrious Japanese Americans gone. "If all of the Japs were removed tomorrow, we'd never miss them because the white farmers can take over and produce everything the Jap grows," the head of the California Grower-Shipper Vegetable Association said. "And we don't want them back when the war ends either."[34]

Under attack across two oceans, Americans were expected to abstain from butter and make bullets. During FDR's January 1942 State of the Union address, he called for production of vast numbers of planes, tanks, ships, and guns necessary to defeat the Axis forces. The Brooklyn Navy Yard in Celler's hometown emerged as a center of an essential wartime industry.

Within a year, yard employment more than doubled to 22,600 workers and its acreage expanded from 198 to 262 so new dry docks could accommodate construction of the *Iowa, Missouri,* and *North Carolina* battleships. In the initial months of US involvement, Yanks suffered crushing defeats because they were inexperienced and ill-equipped. But US factories and shipyards were able to mass produce vehicles and weapons faster than the enemy could destroy them. American industrial might shifted the war momentum. During FDR's State of the Union, 88 percent of the proposed $59 billion federal budget was committed to the war effort.[35] First Lady Eleanor Roosevelt practiced model behavior by rationing. She gave up her nylon stockings and instead wore wool. She rationed sugar too, but Celler complained in January 27 and February 10, 1942, editions of the *New York Times* that Eleanor's good intentions encouraged sugar hoarding by anxious housewives.[36]

News from overseas made clear that Jewish people were targeted for extinction by Nazi Germany and were unwelcome when they tried to leave for British-ruled Palestine or North America. Emanuel Celler's constituents pleaded with him to do something. Consistently during his public life Celler had spoken up for and defended underdogs, whether they were Jewish or Italian immigrants, or the black poor. The congressman was a child of mid-nineteenth-century immigrants, and melting-pot American exceptionalism usually framed his arguments. Now the desperate situation in Europe made Celler reflect intensely on his Jewish heritage. His people needed safe passage to America and a homeland in the Middle East.[37]

Celler personally lobbied President Roosevelt to rescue Jewish refugees. The congressman wrote numerous memos and presented them alone or as the representative of congressional delegations. He forcefully advocated that the United States relax immigration laws on an emergency basis to rescue those fleeing the Holocaust. By 1943, he called President FDR's immigration policy "cold and cruel" and blasted the "glacier-like attitude" of the State Department.[38]

In 1944, Roosevelt invited Celler to the White House. Smiling, the urbane FDR bent toward Celler to whisper a secret. In a recent conversation, British prime minister Winston Churchill said that when the war ended, the British would consent to the establishment of a Jewish homeland in Palestine.[39] (About that time, the allies had landed in Normandy, France, and propelled Nazi Germany into full retreat. Victory in Europe was a year away.)

Churchill told FDR that the first step was to tear up the British white paper on Palestine that restricted Jewish entry. Celler could not betray what FDR told him in confidence, but at every opportunity, the congressman told constituents and friends that he had special knowledge that soon FDR would find a way to open the doors of Palestine to the Jews fleeing murder.[40]

Months later, when Roosevelt reported to Congress on his Yalta conference, he briefed the legislators on his conversations with King Ibn Saud of Saudi Arabia. Celler listened with dismay and disbelief to the president's implied repudiation of the Jewish claim to Palestine. Frustrated and unsure of FDR's true intentions, Celler declared that the president's promises, like pie crusts, were broken.[41]

When FDR died in April 1945, Celler despaired over the prospects of a homeland for Jews in Palestine. Widow Eleanor Roosevelt publicly said the Jewish state remained to the end one of her husband's highest hopes. Celler wondered, that if FDR had been sincere, whether individuals in the State and War departments must have impeded the commander-in-chief.[42] Four decades later, experts—including Celler—who participated in the documentary *Who Shall Live and Who Shall Die?* provided pieces to the puzzle. Jewish organizations sounded alarms warning of a Holocaust in progress, but the State Department shielded the ghastly news from FDR, said advocates.[43] Word eventually got through to the commander-in-chief in 1944 and he acknowledged the crisis. Advocates from the Emergency Committee to Save the Jewish People of Europe said a number of Jewish American leaders persuaded the State Department to ignore the pleas and protests of many groups, including five hundred rabbis who marched on Washington October 6, 1943, and met with Vice President Henry Wallace as FDR exited the White House via a back door.[44] The Jewish leaders who counseled the State Department warned of "the wrong kinds of Jews" who could stir anti-Semitic backlash at home.

A handful of officials from the War Refugee Board told the filmmakers that there were multiple schemes to rescue and settle thousands of Jews: settlers were sent to the Dominican Republic, about one thousand were classified as POWs instead of refugees and sent to Oswego, New York, and placed under military guard except for six hours each day (Eleanor Roosevelt visited the POWs).

Another scheme involved sending thousands of Jews to Turkey, which was a staging area for final settlement in Palestine. The officials regretted that their small rescues were not enough to prevent the Nazi's slaughter of several million Jews.[45]

Celler was elected to his eleventh congressional term in fall 1944. He was an experienced legislator with an unyielding agenda: immigration reform, made urgent by relief for hostages fleeing annihilation; support for winning world wars in Europe and Asia, and the creation of a Jewish homeland in Palestine during the immediate postwar period.

The Allies achieved victory in Europe in May 1945, three weeks after FDR's death. Victory over Japan arrived in August, but not before two atomic bombings convinced the Japanese not to resist and to back away from their vow to defend their island to the last man and woman.

Postwar immediately led to a new concept, Cold War. In this new era, Celler assumed a legislative leadership post and got answers to the Palestine question. Also, Cold War politics influenced and shaped the American immigration debate.

7

Post–World War II, Truman, and the State of Israel

Emanuel Celler gained a House immigration ally in Clare Boothe Luce, a Republican elected by Connecticut voters in 1942. She lashed out against British imperial policy manifested in the fatal end to 267 Palestine-bound Jewish refugees on the *SS Patria* in 1940.[1] In April 1944, she argued that oppressed European Jews should settle in Palestine without restriction.[2] Like Celler's, Luce's immigration views were globally inclusive.

World War II realities incrementally reshaped American leaders' attitudes about immigrants and citizens of color. On December 17, 1943, Congress repealed the Chinese Exclusion Act of 1882.[3] China, which had been defending itself against Japan since the early 1930s, had become America's ally. In July 1943, Luce called for repeal of the Chinese Exclusion Act because the law was unpopular even in its time. Furthermore, one hundred work permits per year for Chinese visitors, Luce said, hardly threatened America's "so-called white civilization."[4] By October Roosevelt agreed to back its repeal. Luce also backed self-determination for citizens of the British colony India, and in America, an end to the ban on immigrants from India. In a few years, the writer, *Vanity Fair* editor, and wife of Time-Life mogul Henry R. Luce would collaborate with Celler on successful South Asian Indian immigration reform legislation.

On January 8, 1943, Emanuel Celler submitted antilynching bill H.R. 820. Six other members of Congress wrote similar bills.[5] Domestic terrorism against

Negroes in the South was a source of embarrassment as the United States was fighting enemies that practiced racial superiority and extermination. Celler and his like-minded colleagues' antilynching bills failed, nevertheless, stymied by what tart-tongued Luce called "lynch-loving Bourbons."[6]

Southern Democratic members of Congress held significant power in Washington. Celler verbally battled with Representative John Rankin of Mississippi, a human volcano of racial and anti-Semitic animus. Once on the House floor, Rankin addressed Celler as "The Jewish Gentleman from New York."

Celler protested the labeling. Rankin retorted: "Does the member from New York object to being called a Jew, or does he object to being called a gentleman? What is the kicking about?"

Rankin ridiculed Celler's relentless opposition to the 1924 Johnson Immigration Act: "They [American Jews] whine about discrimination. Do you know who is being discriminated against? The white, Christian people of America, the ones who created this nation."[7] Rankin also baited race-based immigration foe Adolph Sabath, a fellow congressman who represented Illinois.

Rankin routinely uttered the epithet "nigger" on the House floor (so habitually, that freshman Adam Clayton Powell Jr., an African American from Harlem, took the unusual and ultimately unsuccessful step of protesting and calling for Rankin's censure). In July 1944 when overloaded ammunition resulted in the worst home-front World War II disaster—a horrific explosion that killed 320 sailors at Port Chicago, California—Rankin fought ferociously to reduce monetary benefits to widows and survivors when he realized that two-thirds of the victims were black sailors. Rankin wanted the $5,000 awards cut to $2,000 for Negroes. Congress compromised and reduced the benefits to Negro Port Chicago families to $3,000.[8]

The US military was racially segregated. Pseudo-scientific studies and other propaganda alleged that Negroes were cowardly or mentally inferior for combat. Most Negroes—who by the way were subject to the mandatory draft—were relegated to custodial or service tasks. Eventually, World War II's do-or-die urgency chipped away at Jim Crow conventions. During the Pearl Harbor rout, Doris "Dorie" Miller, a black cook who in Texas hunted squirrels with a rifle but was barred in the navy from handling firearms, took over a 50-caliber antiaircraft gun and shot down four Japanese fighter planes while aboard the battleship *USS West Virginia*. Miller became the first African American to earn a Navy Cross for courage under fire.[9] With the blessing and advocacy of Eleanor Roosevelt, Negro pilots trained in Tuskegee, Alabama. The airmen protected big, slow US bombers from German fighter planes and the Tuskegee Airmen became legendary for their bravery and prowess.

Celler lauded justice for four black Women's Army Corps members whose wrongful convictions for insubordination were reversed in April 1945. The women testified that Lowell General Hospital commandant Colonel Walter H. Crandall told them he wanted no "black" WACs assisting as medical technicians or serving in the Massachusetts hospital motor pool. Also at that time the US Navy reversed itself and granted fourteen honorable discharges to Negro Seabees. The army and navy, said Celler, are "becoming alive to the fact that the public will always react against injustice."[10] Indeed. The nationally circulated *Pittsburgh Courier*, a black weekly, launched a "Double V" campaign. American Negroes were fighting two wars, said the management—one for victory against the Axis enemies, and another for victory over racial segregation and discrimination at home.[11]

In the summer of 1944, Democratic Party leaders replaced FDR's vice president Henry Wallace and brought in Harry Truman of Kansas City. Party leaders knew the commander-in-chief was gravely ill. A closely guarded secret was that FDR was diagnosed with congestive heart failure and very likely would not finish a fourth term, if elected. Party insiders deemed Wallace too liberal, dreamy, impractical, and aloof to be a heartbeat away from the presidency.[12] FDR was not fond of Truman, a loyal protégé of corrupt Kansas City Democratic boss Thomas Joseph "T.J." Pendergast during the 1930s. Truman managed to avoid Pendergast's stench while serving him as an efficient Jackson County, Missouri, official. In 1940, Truman was elected to the US Senate from Missouri and was perceived as a party yes-man, but over time he earned respect in Washington as chairman of a committee that investigated and exposed wasteful military spending and unpreparedness.[13] Truman emerged as a viable running mate because political insiders regarded FDR's preferred vice-presidential choices as too old. FDR met once with his new vice president.

Roosevelt's Republican opponent was New York governor Thomas E. Dewey so the November 1944 election was a battle between two Empire State adversaries. That fall America was blessed with repeated good war news.

Allied forces that stormed Normandy liberated Paris and penetrated German territory in the Rhine. In the Pacific, the Japanese navy was mostly destroyed in battle and General Douglas MacArthur waded ashore to reclaim the Philippines.

FDR defeated Governor Thomas E. Dewey 54–46 percent in the closest of four elections. Indeed, the party insiders accurately predicted. Roosevelt died three months into his new term in April 1945. At that time America and its allies were days, weeks, from ending the world war on one continent. Truman fretted about the future because FDR had kept him in the dark on policy matters. Truman had no knowledge of the Manhattan Project plan to build a nuclear bomb.

Other president-watchers had doubts that Truman, a World War I army artillery captain, failed haberdashery merchant, and farmer was presidential material. Yet after the euphoria of victory in Europe and victory in Japan that spring and summer, Truman had to focus on a rubble-strewn and rearranged world order. Russia and its Soviet Union of satellite countries was America's nominal ally before and during World War II, but postwar it became the passive-aggressive enemy. The totalitarians grabbed Poland and the eastern half of Germany. The western half of Germany stayed aligned with the United States, Britain, and like-minded democratic allies.

In Asia, mainland China became communist. America's Chinese allies fled to the Pacific island Taiwan. These new relationships of East versus West congealed into "Cold War" hostilities without direct warfare. Propaganda and spying were key weapons. On March 5, 1946, British opposition party leader Winston Churchill, speaking in Westminster, Missouri, said an "Iron Curtain" had descended in Eastern Europe.[14]

Also, in the postwar optimism of 1945, most winners and losers established a United Nations. On July 28, the US Senate voted 89–2 to consent to a UN charter. In January 1946, the first General Assembly convened in London. Secretary of State James Byrnes led the US delegation that included Eleanor Roosevelt. That October, the UN met in New York City and the organization accepted $8.5 million from John D. Rockefeller Jr. to build a permanent home there.[15] The one-world-oriented body moved to its permanent New York home in 1949.

Unlike the previous generation of US leaders who had balked at joining a League of Nations, American leaders of this era were fully engaged as facilitators and participants.[16]

In 1945, Truman decided that in order to win the Cold War, America needed to make allies of those who had been, and still were, excluded by reason of their supposed unlikeness to Americans' national origin and race.

The first problem he faced involved displaced persons in Europe. People who were scattered during World War II had to be resettled before Western Europe could stabilize and become secure and self-sufficient US allies in the Cold War.[17]

In 1946, the wealthy and secure United States had an unmatched capacity to accept the displaced, but a great many of the people were from ethnic groups or countries whose immigration the United States limited on historical or racial grounds. Albania, Bulgaria, Estonia, Finland, Greece, Hungary, Latvia, Lithuania, Romania, and Yugoslavia all faced Soviet occupation or control, but their combined annual quota based on the two-decade-old US national origins-inspired immigration law was 3,823 persons.[18] Although China had been an important ally in the war, its allocation was 105 people.

A still-isolationist Congress compromised with the president's demands by allowing refugees to enter the United States if they drew down their country's future quota. The so-called mortgage system meant, for example, that Estonia's full quota of 116 could enter the United States in 1947, with the result that the entire quota for 1947 was used up, and then as more Estonians were admitted, each would be charged against part of their future Estonia quota. In the Estonian case, that would continue up through the year 2146.[19]

Other new nations reshaped the post–World War II globe. The British colony India evolved into a self-governing nation. Since 1930, Mohandas K. (Mahatma) Gandhi waged a campaign for self-rule and nonviolence and civil disobedience tactics against the British rulers. Gandhi and his peers also advocated for the end of the caste system and untouchables code practiced by native elites. Before World War II, Britain gave India a constitution that provided a bicameral federal congress. Immediately after the war, India became a member of the United Nations. Vijaya Lakshmi Pandit, a rare woman diplomat, intrigued Celler: "When I met Madame Vijaya Lakshmi Pandit many years later, before independence had been granted to India and before she had been appointed Ambassador to the United States, I found myself remembering the impotent rage I had felt at the sight of people oppressed by the meanness of poverty. In this cosmopolitan little woman of charm and discernment I could sense that same kind of rage and defiance against the degradation of her people.

"When she asked me to introduce her to President Truman—contrary to the tradition which imposed that responsibility on the British Embassy in Washington—I knew it to be her deliberate act of defiance. When I did introduce her to President Truman, no one caught that gesture or understood that it spelled independence. In that one little act, she bound together for me rage against subjugation and the courage to act against it."[20] At an India League of America meeting, the congressman was asked how he would

diversify his passions—civil rights, labor, trade barriers—and not spread himself too thin.[21] He answered that his interest in India was rooted in interest
in Brooklyn, because it represents all creeds, colors, and equal opportunity.[22]

India's independence had consequences for the United States. A year
before the 1924 Johnson Immigration Act established a preference for so-
called Aryan whites of Anglo-Saxon and Nordic heritages, a US Supreme
Court ruling rejected inclusion of authentic Aryans (Sanskrit translation:
"noble") from India.[23] The expulsion of Oregon resident Bhagat Singh Thind
in 1923 was the test case. The high court agreed that anthropologists considered the Aryan Asians to be the same race as white Americans, nevertheless
there were "unmistakable and profound differences" between Caucasians
from the East and West, said the majority opinion.

The Thind decision resulted in the denaturalization of some people who
had previously become US citizens.

Celler and a colleague observed India and acted preemptively. The Luce-
Celler Act of 1946 was inspired by Clare Boothe Luce's fear that the world's
nonwhite nationalisms would soon become antiwhite nationalisms if non-
white elites were not given more of the privileges afforded to whites. The
Republican congresswoman from Connecticut supported the act to prevent
Indian nationalism from rejecting the institutions and influence of America
and Great Britain, a partnership which she imagined to constitute an "Anglo-
Saxon Empire."

Second, and more important, the Luce-Celler Act of 1946 was hardly
an American bill at all. It was really an Indian nationalist bill. J. J. Singh, an
Indian nationalist living in the United States, submitted the bill to Emanuel
Celler and Clare Boothe Luce's attention and lobbied tirelessly for it. His
intention in passing this bill was not to gain the right to become American,
but to establish India as an independent nation. Singh used the Luce-Celler
Act to secure early international recognition of a secular, united, and independent India. While the British government obstinately refused to transfer
power to the Indian nationalists and refused to recognize the Indian National
Congress as a secular political body representative of Indians across religious,
caste, and ethnic communities, J. J. Singh pulled the levers of the US Congress
to get that recognition written into the US legal code.[24]

The Middle East emerged as strategically important post–War War II and
Cold War real estate. The Arab majority controlled oil, and its region's seas
were the channels to export fuel all over the world. That included car-thirsty

America and Europe, which depended on 80 percent of the region's energy. An official homeland in Palestine for hundreds of thousands of European Jews continued to be a pressing concern. In spring 1945, shortly after Truman took the presidential reins from FDR, Celler led a delegation of senators and congressmen to plead for the Jews in Israel. Truman said, "You know, I haven't been in this job very long, and the Irish have come in to see me for the Irish-Americans, and the Swedes have come to me—to see me about the Swedish-Americans and—the British have come in to see me for the British-Americans, and now the Jews are coming to see me for the Jewish-Americans. When will Americans come in to see me for Americans?"[25]

Before the meeting Celler suspected that Truman might not grasp the life-and-death urgency of placing refugee Jews in Palestine. At the White House meeting, Celler and his colleagues were disturbed by Truman's statement. Yet Celler and his like-minded legislators did not give up on the new president. They continued to brief and lobby him about Palestine. Eventually, Truman was very helpful and very humane in regard to the establishment of a Jewish state in Palestine. On August 31, Truman asked Great Britain to allow one hundred thousand Jewish refugees from Europe to enter Palestine.[26]

Britain, which seized Palestine from Turkey in 1917 and colonized the land for thirty years, was conflicted about agreeing to allow a Jewish nation in Palestine. Arab Palestinians and their kindred neighbors were ferociously against the notion. They vowed war if the Jews got their wish. Weary of World War II, the British wanted to withdraw their fifty thousand troops, and asked the United States whether it could spare one hundred thousand soldiers to keep peace in Palestine while Stalin was mauling Eastern Europe like a ravenous bear.[27] Truman's State and Defense department advisers urged him not to support a Jewish Palestine, because, they said, it was not in America's strategic interest.

Truman however believed he had a moral obligation to support the Jewish state because it was "a basic human problem." When reminded by Defense Secretary James Forrestal that America needed Saudi Arabian oil in the event of war, Truman pushed back that he would make his decision regarding the Middle East based on justice, not oil.[28] On October 9, 1947, Truman supported the UN proposal for autonomous Jewish and Arab Palestinian states.[29] On November 29, the UN General Assembly voted on Palestine partition. The vote was close: thirty-three nations approved, thirteen were against partition, and ten nations abstained. The United States, Soviet Union, and most of Europe were among the "yes" votes. Ten Muslim nations plus India, Greece, and Cuba voted "no."[30] Britain plus nine other nations abstained. Celler recorded the votes—yea, nay, and neutral—on a score sheet.[31]

Truman was committed to the formation of a Jewish state in Palestine although multiple times he demonstrated odd ways of showing his compassion and keeping his promise. Relentless lobbying by Jewish American leaders and the public provoked intemperate responses from the president. Citizens—100,000 in 1947—wrote letters pleading for a Jewish Palestine.

Exasperated, Truman wrote to Ed Flynn, an aide, "I don't believe there is any possible way of pleasing our Jewish friends." To his Cabinet, Truman fumed, "Jesus Christ couldn't please them when He was on earth, so how could anyone expect that I would have any luck?"[32] Truman was so agitated he tried to avoid meeting with Zionist leader and elder Chaim Weizmann, who had made an overseas trip to meet the president. Truman's closest Jewish American friend and former Kansas City business partner Eddie Jacobson intervened and persuaded the president to meet seventy-three-year-old Weizmann.

Inside the White House, Jacobson urged Truman to meet the ailing man who had "traveled thousands of miles just to see you and plead the cause of my people." Jacobson reminded Truman that Weizmann was unlike American Jewish leaders who pummeled him with demands and insults. Truman, sitting with his back to his friend, drummed his great desk and then swung around, looked Jacobson in the eye, and said, "You win, you bald-headed son of a bitch. I will see him."[33]

Weizmann's forty-five-minute March 1948 meeting with Truman was cordial. The Zionist leader believed Truman did not waver from his promise to support a split Palestine that provided land for a Jewish nation. Yet in less than a week, the Truman administration appeared to reverse its position favoring the Jewish Palestine state.

US ambassador Warren Austin told the UN General Assembly that America recommended substituting a temporary UN trusteeship over Palestine instead of the partition plan. Truman insisted he had not changed his position and blamed the policy contradiction on Secretary of State George Marshall's unawareness about the Weizmann meeting (Marshall was visiting the West Coast on other official business), and Austin releasing a statement that was not cleared by the White House.

Either way, Truman looked like a double-crosser, and he acknowledged as much to adviser Clark Clifford: "I don't understand this. How could this have happened! I assured Chaim Weizmann . . . he must think I'm a shit ass."[34]

No more shameful decision in international politics, Celler said, had ever been made.[35] Through the month of April, Truman strained mightily to repair the diplomatic damage. Edwin M. Wright, a US State Department adviser, called Celler a "run-of-the-mill Zionist" who led a delegation that met with Truman in 1946. Celler and company said New York governor and the last

GOP presidential nominee Thomas Dewey promised he would support a State of Israel. Celler pounded on the president's desk and said, "And if you don't come out for a Jewish state we'll run you out of town." Foreign policy, according to Wright, was not based on what was going on in the Middle East, but what was going on in the United States.[36] Truman feared his secretary of state would resign, but George Marshall stayed put. The British mandate in Palestine was to expire on May 12.

On May 14, 1948, the existence of a new Jewish state was to be proclaimed at midnight in Jerusalem, 6 p.m. Washington time. That afternoon, Marshall called Truman to say he could not support the position that as president he wished to take, but Marshall promised he would not publicly oppose Truman. The president's aide Clark Clifford hurriedly called the Jewish Agency in Washington to alert its staff that US recognition would occur that day. A Jewish nation was about to return to the Middle East after a two-thousand-year exile yet American officials did not know the country's name. At midnight, the new Jewish state was declared on schedule.

Eleven minutes passed. Then a White House official announced the United States' de facto recognition of the new nation named Israel. America was the first country to recognize Israel.[37] Chaim Weizmann would become its inaugural president.

The American delegation at the United Nations was caught off guard by the announcement, that is, except for Ambassador Austin, who was notified in advance about Truman's prerogative and went home without briefing his colleagues. Marshall dispatched Dean Rusk, head of UN affairs, to New York in order to keep the delegation from quitting en masse.[38]

Israel's birth marked the climax of a fifteen-year campaign by Emanuel Celler. Beginning in 1933 he had recognized Hitler's treachery toward German Jews. Celler's New York constituents that included Jewish religious leaders had angrily pressured the congressman to get results. Celler pleaded with the powers in Washington to make exceptions and bring refugees facing persecution and certain execution to America, the land where 75 percent of American Jews were of Eastern European heritage.[39]

Understanding that his options in America were limited, Celler also raised awareness by pressing leaders to persuade British allies to have Jewish refugees relocate to predominantly Arab Palestine. Celler harangued FDR and State Department leaders. The congressman from Brooklyn could not tell whether President Roosevelt heard him but could not act, or tuned him out with no intention of helping the Jews.

After FDR's death, successor Truman was overwhelmed and annoyed when Celler led a New York congressional delegation in 1945 to lobby for persuading Britain to let more Jewish refugees into Palestine. Truman, the coarse midwesterner, proved to be a principled and resolute supporter of the Jewish state even though the journey to that destination was a roller-coaster ride of misunderstandings, tense debates, perceived betrayals and makeups.

────── • ──────

People danced in the streets of Brooklyn and the Bronx upon hearing the news of a state of Israel. That evening in Washington over the Jewish Agency on Massachusetts Avenue, a pale blue and white flag bearing the Star of David in the center was unfurled. Celebrations were passionate but short lived. Israel immediately came under attack by five Arab nations—Lebanon, Syria, Iraq, Egypt, and Saudi Arabia, which sent a unit that fought under the Egyptian command. Before Truman's decision to recognize Jewish Palestine, Marshall and Forrestal warned that the Arabs had the numbers to push the Jews into the sea and strangle their nation before it could begin living. Egypt, Jordan, Syria, Lebanon, Iraq, and Saudi Arabia invaded but failed to destroy the Jewish state. For months, Truman refused to lift a US embargo on arms shipments to Israel. Also, in the United Nations, the United States supported mediation and compromise that infant Israel opposed.[40]

The Jews on the battlefield were mostly on their own during the nascent months of their independence. The Israeli military's courage, cunning, and victory changed many American minds, Celler told an American Jewish Committee interviewer Lawrence Rubin in 1970: "I would say—and I gather this from conversations of members of Congress of all faiths, heard in the cloakrooms, that the image of the Jew has been greatly heightened in the Gentile mind. No longer do they look upon the Jew as a mere pants peddler or a junk dealer or a Fagin or a Shylock; they look upon the Jew as an upstanding character of great courage, and as a worthy descendant of the Maccabees, as a worthy descendant of those who fought at Masada."[41]

Generals that included Yigal Alion and Yitzak Rabin told David Ben-Gurion that with 19,000 fully mobilized fighters Israel had a 50–50 chance of success against their invaders. The Jews lost nearly 1 percent of their population on the battlefield (6,400 of 650,000) during 1948–1949 yet they prevailed.

In 1949, victorious Israel signed separate armistices with five of the six invading Arab countries. Iraq did not sign an agreement but withdrew its troops.[42] With a tenuous peace achieved, Congressman Emanuel Celler prepared to visit the new nation whose creation he had lobbied.

8

Antitrust, Cold War, Incremental Immigration

Emanuel Celler emerged as the chief House sponsor of President Truman's extensive 1948 civil rights proposals. No president before Truman gave a special message on civil rights, a message that particularly distressed southern Democrats. "Our first goal," said the president January 7, "is to secure fully the essential human rights of our citizens." For decades Celler had been a rare voice advocating for these policies. Now he had a kindred soul in the executive branch.[1] First, however, Truman served the remaining three years and eight months of the late Franklin D. Roosevelt's fourth term, then pivoted to run for president under his own steam in 1948. Truman was an underdog, despite his monumental decisions to drop nuclear bombs on the Japanese cities Hiroshima and Nagasaki three days apart in August 1945 that resulted in instant, mass destruction of lives. Five days later, World War II ended in the Pacific.[2] In addition, Truman supported the partition of the former British colony Palestine that in spring 1948 created Israel and the restoration of a Jewish nation in the Middle East.

Truman faced a formidable Republican opponent in Thomas Dewey, governor of what was then America's most populous state, New York. Dewey in 1944 had challenged sickly incumbent FDR, but lost. In that case, most American voters were not ready to switch leaders during a climatic war, much like voters' decision four score years before in 1864 to stay the course and reelect embattled president Abraham Lincoln because his Union forces gained the upper hand after three and a half years of Civil War.[3] In addition to Dewey of the Empire State, two men who had split from the Democrats challenged Truman. Henry Wallace—FDR's former vice president, whom Democratic bosses dumped and replaced with Truman in 1944—ran as a Progressive Party candidate. At the June Democratic Convention, southern Democrats stormed out of the meeting to protest a civil rights plank added to the party platform.[4] US senator Strom Thurmond of South Carolina, a committed segregationist, ran as the choice of the new Dixiecrat Party. Truman appeared surrounded—by the GOP adversary from the Empire State, and by smaller yet potent splinter party opponents who could weaken him. Celler backed Truman and was a convention delegate. He had voiced concerns about Truman's Palestine policies but called "absurd" suggestions he would abandon Truman.[5]

Election 1948 produced the lowest presidential turnout in twenty-four years. Fifty-one percent of Americans voted, compared to 49 percent in 1924.[6] But once all the votes were counted, Truman won just under 50 percent of ballots cast compared to 45 percent for Dewey. Combined, Dixiecrat Thurmond and Progressive candidate Wallace earned 5 percent of the votes. The electoral college tally was Truman 303, Dewey 189, and Thurmond 39.[7] A jubilant Truman held up a predawn edition of the *Chicago Tribune* that carried the banner headline "Dewey defeats Truman." Later *Tribune* editions at sunrise carried a single right-column head that corrected the error and announced the Truman victory. Truman won 24.2 million of 48.5 million total votes. Dewey earned 22 million votes, about what he had scored in his 1944 run against FDR. He won Northeast states New York, New Jersey, Connecticut, Pennsylvania, Maryland, and New Hampshire, but lost many Midwest states he had won in 1944. Dewey forfeited 75 electoral college votes that he had won in 1944.

———— • ————

Dewey in essence won key battles—he dominated East Coast states, including New York and Pennsylvania—but lost the Midwest, which included Illinois, among states he'd won during his 1944 presidential run. New York, Pennsylvania, and Illinois contained 65 percent of the American Jewish population. Dewey won two of three states, including Emanuel Celler's home New York. Celler breezed to victory during his Fifteenth Congressional District election. He routed Republican challenger Henry D. Dorfman 81 to 19 percent. Overall, Democrats flipped the House of Representatives and took control, gaining seventy-five seats, the largest boost since the 1932 FDR election.

Truman, who complained bitterly of a do-nothing Republican majority that blocked his initiatives, now had majority legislative allies. Among them was Estes Kefauver, a House member from Tennessee since 1939. In his first campaign for the US Senate, he had achieved an upset victory over Judge John A. Mitchell, the candidate of the Memphis-based political machine of Democratic boss Edward H. Crump. Kefauver assembled a coalition of labor, women's, African American, and professional groups as his chief support-ers. The cum laude Yale Law graduate campaigned in a coonskin cap (his great-grandfather ran unsuccessfully against Davey Crockett) after Crump attacked him as a "pet coon."[8]

Because of the Democratic Party's congressional landslide, Celler gained a leadership post. In January 1949, he assumed chairmanship of the Judiciary Committee.[9] He also became chairman of the Monopoly Subcommittee of the House Judiciary Committee. That year, 1949, he began an investigation of the insurance industry and after that scrutiny of large acquisitions in manufacturing and mining. Through the 1950s and 1960s mergers accelerated and scores of companies disappeared from the Fortune 500 list.[10] With time, Celler's committee accelerated its activities, averaging fourteen hearings or reports per Congress from 1955 to 1962.

By 1950, Celler and Kefauver cosponsored House and Senate legislation to curb business excesses. The Celler-Kefauver Anti-Merger Act of 1950 rein-forced the 1914 Clayton Antitrust Act that prohibited manufacturers from selling only to dealers and contractors who agreed to reject the products of business rivals. The Celler-Kefauver Act limited any corporate mergers and joint ventures that reduced competition. By the twenty-first century, these laws were enforced by the Federal Trade Commission and the antitrust divi-sion of the Department of Justice.[11]

Celler and Kefauver had similar skepticism toward the consolidation of large banks. John J. McCloy, chairman/president of Rockefeller-owned Chase Bank, persuaded J. Stewart Baker, chairman of the House of Mor-gan-owned Manhattan Bank, to merge the two institutions into Chase Manhattan Bank, which with resources of $7.6 billion would make it Amer-ica's second-largest bank (San Francisco-based Bank of America was No. 1 with $8.3 billion in assets).

"This is too big a merger," Celler told reporters. "It would give an all-powerful oligarchy a stranglehold on New York banking." McCloy, whose legacy was chairman of the post–World War II American century—the 1940s to 1970s when America's leaders rejected isolationism and embraced public service and realpolitik over ideology—because of roles as adviser to US presi-dents and chairman of banks, corporate boards, and philanthropies, disputed

Celler's criticisms. A merged Chase Manhattan, said McCloy, would have 87 offices out of 560 operated by fifty-seven banks in Metropolitan New York.

Furthermore, with 14,000 commercial US banks, "It's really hard," he said, "to conceive of any industry in the country where competition is keener."[12] McCloy's merger attempt succeeded and it triggered an explosion of bank mergers nationwide.[13] Three months after the Chase merger, Celler introduced a bill that specifically subjects banks to the Clayton Antitrust Act. McCloy made multiple trips to Washington to testify against Celler's bill. In 1960, Congress passed the Bank Merger Act. All federally insured banks were subjected to congressional approval.[14]

In addition to banks, Celler was a critic of sports monopolies. In 1951, Celler, chairman of the House subcommittee on Antitrust and Monopolies, initiated an inquiry into Major League Baseball. Celler told reporters that the committee's purpose was to "help baseball against itself." There was player unrest and a growing demand for newer franchises (there were no West Coast teams and the westernmost clubs were St. Louis and Kansas City). Unlike Celler, few of the House members appeared to understand the testimony, wrote author David George Surdam in *The Big Leagues Go to Washington* (2015), and the other committee members made dubious comments and some hearings lapsed into farce.[15] League owners resisted releasing financial records and retained an antitrust exemption. The leagues were considered small businesses. They still are in the twenty-first century, although how "small" is $10 billion annual enterprise MLB, $14 billion National Football League, and $8 billion National Basketball Association? Despite striking out at the 1951 hearings, Celler remained skeptical through the end of his service in Congress in the early 1970s. With other legislators he introduced bills seeking to strip professional sports of antitrust exemptions.[16]

⎯⎯⎯⎯ • ⎯⎯⎯⎯

For Americans, World War II was a five-year-old memory. Their time to focus on civilian life and even domestic tranquility was disrupted again. On June 25, 1950, Soviet-supported North Korean soldiers crossed the 38th Parallel and invaded South Korea. The following day President Truman authorized the US Navy and Air Force to assist South Korean troops defending their territory.[17]

On June 27, the UN Security Council adopted a resolution that called for armed intervention in Korea on the eve of the collapse of Seoul—South Korea's capital and largest city—to invading communists. The Soviet representative was absent during the Security Council vote. Five days after North Korean aggression began, Truman sent US ground troops to South Korea.

He also signed a bill that extended the draft one year and ordered the US Navy to blockade the Korean coast. World War II had ended five years before and during the new era of Cold War a Soviet satellite country induced heat.

There was no declaration of war from Congress; US military activity was labeled a "police action." General Douglas MacArthur in July was named to command UN peacekeeping troops in Korea. On September 15, UN troops landed in Inchon. MacArthur-led forces' daring military maneuver behind enemy line routed the North Koreans.

The Allies then pressed on toward Seoul. They recaptured the capital in nine days, on September 26.[18] On September 29, US-backed South Korean soldiers reached the 38th Parallel. A week later, October 7, UN forces crossed the border and invaded North Korea. On October 11, leaders in mainland Communist China denounced the United States for entering North Korea and vowed that they would not "stand idly by." On October 20, US troops captured the North Korean capital Pyongyang after a two-day battle. MacArthur's forces reached the Yalu River that separated North Korea and China. In response, Chinese soldiers attacked on November 6, but pulled back as an apparent warning.[19] The Chinese followed up with a massive counteroffensive—two hundred thousand troops were sent in—November 26. UN troops retreated and abandoned Pyongyang on December 5; however, the same UN forces recaptured Seoul in March.[20]

Commander-in-Chief Truman committed to averting another world war by managing little skirmishes under Cold War rules of engagement. Truman's intent was to negotiate a truce. MacArthur had other ideas. In an April 5 letter to House Minority Leader Joseph Martin, R-Massachusetts, the general said, "There is no substitute for victory" as far as Korea was concerned. MacArthur disregarded Truman's orders to not discuss war in public. Six days later, Truman relieved MacArthur of his command in the Far East and replaced him with General Matthew Ridgway.[21]

Hawks who wanted to escalate the fighting denounced Truman's firing of MacArthur. Celler supported the Truman administration: "Our aim is peace without appeasement and with honor. The only road to peace for the world is collective security and the administration has consistently followed this course," said the congressman during a June radio broadcast debate with US senator William E. Jenner, an Indiana Republican.[22] At the same time, dovish observers praised the president for reining in the general. Peace talks began in July 1951 but deadlocked. Low-level fighting dragged on for two more years.

Senator Estes Kefauver was a kindred soul to Celler. Their shared interests included civil rights, consumer protection, and regulation of monopolies. Both men cultivated personas as earnest advocates and protectors of common citizens. If Celler was the unrelenting bulldog, Kefauver was the authentic political maverick of the middle third of the twentieth century.

Among his bold acts was leading televised corruption hearings in May 1951 that looked into the activities of organized crime. Testimony by reputed underworld figures Joe Adonis and Frank Costello caused a sensation. Virginia Hill, girlfriend of gangster Bugsy Siegel, also testified. She showed up wearing a $5,000 silver-blue mink coat. "You bastards," roared an agitated Hill. "I hope a goddamn atom bomb falls on every goddamn one of you."[23]

On April 11 and April 14, 1951, Emanuel Celler exchanged letters with *Brooklyn Eagle* editor Thomas N. Schroth.[24] The editor invited the congressman to write a series of articles after he returned from an upcoming second trip to Israel. Celler made his first visit in October 1948, five months after independence and an immediate war with seven Arab neighbors. Stella accompanied him abroad. On that trip, the Cellers arrived in a land of 8,000 square miles, about the size of New Jersey, populated with 650,000 citizens.[25] Celler accepted Schroth's invitation to report from the desert. The Cellers' follow-up visit was sponsored by the Magan David Adom Mission (Israel's Red Cross).[26] The *Brooklyn Eagle* series on Israel began June 10 with the headline, "1.3 million turn desert into nation." An editor's note said in 1948, Celler made an extensive trip through Israel for the Magan David Adom Mission.

Celler wrote: "This is the year 5711 in the life of the Jews—a people who possessed nationhood, lost it for 2000 years, and regained it again only three short years ago." The 800-word account included a picture of Celler with his wife. An illustration of New Jersey placed inside trapezoid-shaped Israel helped to describe their similar land mass. Part two on June 11 was titled, "Jews for centuries sought a homeland," a two-line head. The third installment on June 12 was under the banner headline, "Israel is a democratic nation with rights for all."

Celler's fourth dispatch on June 13 arguably was his most exuberant, "Enthusiasm and energy mark growth of state of Israel: People are indomitable despite war and nature." He wrote, "There is a climate of energy and vigor which I encountered in Israel, which in part expresses the almost miraculous strides Israel has made in the three years of statehood. . . . They were fighting a war, building a structure of government, hewing out roads, building villages and settlements, draining the marshes, creating new industries, writing books, singing songs, producing operas, painting, exploring new scientific fronts—all at the same time."[27]

Part five on June 14 focused on education, headlined "Israel's school gains cited: 125 new ones erected in year, Celler reports." The congressman wrote, "Teachers are the largest professional group in Israel, but her need for new teachers increases rapidly.... Education is free, universal and compulsory."[28] Part six of the series June 15 bore the cautionary headline, "Israel divides resources: Country's progress spurs Arab leaders." Celler wrote, "The two most acute problems that face Israel are military and economic. Humiliation and disgrace suffered by the Arabs in their defeat at the hands of the Israelis are spurring the Arab leaders to redeem themselves before their people."[29] Hostility from Arab neighbors, surrounding Israel from the Atlantic to the Indian oceans, would be unrelenting.

The so-called Israel miracle that Celler praised was indeed based on promise, but also denial. "The nation I am born into has erased Palestine from the face of the earth," explained author Ari Shavit six decades later. "Bulldozers razed Palestinian villages, warrants confiscated Palestinian land, laws revoked Palestinian citizenship and annulled their homeland."[30]

Young Israel had no time for guilt and compassion as it welcomed nearly 300,000 European refugees while expelling twice as many Palestinian natives. Shavit acknowledged that neighbor Arab states hostile to Israel offered no help to Palestinian brothers and sisters who did not have nation concept or a mature and recognized national movement.[31] Still, in order for the nation of Israel to bloom in the desert, 700,000 human beings lost their homes and homeland, a reality Celler the visitor and correspondent conveniently downplayed.[32]

Celler's series finale, part seven on June 17, explained why the new nation's population doubled in three years, "Israel harbors homeless Jews," read the two-line head. Celler wrote that based on a 1950 estimate, 287,500 Central and Eastern European Jews had emigrated to Israel. The breakdown went like this: Bulgaria, 7,000; Czechoslovakia, 17,000; Hungary, 160,000; Poland, 65,000; Romania, 35,000; and Yugoslavia, 3,500. In addition, Celler noted, 200,000 Jews came from North Africa, Yemen, and Iraq. The entire Yemeni community—44,000—was brought to Israel by air, a transfer that took eighteen months. Among the European immigrants, practically all Bulgarian and Yugoslavian Jewry resettled in Israel.[33]

Celler also noted that he had initiated a June 1948 Displaced Persons Act in America that resulted in 48,000 Jews entering the United States. President Truman wanted a more inclusive act. He called the measure "flagrantly discriminatory" and anti-Semitic and accused the Congress of dragging its feet.[34] One million people liberated by allied forces remained in limbo in West Germany, Austria, and Italy, afraid to return to their homes. The people waited in refugee camps. "The only civilized route," said Truman, "is to allow these people to take new roots in friendly soil."[35] The first displaced persons ship reached New York Harbor on October 30, 1948. It came from Bremerhaven, Germany, and was filled with 813 men, women, and children. A "WELCOME TO AMERICA" banner greeted the seafarers.[36] Celler's final *Brooklyn Eagle* dispatch said Truman and Congress intended to extend the law six months, until 1951.

On March 30, 1952, Truman announced that he would not seek reelection in the fall. He was about to complete nearly two tumultuous terms, as stand-in for FDR's unprecedented fourth term, and then his surprise 1948 election. Truman served nearly eight years but was exempt from the Twenty-Second Amendment that limited future presidents to two, 4-year terms. He was weary of Cold War politics that included the unresolved Korean military conflict. Truman's public approval ratings were dismal, 23 percent in January, according to the *Congressional Quarterly* weekly report. Estes Kefauver challenged Truman for the Democratic nomination and handily defeated the incumbent in the winter New Hampshire primary.

Dwight D. Eisenhower, World War II hero commander, at that time president of Columbia University, was an anticipated, formidable Republican challenger for the White House. So was Senator Robert Taft of Ohio, conservative Republican and son of the twenty-seventh president, Howard Taft.[37]

———— • ————

US senator Pat McCarran of Nevada was among the most reactionary of the members in that upper chamber.[38] Even more than Senate colleague Joseph McCarthy, McCarran railed against alleged communist sympathizers in the State Department and also said a "traitorous" Protestant elite should be replaced by American Irish Catholic leaders.[39] In the climate of anticommunism he proposed legislation that would restrict immigration. That spring, the McCarran-Walter Act retained the ethnic quota structure of the 1924 Johnson-Reed National Origins law that Celler had unsuccessfully fought. McCarran's law repealed and recodified scores of immigration laws that had evolved—because of tweaks by Celler and like-minded colleagues—helter-skelter over the years. Senator Hubert Humphrey of Minnesota attempted to substitute the 1950 US Census as the baseline to determine who was American. The Senate rejected Humphrey's proposal and the 1920 census—far less ethnically and racially diverse compared to the previous count—was used as the measure.[40]

Because of anxiety over Mexican migration, McCarran-Walter included a so-called "wetback provision" that made it a felony to bring into the United States or induce persons who were ineligible for entry. Black immigration was cut from Africa and the West Indies too. Quotas were set for persons from the nearby British West Indies, whose residents had formerly qualified under European parent-country quotas.[41] The law did remove racial prohibitions on naturalization and immigration. For the first time in American history, the federal government granted Asians opportunities to become US citizens. An "Asia Pacific" triangle established an annual quota of one hundred from each nation.[42] McCarran-Walter passed the House and Senate and moved to the president's desk. On June 25, 1952, Truman vetoed the bill, condemning it as an insult to the Italians, Greeks, and Turks with whom the United States had just formed NATO, the North Atlantic Treaty Organization alliance. Truman also said the notion of protecting America against Eastern Europe was abhorrent and absurd: "The countries of Eastern Europe have fallen under the Communist yoke—they are silenced, fenced off by barbed wire and minefields—no one passes their borders but at the risk of their life. We do not need to be protected against immigrants of other countries."[43] Two days later, June 27, 1952, the Senate overrode the president and McCarran-Walter became law.[44]

Celler valiantly fought the McCarran-Walter legislation before it became law. In February 1951, Celler introduced an omnibus bill "to revise the laws related to immigration, naturalization and nationality."[45] Celler's proposal did not limit immigration from European colonies in the Western Hemisphere (Caribbean) that were populated predominantly by people of color. Celler also advocated for annual distribution of 7,000 unused quotas for the benefit of low-quota countries. "Each year almost one-half of the sum total of annual quotas, numbering slightly over 154,000, remain unused because some of the countries which have large quotas at their disposal simply do not send us their emigrants," said the congressman from Brooklyn. "On the other hand, natives of such countries as Italy, Greece, Spain, Portugal, Turkey, Austria, Egypt and Poland have to wait upwards of eight to 10 years until their turn on the very long waiting lists is reached."[46]

Through the spring of 1952, Celler refused to cease his diatribes against the McCarran and Walter immigration bills. Celler pointed out discrimination toward Asians in Walter's H.R. 5678 and protested the provision that conferred upon the president the right to suspend immigration at will. Celler explained he could accept presidential suspension in time of war, in time of extreme emergence, but not in times of peace. That month, although without success, Celler introduced amendments to liberalize the Walter bill.[47] In condemning the ethnically discriminatory aspects of McCarran-Walter, Celler appealed to wartime patriotism: "If you look at the casualty lists coming from Korea you will see what? Only British or German names? Indeed no. You will see many names of those who came from southern and eastern Europe . . . These diverse names belong to honored dead and wounded. Why should their people be so discriminated against by virtue of the national origins theory?"[48] Celler fought relentlessly yet suffered a bitter defeat. McCarran and Walter did all they could to exclude Celler from the immigration debate. When Celler asked to be allowed to explain a reform bill that would have overturned national origins quotas, McCarran, who chaired the hearing, gave him three minutes to testify, an insult to a full committee chairman.[49] Yet despite the passage of McCarran-Walter—which overrode Truman's veto—the congressman from Brooklyn resumed his fight for liberalized immigration.

Truman was a lame-duck president as he continued to fight the immigration law. Three months later, the president appointed a commission on immigration and naturalization. "Whom We Shall Welcome," the report published in January 1953, during Truman's final days in office, said America's immigration policies had "frustrated and handicapped . . . American foreign policy" and called racially discriminatory quotas a "major disruptive influence."[50]

Many other Americans began to see all-restrictive, race-based policy as inconsistent with and contrary to postwar foreign and domestic policy goals. They worried that newly independent Southeast Asian countries and former European colonies in Africa would reject alliances with a United States whose laws they considered racially derogatory and would join the Soviet Union instead.[51] The commission recommended increasing the numbers allowed to immigrate and replacing the existing quota system with another that did not discriminate on the basis of race, ethnicity, or creed.

Celler wholeheartedly agreed. His vision was a coexistence of pragmatism and idealism. Celler represented the multiethnic Fifteenth Congressional District of Brooklyn, New York, and had no interest in alienating his electors. Numerous constituents exhorted him to adopt a liberal stance on immigration, noted Canadian scholar Bernard Lemelin in a 1994 journal article. Constituent Mary Liroff pressed Celler to concentrate his efforts on liberalizing the Displaced Persons Act of 1948.[52] Celler was sensitive to distress over McCarran-Walter bills that limited Caribbean immigration from

British-controlled islands despite Britain's favored immigration status. "I know in my own district that the groups representing the National Association for the Advancement of Colored People and the Urban League," said Celler, "are very much disturbed by it."[53]

Celler's involvement in immigration was not dictated solely by local interest. He was a staunch defender of Truman's foreign policy. Celler justified his opposition to the discriminatory provision in McCarran-Walter legislation toward Asians because America's image could be severely tarnished.

"To my mind, that clause will wound the sensibilities of the people of Asia, people whose friendship we are endeavoring now to cultivate," said Celler. "It will be grist to the communist mill. It will be bruited about throughout all Asia that we are discriminating violently against these peoples."[54] In the early years of Cold War strategy, Celler surmised that race-neutral US immigration policy was in America's best interest.

At the Republican National Convention in Chicago on July 7, Eisenhower defeated Taft to win the GOP nomination on the first ballot. Senator Richard M. Nixon of California became Eisenhower's running mate. The GOP platform proposed a balanced budget and a reduced national debt.[55] The Democratic National Convention, also in Chicago, opened July 21 and lasted six days. Governor Adlai Stevenson of Illinois emerged as the nominee on the third ballot. He beat Kefauver, who had won thirteen of fifteen winter and spring primaries, losing only in Florida and Washington, DC.[56] Truman, big-city political bosses, and conservative southern Democrats combined to block the maverick's selection and swing the convention to Stevenson. John Sparkman of Alabama was picked as Stevenson's running mate.[57] On Election Day, November 4, Eisenhower defeated Stevenson 55 to 45 percent and handily won the electoral college 442 to 89. Amiable "I like Ike" Eisenhower also had long coattails. The GOP regained control of the House of Representatives and held a slim 221- to 213-seat advantage.

Celler's sixteenth reelection campaign was a rematch against Republican Henry D. Dorfman. As in 1952, Celler won handily 74 to 22 percent. Two American Labor Party candidates claimed the remaining 4 percent of votes. However, the slight GOP power shift advantage in the House resulted in Celler losing his Judiciary Committee chairmanship. Chauncey W. Reed of Illinois replaced Celler as chairman during the 83rd Congress from 1953 to 1955.[58] Republicans also squeezed Celler out of a seat on an "alien watchdog" committee that addressed immigration reform.[59]

At age sixty-four, Emanuel Celler's political career appeared to be in decline. Yet that did not mean the congressional bulldog would give up the fight.

Figure 1: President Lyndon B. Johnson (*seated*) signing the 1964 Civil Rights Act on July 2 in the East Room of the White House. Emanuel Celler, House floor manager of the legislation, stood at LBJ's shoulder (*right*). The Rev. Dr. Martin Luther King Jr. stood behind the president and peered over LBJ's shoulder. *LBJ Library photo by Cecil Stoughton*

Figure 2 and Figure 3: The Cellers, wife Stella, oldest daughter Jane, and Emanuel holding youngest daughter Judith in 1927. The family is on the deck of a ship about to embark on a trip to Europe. *Bain Photo Agency image, Jill Rifkin Collection*

Figure 4: Sumner Avenue, the Brooklyn street where Celler grew up. The Williamsburg neighborhood street was named for Charles Sumner, the Massachusetts US senator and abolitionist. In 1987, Sumner Avenue was renamed Marcus Garvey Boulevard. *Brooklyn Public Library-Brooklyn Collection*

Figure 5: Harlan Fiske Stone, Celler's professor at Columbia University School of Law. Stone would later become an associate justice of the US Supreme Court in 1925. A few years later, Celler joined his mentor in Washington, but in the other branch of government. In 1941, Stone ascended to chief justice and served until his death in 1946. *Columbia Law School Collection*

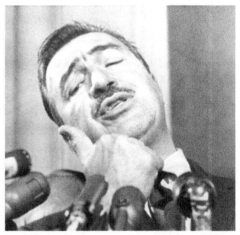

Figure 6: Adam Clayton Powell Jr. was the wily African American congressman from New York. Colleague Celler chaired the special committee that reached this conclusion: Powell, reelected to his seat by Harlem constituents, could not be banished by Congress for alleged indiscretions; however, he could be stripped of his powerful committee chairmanship. The House ignored the Celler Committee recommendation and Powell was removed. Powell returned after the US Supreme Court ruled that act was unconstitutional. *Collection of the US House of Representatives*

Figure 7: John Rankin of Mississippi was a Celler foe. Rankin was an over-the-top race-baiter and bigot. Celler challenged Rankin's rants on the House floor; New York delegation colleague Adam Clayton Powell Jr. wanted Rankin censured. Margaret Brisnine's portrait was in recognition of Rankin's service on the War Legislation Committee, which ultimately became the Veterans' Affairs Committee. *Collection of the US House of Representatives*

Figure 8: Clare Boothe Luce, Republican representing Connecticut, partnered with Celler on legislation that allowed immigrants from India to become US citizens. India, the former British colony, by the late 1940s emerged as the world's biggest Democratic nation. Luce was the wife of Time-Life media mogul Henry Luce. *Collection of the US House of Representatives*

Figure 9: Estes Kefauver of Tennessee was Celler's Senate ally in cosponsoring legislation that regulated big business and broke up monopolies. Kefauver ran for president in 1960, but the Democrat lost the primary to John F. Kennedy. *Collection of the US House of Representatives*

Figure 10: Francis Eugene Walter of Pennsylvania was Celler's Democratic foe regarding immigration reform. Walter was cosponsor of the 1952 McCarran-Walter Act that in large part restored the immigration race-based national origins model of 1924 that Celler loathed. When immigration subcommittee chairman Walter died in 1963, Celler pushed quickly—and successfully—for immigration reform. *Collection of the US House of Representatives*

Figure 11: Michael A. Feighan of Ohio was Celler's opponent during the 1960s immigration reform process. Feighan, a conservative Democrat, eventually yielded leadership of the legislation to Celler, the tenacious liberal Democrat. *Collection of the US House of Representatives*

Figure 12: House Rules Committee chairman Howard W. Smith's portrait was painted by Victor Lallier. "Judge" Smith, a Virginia Democrat, was a Celler adversary. Both committee chairmen waged an epic battle over the 1964 civil rights bill. Smith's tactical move to kill the legislation failed. Because Smith was "one of Congress' most notorious bigots," reported the *New York Times* in 1995, who "used his chairmanship to impede civil rights legislation," the Congressional Black Caucus and other House members had Smith's portrait removed from the hearing room. *Collection of the US House of Representatives*

Figure 13: Edna Kelly of Brooklyn was the first woman elected the New York congressional delegation. She was an anti-communist foreign policy expert. When gerrymandered congressional boundaries were redrawn under court order, incumbents Kelly and Celler had to compete for the same seat. Celler won and Kelly declined an offer from President Lyndon B. Johnson to become treasury secretary. *Collection of the US House of Representatives*

Figure 14: Celler, an avid opera-goer, walking to the Metropolitan Opera House in Manhattan. Although he loved the performances, Celler believed the former house on Broadway at West 39th Street was an architectural monstrosity. In 1967, he scolded fans who wanted to save the structure from demolition: "Why the sudden urge? Is it publicity? Some of them probably think Puccini is a name for spaghetti and that Richard Wagner was a baseball player." *Brooklyn Public Library-Brooklyn Collection*

Figure 15: Stella and Emanuel Celler at their fiftieth wedding anniversary in June 30, 1964. The couple married two days after the 1914 incident that ignited World War I, and their golden anniversary occurred two days before one of the congressman's greatest accomplishments, the Civil Rights Act. *Jill Rifkin Collection*

Figure 16: Elizabeth Holtzman challenged Celler in 1972 and pulled off one of the most spectacular upsets in House of Representatives history. Celler lost in the June Democratic primary by 600 votes out of 35,000 cast. Holtzman convinced enough voters that the octogenarian congressman was "too tired" to do the job. She became a member of the Watergate committee that investigated President Richard M. Nixon and his administration. Had Celler been reelected to a twenty-fifth term, he would have chaired the House Judiciary Committee investigation of Nixon. *Collection of the US House of Representatives*

Figure 17: Emanuel Celler's Judiciary Committee portrait was unveiled on March 19, 1963, coinciding with his fortieth anniversary in the House of Representatives. Joseph Margulies was the painter. Celler said the artist created a "painted biography" reflecting his character and personality. *Collection of the US House of Representatives*

Figure 18: Celler riding US Capitol subway system train. At that time, the two-car train moved representatives from their offices in the Rayburn House building to the Capitol. *Jill Rifkin Collection*

9

You Never Leave Brooklyn, Early 1950s

A Cold War against new nemesis Russia and its Soviet Union of Eastern European satellite countries prompted a communist red scare in America. By 1947, the House Un-American Activities Committee—launched in 1938—convened new investigations. There were sensational hearings investigating alleged communist mind control inside the Hollywood moviemaking industry. The next year Whitaker Chambers, who had participated in the American Communist Party but later disassociated, testified before HUAC and accused Alger Hiss, a US State Department official, of government espionage. Emanuel Celler's anti-Semitic, race-baiting nemesis and colleague John E. Rankin of Mississippi used parliamentary tricks to make HUAC a permanent congressional committee.[1] At the same time, he blunted investigations into KKK activity, making that society off-limits to scrutiny for committing undemocratic, domestic terrorism.

Two years after the end of World War II, federal agents combed New York City in search of former Nazis and Russian spies seeking to gain an edge on scientists and technology. *The House on Carroll Street*, a movie set in Brooklyn, later depicted that cat-and-mouse game.[2] When the Soviets in 1949 conducted a test explosion of an atomic bomb, the Red Scare in America intensified. Two self-confessed spies accused Julius and Ethel Rosenberg of being at the center of the spy ring that sold nuclear weapons secrets to the enemy. The couple insisted they were innocent, despite offers of leniency by prosecutors if they admitted guilt. The Rosenbergs were sentenced to death in 1951.[3]

Samuel Dickstein, chairman of the House Immigration Committee, a Celler ally and co-New York delegation colleague, was a Soviet spy. In the late 1930s, Dickstein hunted Nazis for the Soviets. At that time America and the Soviet Union were allies in destroying the Nazi German threat. The Soviets secretly paid Dickstein to serve as their agent.[4] Post–World War II, Dickstein was a New York state supreme court justice with no indication of communist sympathies. In 1950, he upheld the refusal of the Concourse Plaza Hotel in the Bronx to rent a ballroom to the leftist American Labor Party for an event in honor of actor and singer Paul Robeson.[5]

Neighbors accused neighbors of "red" activities or dismissed others as well-meaning "pinko" communist and socialist sympathizers. Such labels were political kisses of death. California US representative Richard Nixon won a US Senate seat in 1950 by strongly hinting that his opponent Helen Gahagan Douglas, liberal congresswoman from a heavily minority Los Angeles district and a former actress, was the "pink lady."[6] Douglas embodied the Hollywood liberalism denounced in Nixon's House Committee on Un-American Activities. Gahagan voted against renewed funding for HUAC and against a contempt citation for the Hollywood Ten, screenwriters and directors who were reluctant witnesses accused of communist sympathies. Nixon portrayed his opponent as at best a communist dupe and at worst a secret agent of the Kremlin.[7]

Citizens were in a panic during six months of ominous events: The fall of mainland China to communist rule, the Alger Hiss and Rosenberg spy cases, evidence that the Soviet Union joined the United States as exclusive owners of atom bombs, and Soviet-backed North Koreans invading democratic, US-supported South Korea.

Joseph McCarthy, forty-one, of Wisconsin was rated the worst US senator according to a poll of congressional correspondents.[8] Father Edmund A. Walsh of Georgetown University encouraged McCarthy to rage against the red threat and McCarthy found his issue. On February 9, 1950, he embarked on a red hunt.[9] This was at a time US communist membership was in steep decline, said FBI director J. Edgar Hoover. He told *American Legion* magazine that Communist Party membership declined 200 percent in six years, from 74,000 members in 1947 to 24,000 in 1953.[10] Red hunters received a boost when the Smith Act was upheld as constitutional. Communist influence said Hoover declined in direct ratio to the member numbers.

Yet McCarthy persisted. He gave a speech in West Virginia in which he claimed to hold a list of 205 mostly State Department employees who were communist plants. When challenged, McCarthy declined to verify his allegations. The senator repeated his red-baiting out West in Salt Lake City and Reno, Nevada. McCarthy gradually reduced the numbers on his lists of communist infiltrators but continued to rebuff attempts to verify his charges.[11]

McCarthy continued his stunts because his strategy worked. He could stop in remote areas and smear public servants. Local press and wire service journalists often would report or broadcast his charges without checking the facts. Exceptions included McCarthy's home state newspapers, the *Milwaukee Journal* and *Capital Times* of Madison, which often ran disclaimers next to the senator's charges, and the *Washington Post*, where editorial cartoonist Herbert Block ("Herblock") drew a barrel of tar and labeled the container "McCarthyism."[12] The phrase stuck.

Soon, McCarthy alleged that even the revered army general George C. Marshall was a communist sympathizer. Republican colleagues were reluctant to criticize the junior senator from Wisconsin. While campaigning for president in 1952, Dwight Eisenhower intended to pay tribute to Secretary of State and General George C. Marshall at a GOP rally in Milwaukee. At the last minute, he declined because he did not want to stoke hard feelings in McCarthy's home state.[13]

The Wisconsin senator allegedly singled out and smeared Emanuel Celler, the unapologetic liberal from New York. Celler was told that the index of the Committee on Un-American Activities contained a reference to "Celler, Emanuel, M.C."[14] There was no evidence in the copious Library of Congress Celler papers of any face-to-face clashes between the congressman and the senator from Wisconsin. McCarthy however did tangle with colleague US senator Herbert Lehman of New York, Celler's ally, and reflexively challenged McCarthy's smears. For example, during a long speech on the Senate floor at a lectern piled high with so-called cases, McCarthy claimed he cataloged lists of communist sympathizers working in government. Lehman recognized one of McCarthy's "cases" was false. Lehman rose from his seat, reminded the Senate of McCarthy's promise to let any senator examine the evidence, and walked down the aisle and stood in front of McCarthy with his hand out. Both men stared at each other.

"Go back to your seat old man," growled McCarthy. Lehman, seventy-three, looked around the chamber for support but instead received silence and lowered eyes.[15]

Celler meanwhile confronted McCarthy and McCarthyism from a distance, on radio and television, in publications, and at public forums. "Our greatest internal danger," Celler told the Federal Bar Association, "is that of the paralysis of fear gripping this country . . . We are surrounded by distrust—distrust of ourselves, distrust of our Bill of Rights, distrust of law. In this distrust of the law to protect us internally, we fashion more laws which in turn, we again distrust . . . I have talked with many of my constituents—student, worker, businessman, housewife—and many of them are afraid; afraid, not of any spy lurking under a bed, or in a closet, or in the guise of an instructor (they do not feel that the Communist ideology is a passionate-eyed brunette whose charms are irresistible), but they are afraid of being accused of heresy should they depart from the expression of any but the most orthodox of opinions. In short they are afraid to speak their minds."[16]

Then in July at the Democratic National Convention, Celler pleaded that the party add an anti-McCarthyism plank to its platform. The previous month McCarthy delivered the keynote speech at the GOP convention. "My good friends," said the senator, "I said one communist in a defense plant is one communist too many [applause]; one communist on the faculty of one university is one communist too many [applause]; one communist among the American advisers at Yalta is one communist too many, and even if there were only one communist in the State Department, that would still be one communist too many."[17]

"I offer it soberly," said Celler to committee members, "because it is a sobering and fearful thing that this kind of plank in a national party platform has become a necessity." It said:

> The Democratic Party will never desert the freedoms of our people under the guise of pretending to protect them. We pledge to fight the dark and reactionary forces high in the counsels of the Republican Party which have made political capital out of the techniques of character assassination by innuendo and who have adopted the dishonoring and dishonorable concept of guilt by association. We shall wipe out the climate of fear which has led good men of good will to avoid freedom of expression and assembly.
>
> We pledge ourselves to reinvigorate our fundamental precept that a man is innocent until proven guilty. We believe firmly that Communism internally and externally can and must be fought without resort to the Communist tactics of suppression of all individual freedom. It is this respect for the individual and his rights as an individual which compels our abhorrence of Communism. Communism which feeds on aggression, hatred, and the imprisonment of men's minds and souls shall not take root in the United States. To that end we pledge our every resource.[18]

Celler's criticism of McCarthy boiled over occasionally. Once Celler said that it would be a misfortune if someone were to throw Senator McCarthy into the Potomac River, but "if someone were to fish him out that would be a calamity."[19]

Also, while addressing two hundred constituents at Brooklyn's Aperion Manor on Kings Highway, the congressman scolded the crowd for being apathetic about McCarthy and said, "I am sure [President Eisenhower] hates his guts, and I do too." Still, Celler's mail regarding McCarthy favored the Wisconsin senator 3–1 in 1954, the year McCarthy was eventually rebuked and discredited by the Senate and CBS News.[20]

———————•———————

On August 8, 1951, Richard J. Walsh Sr. sent a letter to Celler in Washington. Walsh was the second husband of writer Pearl S. Buck, and established book publisher John Day Company of New York City in 1926.[21] John Day published Buck's *The Good Earth* and the historical novel about China won a 1932 Pulitzer Prize for fiction. In 1938 her body of literary work earned Buck a Nobel Prize. R. J. Walsh wrote to Celler: "Reading this piece about you by Tex (McCrary) and Jinx (Falkenburg) made us wonder whether you might some time to write the story of your life. Perhaps you have already planned this with some publisher. If not, shouldn't you and I discuss it together some time?"[22]

On August 9, Celler replied: "It sounds like it might be a lot of fun. Let's get together and talk about it."[23] On September 14, Walsh received a letter written on House of Representatives letterhead from Bess Effrat Dick, Celler's chief clerk:

> Dear Mr. Walsh,
>
> Congressman Celler talked with me about the possibility of writing a book about him, the central themes of which would be his views and comments on issues of public concern and interest.
>
> I shall appreciate an opportunity to discuss this with you. Should you contemplate a trip to D.C. shortly, we could arrange for a meeting mutually convenient; otherwise, I shall be pleased to discuss this matter with you in New York.[24]

In a September 24 follow-up note to Miss Dick, Walsh said he would be visiting Washington, DC, on October 23 and he did indeed want to talk to her about the possibility of a book by Celler. In a September 28 reply, Miss Dick said she was pleased to learn he was arriving in Washington on Tuesday, October 23. She instructed Walsh to come to Room 346 of the Old House

Office Building.[25] On October 24, Richard J. Walsh Sr., John Day Company president, sent this memo to his son and employee Richard J. Walsh Jr.:

> As a result of my call at Representative Celler's office yesterday, I feel quite encouraged about the book we have proposed. His chief clerk, Miss Bess Effrat Dick, with whom I had a long talk, will probably be able to collaborate successfully with him.
>
> It was his own suggestion that she should do so, and I could see that she has done a lot of thinking and has a good idea of how to go about it. She has been with him 10 years and she proposes to do a great deal of research about the previous years.
>
> He has been in Congress since March 1923, the ninth-oldest representative in point of service, although he is only 63. Miss Dick's plan is to cover the events of 30 years in our national and international life, in the human terms of Celler's experience. Thus, the book would begin with his entrance into Congress in 1923, and the events of his boyhood and youth would gradually be revealed by flashbacks.
>
> She will prepare an outline and several chapters which we should see early next year [1952]. She said that she would be very open to criticisms and suggestions, and I think she will.
>
> I had a little talk with Celler himself and he is beginning to get interested in the book, as he was not when I first talked to him in New York.
>
> I have suggested that we aim at publication March 4, 1953, the 30th anniversary of his entrance into Congress.
>
> Incidentally, he came out to see me, only briefly, because he was presiding over the hearing being held by the Judiciary Committee on baseball. Branch Rickey [Brooklyn Dodgers owner] was testifying and at Celler's suggestion I went in and listened for five minutes.[26]

That same day Walsh Sr. also sent a memo to employee Paul S. Ericsson:

> You will note from the attached that your suggestion of a book by Congressman Celler may work out. Miss Dick tells me that there was an interview with him in the *New York Post* a few years ago, of which she has no copy, and which would be useful as biographical background. Do you think you could locate this, either in the public library or the morgue of the *Post*, and if it is worth having, get a photo static copy of it (the *Post* says it has no index record).

On October 26, Bess Effrat Dick answered Paul S. Ericsson's inquiry: "It is a guess of mine that it appeared in the *New York Post*; possibly it appeared in the now-defunct *P.M.*"[27]

Actually, the article Walsh and Dick were looking for was the Tex and Jinx gossip column published in the *New York Herald Tribune*, not the *Post* or *P.M.* or the *Mirror*.[28] Tex McCrary, World War II veteran turned journalist, and Jinx Falkenberg, model/actress/athlete, were a husband-wife media team with radio and TV talk show, and a syndicated newspaper column.

————————•————————

On March 3, 1953, in Washington, Celler was recognized inside the Capitol for thirty years of service in Congress. "Manny Celler is a fighting liberal," said colleague Louis B. Heller of the Seventh Congressional District. "He has fought the battle of the working people. He has fought the battle against the power of big business monopoly. He has fought for traveling in the defense of free expression. Press, free assembly, and for all civil liberties which make up our democracy. In recent years he has been one of the staunchest advocates of the United Nations and has espoused the causes of independence for Israel and India."

Heller recalled that he met Celler in June 1922 when the honoree made his first run for Congress. Celler spoke at his Boys High School graduation ceremony and left an indelible impression.

In 1942, Heller said he ran for New York state senate on the Democratic Party ticket. Celler was well established and projected to be reelected by at least a 2 to 1 margin. Heller believed that Celler waged a vigorous campaign in order to bring him along on his bandwagon and introduce him to the voters. Heller was grateful:

> When he first came here, he was quickly plunged into the fierce controversy then raging over the question of immigration. He is still in the midst of that controversy today—but how the world has changed during those 30 years. In a sense, Manny Celler has never left Brooklyn and the millions of people that make up that community—the Jews, the Irish, the Italians, and other nationality groups.[29]

The next day, March 4, *You Never Leave Brooklyn*, Celler's autobiography, was published by the John Day Company. Publishing trade magazine *Kirkus Reviews* offered an advance critique on February 1: "Mr. Celler is no great shakes as a writer, but his book can be recommended as a simple, modest self-portrait of an able congressman who has almost always been on the side of the angels."

William S. White, a member of the *New York Times* Washington bureau, reviewed Celler's autobiography March 15 for the Sunday Book Review. White's piece was headlined "A Sturdy Foe of Cant":[30]

He has been told, he says, that in the index of the House Committee on Un-American Activities, there is a reference to "Celler, Emanuel, M.C." That does not disturb him, he says. "What is disturbing was the hesitation—no, stronger than that—the reluctance in me to state publicly that I have been indexed by the Un-American Activities Committee. I knew that in that reluctance I was facing fear [...]

One of his happiest days came with the creation of Israel, and then in due course he went out to see the new country where, as he says, he was privileged to "touch the raw material of history."[31]

On the Sunday of the *New York Times* review, the publishing trade magazine *Booklist* called the autobiography "A lively, readable book."[32] On Monday, March 23, W. S. White wrote a 750-word review for the *New York Herald Tribune*.[33]

The Nation magazine weighed in March 28 with this critique: "Reading that is easy and pleasing but never satisfying with both Celler's personality and the Brooklyn he typifies being treated only sketchily and inadequately. In short, one is left feeling that Celler has a much better story to narrate than the one he has actually told."

That same day, the *New Yorker* magazine published a brief 140-word review. *You Never Leave Brooklyn* was also reviewed by the *Springfield Republican* of Massachusetts on April 19, the Harvard Law School *Record* on May 21, and the June *U.S. Quarterly Book Review*, which said: "Mr. Celler's is an honest, sincere and frank book, a reflection of the personality behind it. He writes in a direct, simple style well suited to his purpose and to the general reader."[34]

Three months after publication, R. J. Walsh sent this progress report to Celler on June 24:

The number of copies of the book sold through last week was 1,725. This is not good, but I will say it is better than some of the books on our spring list. Three hundred more than we have sold of "Heresy Yes, Conspiracy, No," which has had very wide publicity all over the country . . . Whereas the distressing fact is that we have had to take back order credit this month nearly as many copies of yours as we have sold . . . I am at it long enough to know it has not caught on. Reviewers feel that the book does not contain enough material to be regarded as full-scale biography.

(1) We have not succeeded in lifting it out of the local Brooklyn atmosphere to the national and international levels, in spite of the fact that you richly deserve to be thought of on those levels because of your ideas and your accomplishments.

(2) Perhaps, after all, it was a mistake to say in the title that "You Never Leave Brooklyn," although everybody thought that would make a good title.[35]

Celler wanted to write a follow-up book. On September 14, 1953, a member of the congressman's staff corresponded with Richard J. Walsh:

He [Celler] wanted you to know he is leaving with his wife and Mrs. [Bess Effrat] Dick on November 5 on a journey that practically amounts to a trip around the world. He will be traveling under the auspices of the U.S. State Department with the dual purpose of making a study of the refugee problem and the effectiveness of the point four programs. His itinerary in this order is: Israel, Pakistan, Karachi, Bombay, New Delhi, Kashmir, Ankara, Calcutta, Malaya, Siam, Singapore, Manila, Hong Kong, Formosa and Tokyo. Mr. Celler expects that he will have material for a book when he returns. Would John Day be interested?[36]

The John Day Company passed on Celler's pitch. Instead, in 1954 Celler and publisher focused on selling off surplus stock of You Never Leave Brooklyn at a 75 percent remainder discount.[37]

10

Suez-cide and Civil Rights, 1950s

Emanuel Celler in September 1953 asked Representative Harold H. Velde that the House Un-American Activities Committee hold a public hearing at which friends of the late rabbis Stephen S. Wise and Judah L. Magness could reply to charges linking the names to communist activities.[1] Velde, an Illinois Republican, chaired the House Un-American Activities Committee in 1953. Despite the communist scare that chilled many Americans, others who were hot with rage pushed back. Louis Harap, editor of *Jewish Life* magazine, was subpoenaed to appear before the committee. Harap sparred with Velde and other House committee members and asserted that their actions were threats to democracy.[2]

On June 7, 1954, Celler was the subject of a WNYC radio interview. Journalist Gabe Pressman of the *New York World-Telegram & Sun* and four campus journalists, Martin Birmingham (*Washington Square Bulletin*), Fred Goldsweig (*Heights Daily News* of New York University), Ursala Mahoney (*Hunter College Arrow*), and Andrew Meisels (*City College Observation Post*), quizzed the congressman. Celler blasted McCarthy: "In the name of uncovering a communist conspiracy, he threatens the stability of our government. McCarthy invites anarchy. He shouts defiance to President Eisenhower. McCarthy is a demagogue who must be curbed and cut down to size by the Senate. But the Senate is controlled by Republicans and they are loathe to act. Eisenhower is taking the middle road by appeasing McCarthy, but he should remember, most accidents happen in the middle of the road."[3]

Celler told the campus journalists that he drafted a House Resolution urging the attorney general and Justice Department to take action and ferret out spies and informants, because they—not McCarthy—were qualified to investigate. McCarthy's committee investigations set him up above the law. "The attorney general would not have trouble finding these people," said Celler. It was "nonsense," said the congressman that McCarthy's GOP allies said the senator was doing a good job.[4]

By that time, McCarthy's reckless, red-baiting antics were wearing thin. Edward R. Murrow, his producer Fred Friendly, and CBS News profiled the senator in an unflattering *See It Now* TV episode. On March 25, 1953, McCarthy tried to block the appointment of Charles E. "Chip" Bohlen as US ambassador to the USSR because of the Eisenhower appointee's ties to the FDR and Truman administrations.[5]

US senator Herbert Lehman of New York, a friend and colleague of Celler, sparred with McCarthy for years on the Senate floor. In February 1951, Lehman told colleagues that McCarthy should not have been appointed chairman of the appropriations subcommittee that considered the State Department's budget because of the Wisconsin senator's bias.[6] In testy exchanges with McCarthy in June and July 1953, Lehman accused the Wisconsin senator of intimidation tactics and innuendo because McCarthy read into the record a sympathetic letter Lehman wrote to Alger Hiss, before that official and alleged communist spy was convicted of perjury. "The tactics of fear and smear demonstrated here today, as they have been on occasion," said Lehman on the Senate floor, "are a rebuke, not to me . . . but to all those of us who tolerate such tactics. The senator read a letter which I wrote in 1948 to Alger Hiss, months before there was any real evidence against him. That letter was trotted out in the 1950 campaign, when I was running for the second time for Senate. The people of New York showed what they thought of me. I have no apologies to make for [the letter] I was re-elected with a 300,000-vote plurality. Hiss was recognized for his work as president of the Carnegie Endowment for International Peace by Secretary of State John Foster Dulles."

McCarthy asked Lehman, when he was director of the United Nations Relief and Rehabilitation Administration (UNRRA), did he "put in positions of power" David Weintraub, Irving Kaplan, and Joel Gordon, two of the men accused communists and the other who refused to testify at a congressional committee? Lehman's answer: "It has 20,000 people worldwide, doing God's work. Of course there were communists in the UNRRA. It was an international organization whose members included many communist countries. I had no reason to suppose that Americans serving in UNRRA were communist sympathizers."

McCarthy: "I am not accusing [Lehman] of being a communist or a sympathizer."

Lehman: "I thank [McCarthy]. That is a very generous concession," and the Senate audience laughed uproariously.[7]

In November, McCarthy lashed out at the Truman administration, alleging it was "crawling" with communists. The day before the senator made that statement, Eisenhower referenced McCarthy and said people accused of disloyalty and spying had the right to confront their accusers face-to-face.[8] At a Senate hearing in April 1954, McCarthy attacked army operations at Fort Monmouth, New Jersey.[9]

US senator Robert C. Hendrickson of New Jersey, a determined anti-communist, was among the first members of Congress like Lehman to publicly challenge McCarthy's conduct.[10] Hendrickson was a member of the Senate Judiciary Committee who consulted with Celler, chairman of the parallel House committee. Hendrickson was also an advocate of ending racial segregation in public housing and restricting the use of injunctions against labor unions.[11]

Amid credible Cold War tensions and wariness about communism, lawmakers condemned McCarthy during congressional hearings in December 1954 and discredited his tactics. McCarthy's spotlight dimmed. During the November 1954 midterm elections, Democrats regained control of both chambers—the Senate by a one-seat majority and the House by twenty-nine seats. Celler's two-year exile from chairmanship of the Judiciary Committee ended. He resumed that leadership role in January 1955.

———————— • ————————

In the months before the midterm election Celler attempted—with little success—to loosen retightened immigration rules. President Eisenhower reviewed the Refugee Act of 1953 and urged the adoption of ten amendments. Congress, said the president, "would permit effective administration of the act by the executive branch of government and greatly aid the success of the program."[12] Eisenhower's suggested amendments included a proposal that immigration officials redirect unused quota numbers in various categories, possibly for orphans, on a worldwide basis; that definitions of the terms "refugee," "resettlement," "escapee," and "expellee" be liberalized; that requirement of a passport be waived where feasible; and that organizational sponsorship be accepted as sufficient for entry.[13] As the Cold War escalated Eisenhower practiced "mortgaging" immigration quota slots in order to manage frequent refugee crises. Mortgaging meant, for example, if Estonia's annual US immigration quota of 116 was already used up that year, additional refugees could be allowed in and the extra people would be charged against the next year's quota, similar to a loan.[14] The Soviet Union raised the stakes on this rivalry by refusing to allow people to leave the countries it controlled; that increased pressure on the United States to admit anyone who could get out.[15] Over a round of golf, Eisenhower pitched a plan to admit an additional 240,000 European immigrants within two years to adversaries Senator Pat McCarran, D-Nevada, Representative Francis Walter, D-Pennsylvania (coauthors of the previous year's McCarran-Walter Act), plus Celler, an advocate of the change.[16]

"Multer only Democrat opposing Red ban in final House vote," read one *Brooklyn Eagle* headline August 18, 1954. Abraham J. Multer, one of two House members who voted against the original bill outlawing the Communist Party, was the only Democrat in the House and the only Brooklyn representative to vote against the Senate-approved amendment making communist membership a felony. Representatives Francis E. Dorn and John H. Ray, Brooklyn's two Republicans, and Emanuel Celler and John Rooney, Democrats, voted in favor of the amendment. Multer and ninety-nine GOP members opposed it.[17]

The vote placed Celler, a frequent critic of some congressional investigations, on the same side—in favor of making communists felons—as Martin Dies, former chairman of HUAC. Joining them was Lester Holtzman, a Queens Democrat, who had interceded for Major Irving Peress, the dentist promoted and discharged from the army after his case was questioned by Senator Joseph McCarthy. Among those opposed to the amendment included Harold Velde, HUAC chairman at the time.[18]

America's entry into World War II resulted in an acute shortage of farm labor. Mexican migrant workers were recruited by the US government via a Bracero—Spanish for "arms"—program. Bracero policy was to work the Mexicans hard, pay them cheaply, and then return them across the Rio Grande and Tijuana borders when their labor was no longer needed. Mexican laborers were too poor to qualify as immigrants under the highly regulated, congressionally approved program.[19] During the war years the program expanded. It began in September 1942 in California with 1,500 migrant workers, then expanded to 52,000 in 1943 and to 120,000 by 1945.[20] Braceros labored in twenty-one states and harvested sugar beets, tomatoes, peaches, plums, and cotton valued at $432 million. The workers also worked on the railroads as section hands and maintenance laborers to transport military freight and personnel.[21] After the war, many employers favored these "wetback" laborers because they functioned without paperwork or minimum wage requirements. An illegal workforce grew and the US government winked at it.[22] By the 1950s, US officials realized that Mexican migrants were not behaving as expected. Many were staying in the United States and instead of stabilizing, the population was growing rapidly, especially near the Southern California border. Federal policy began to focus on curtailing illegal traffic along the southern border.

———————————

At the same time, Europe abandoned coal to heat homes and power vehicles. That continent's preferred fuel was oil, and most of the supply came from the Middle East, which included Saudi Arabia and Iraq. Egypt, a more densely populated area without oil, was strategically important. It maintained the Suez Canal where oil tanker ships anchored before traversing from the Middle East to Europe.[23] British and French companies built the canal that opened in 1869. Both countries maintained the waterway and both agreed to hand over the canal to Egypt and withdraw their armies. In addition to the canal, Egypt was committed to building an Aswan Dam so its peoples would have a reliable water supply. By 1956, the Eisenhower administration was concerned that President Gamal Abdel Nasser of Egypt was seeking Soviet Union–financed aid. Nasser was a coy, cagy, and charismatic character. He flirted with the Americans, then teased communist suitors. Egypt also was an enemy of the fledgling state of Israel. Throughout 1955 and the early months of 1956 both countries' armies engaged in continuing, lethal border clashes while both governments pointed fingers accusing each other of provocations. Although Israel was an eight-year-old democracy that harmonized with America's values, US policy leaders still expressed skittishness about arming Israel's military at the risk of offending Middle Eastern oil suppliers.

President Eisenhower had a heart attack in fall 1955. He recovered. Eight months later, the sixty-four-year-old president underwent surgery to remove an intestinal blockage. He was hospitalized for weeks with limited access to visitors when he returned to the White House. Middle East policy was left in the hands of Secretary of State John Foster Dulles, who altered relations to an anti-Nasser stance that included US reluctance to finance the Aswan Dam. Nasser in turn negotiated with the USSR and China's communist governments.

Egypt ally Saudi Arabia received US military aid—for example, eighteen Walker Bulldog army tanks. Israel, meanwhile, was approved for twenty-one army surplus half-track vehicles (with caterpillar treads in the rear and conventional front wheels).[24] In May, unbeknown to the White House or the State Department, a customs official blocked the shipment because the vehicles were covered by an invalid export license.

The Israeli embassy did not raise objections about the misunderstanding. But Senate Democrats Hubert Humphrey of Minnesota and Paul Douglas of Illinois accused the Eisenhower administration of pro-Arab favoritism. Recalling the February sale of tanks to the Saudis, Celler called the customs incident "part of a studied purpose of the State Department to hamstring and hurt Israel."[25]

———— • ————

At the Republican National Convention in San Francisco August 20–23, Eisenhower accepted the party's nomination by acclamation for reelection. His repeat running mate was Richard Nixon. Unlike the unanimous GOP gathering, the Democratic National Convention in Chicago August 13–17 was competitive. Adlai Stevenson, 1952 nominee, campaigned again to be the presidential candidate and was challenged by Governor W. Averell Harriman of New York, Senator Lyndon B. Johnson of Texas, and Senator Stuart Symington of Missouri. Delegates elected Stevenson on the first ballot. Stevenson did not reselect his 1952 running mate John Sparkman. A "free vote" ensued and after three ballot rounds, maverick senator Estes Kefauver of Tennessee, a Celler ally, defeated John F. Kennedy of Massachusetts.[26]

———— • ————

As American political leaders and voters prepared for fall elections, a dispute in the Middle East had the potential to spin out of control into a near world war like the Korean conflict that had been settled in 1953. This time, on July 26, Egyptian president Gamal Abdel Nasser nationalized the Suez Canal in retaliation for the United States withdrawing promised funds to build an Aswan Dam.[27] With the seizure, Nasser offered to compensate the British and French, but their diplomats reacted with outrage. Nasser in turn expressed indignation at continued colonial influence.[28] US officials suspected that Nasser was double dealing and courting the Soviet Union for aid. The Eisenhower administration monitored the conflict from across the Atlantic and then tried to broker a diplomatic agreement among Britain, France, and Egypt. Eisenhower wanted to circumvent any Soviet Union involvement in the Suez region. The US offer was a Suez Canal Users Association that included eighteen maritime nations and called for the British and French to be equal partners in operating the canal. That idea failed.[29]

From August through most of October, British prime minister Anthony Eden repeatedly hinted that he might use force against Egypt. Furthermore, British and French leaders held secret military consultations with Israel. On October 29—eight days before the US presidential election—Israel invaded Egypt and placed ground forces within ten miles of the canal.

In a moment of attempted levity and spontaneous angst over US policy in the Middle East, Celler called the military confrontations "a Suez-cide."[30] This was because the Middle East lunged toward possible World War III and six nation players starred in roles as double dealers, instigators, and negotiators. On Halloween, Nasser's military sank a 320-foot ship that effectively blocked the Suez Canal. The act was a response to British and French bombings. Egypt scuttled thirty-two additional ships in the canal. That same day Eisenhower in a televised broadcast said the United States was not consulted by its allies and did not know of advance war plans. Furthermore, said the commander-in-chief, there would be no US military involvement in the Suez crisis.[31] The United States did, however, operate as a negotiator. On Monday, November 5, a ceasefire was achieved among Britain, France, and surrogate Israel vs. Egypt. A United Nations force was dispatched to prevent more clashes between Egypt and Israel.[32]

At the brink, the USSR warned it was prepared to use military force against the British-French-Israeli military inside Egypt. The United States believed the Soviets were bluffing, since they had been negotiating partners in the dispute; however, just in case, Eisenhower placed American military units on worldwide alert. Then the protagonists came to their senses and pulled back. Every nation was tarnished in the near-group suicide event. Egypt and its military were humiliated and the temporarily shut canal meant lost revenue; Israel proved its toughness but hardened the animosity of the Arabs surrounding them; Britain was foolish for invading and so was France, who in addition lost influence in the region; the USSR gained minimal influence in the oil-rich Middle East; and the United States had to patch up bruised relations with Western allies and face cool relations with Arab states.[33]

On Election Day, November 6, Eisenhower and Nixon easily defeated the Stevenson-Kefauver ticket 457–73 in the electoral college. Meanwhile, control of the US Senate flipped into Democratic control, like the majority Democratic House in which Celler continued as Judiciary Committee chairman.

As the Suez conflict raged in fall 1956, the Soviet Union invaded Hungary to squelch student pro-democracy demonstrations. The bloody crackdown in Hungary became a full-blown international crisis. Thousands of refugees sought safe harbor in America. The Eisenhower administration offered to admit individuals who wanted to leave the communist satellite.

Once again, realpolitik tested America's ethnically restrictive immigration law. Hungary was an Eastern European country that was not on the preferred list based on national origins set in 1924 by the Johnson-Reed immigration act and reaffirmed in 1952 by the McCarran-Walter immigration act. Hungary sent the largest bloc of Jewish refugees—160,000—to the new state of Israel. Of 200,000 Hungarians who fled the failed 1956 revolution and crackdown, 6,500 were initially authorized entry into the United States.[34]

The Eisenhower administration watched, and southern members of Congress also observed a Negro civil rights revolution begin, gain momentum, and then command national attention. In May 1954, the US Supreme Court ruled in *Brown vs. Board of Education* that racially segregated "separate but equal" public schools were unconstitutional. Linda Brown, a schoolgirl from Topeka, Kansas, was the plaintiff who sued the local board of education. The NAACP, led by Charles Hamilton Houston, worked for decades gathering evidence for an opportunity such as the Topeka case. Thurgood Marshall successfully argued the case before the high court.

The court victory that spring was tempered a year later in 1955 by a horrific homicide during the summer. The mother of Chicagoan Emmett Till, fourteen, sent him to Money, Mississippi, to spend time with cousins and other family. Emmett and his male cousins walked to a country store to purchase candy. A young white woman worked the store counter. According to numerous historical accounts, the local boys dared Emmett, the city slicker, to talk to the woman. Emmett allegedly whistled at the brunette-haired female.[35] The woman went home and complained to her husband. That night a carload of white men arrived at the home hosting Emmett and took the boy away against his will. Days later Emmett Till's bloated, beaten, and bound corpse was found in a river. Local law enforcement officials dismissed reports of a murdered Negro teen as fiction. It took cunning and guile to get Emmett's body out of Mississippi and back to Chicago. The outraged mother Mamie Till demanded that the funeral parlor display her son's hideous remains in an open casket so America could see what had happened in the Jim Crow South. (In 2017, Carolyn Bryant Donham, eighty-two, told Duke University professor Timothy B. Tyson that Emmett did not touch her inappropriately or utter vulgar comments. "That part is not true," Donham told the author of *The Blood of Emmett Till*, published that January.)[36]

Months later in fall 1955, Rosa Parks was returning from her seamstress job and sat in the segregated section of a Montgomery, Alabama, public bus. When all of the "white" seats were taken, the bus driver instructed Parks to give up her "colored" seat to a white passenger. She replied no. Parks, a modest woman who had attended Quaker freedom schools as a child and practiced nonviolent resistance, was the perfect plaintiff for an NAACP challenge. Black leaders in Montgomery agreed to stage a boycott against the bus company, which was working Negroes' primary mode of transportation. A new minister in town, the Rev. Dr. Martin Luther King Jr., was unanimously elected leader of the boycott effort. Mythology holds that King was selected because special qualities were recognized in him. It is more likely true that the choice was made because King had not been compromised in his dealings with whites or weakened in factional disputes with the local blacks.[37] African Americans in Montgomery displayed amazing discipline. They virtually stayed off the buses for a year and financially crippled the bus company. In fall 1956, King with a Negro coalition and white Montgomery leaders agreed to desegregate the bus service. It was another legal victory for Negroes, with more challenges to southern racial segregation to come.

In early 1956, Herbert Brownell, Eisenhower's attorney general, drafted a civil rights bill that included establishment of a federal Civil Rights Commission, plus a Civil Rights Division within the US Department of Justice.[38] Emanuel Celler, chairman of the House Judiciary Committee, took Brownell's draft and wrote the House version of a bill. Celler believed the proposal was weak and compared the administration's draft to "a bean shooter when you should use a gun." Nevertheless, he shepherded that bill through the House.[39]

Celler's adversary Howard W. Smith of Virginia tried numerous tactics to scuttle the bill he dismissed as "civil wrongs."[40] Even in its weakened form, the 1957 civil rights bill carried some teeth. It included federal penalties for those who violently obstructed school desegregation orders or who fled across state lines after bombing schools and churches. The bill also required state officials to preserve for federal investigators election records that documented voter discrimination.[41] Smith tried to hold the bill hostage in his Rules Committee but Judiciary Committee chairman Celler dislodged it by filing a rarely used discharge petition.

House Speaker Sam Rayburn of Texas invited House members to sign the petition. Rayburn's choice marked the first open break with his southern colleague Smith.

Instead of lashing out at the speaker, Smith channeled his fury at Celler and alleged that the liberal, civil rights advocate had "dillied, dallied and delayed" the bill in his committee for months. Smith also complained that the bill would return the South back to the carpetbag governments of the post–Civil War Reconstruction era because federal registrars would dictate to southerners again.[42]

The civil rights bill—the first of its kind in the twentieth century— passed the House in April. The last federal civil rights law passed in 1875 during Reconstruction. That law—pushed through by radical northern Republicans—guaranteed Negroes the right to use public accommodations in the South.[43] The disputed 1876 US presidential election resulted in the end of southern Reconstruction in 1877. Once federal officials withdrew from southern states, civil rights for Negroes lacked enforcement power. In 1883, a US Supreme Court majority said the Thirteenth Amendment freed enslaved Negroes but did not guarantee federal protection from states that denied Negro individuals access to inns, theaters, and public conveyances.[44]

The civil rights bill faced solid opposition from white southern House members. On March 12, 1956, a month before the civil rights bill vote, ninety-six southern congressmen issued a declaration of protest against the US Supreme Court *Brown vs. Board of Education* school desegregation ruling. After the spring 1954 ruling, Kansas's neighboring states desegregated with little fanfare. The political leaders of southern states meanwhile vowed massive resistance to integration. The court's decision, said the southern bloc, usurped the states' authority to run public schools.

Furthermore, they added, the court's unwarranted exercise of power was destroying the "amicable relations between the white and Negro races that have been created through 90 years of patient effort by the good people of both races."[45] The massive resistance bloc appeared deaf, dumb, and blind to ninety years of domestic terrorism toward blacks through Ku Klux Klan intimidation, lynching, and slavery-like sharecropping.

When the House bill moved to the Senate, anti–civil rights members including Mississippi's James Eastland, Harry Byrd of Virginia, and Strom Thurmond of South Carolina were waiting. The Senate Majority Leader, fellow southern Democrat Lyndon B. Johnson of Texas, engineered a compromise to get the bill passed. The House version of the bill asked for nonjury trials of state election officials held in contempt of court. The reasoning of northern representatives was that in the South, no white jury would convict officials because they denied blacks their voting rights. Southern senators balked at the House bill and threatened filibusters. Indeed, Thurmond set a

filibuster record of twenty-four hours and twenty-seven minutes of continu-
ous talking in an effort to block the bill.[46]

In an act that LBJ biographer Robert Caro called "legislative power and
genius," Johnson linked civil rights with a publicly funded dam project for
the Pacific Northwest. With that tactic, he persuaded northern senators to
accept a public instead of private utility to build the dam, and southern senators agreed if a jury trial amendment were added to the civil rights bill, they
would end their opposition.[47] The civil rights bill passed 72–18 on August 7.
Three weeks later, on August 29, Eisenhower signed the Civil Rights Act of
1957. In a Western Union telegram to Celler, H. H. Bookbinder, an official
with the AFL-CIO, wrote, "Congratulations on the final civil rights victory.
You can be mighty proud of your decisive role." And in a letter, Ethel Payne,
Washington correspondent with the *Chicago Defender* and Sengstacke Newspapers, thanked Celler for his "able conduct in guiding H.R. 627 through to
successful conclusion by an overwhelming margin."[48]

The civil rights community, most prominently the NAACP, was unhappy
with the diluted bill. Its leaders vowed to fight the senators who signed
off on the jury trial addition. However, when the bill passed the Senate,
NAACP leaders Roy Wilkins and Clarence Mitchell changed their positions
and argued in favor of the law. Civil rights advocates, Wilkins and Mitchell
explained, could not afford to oppose the first civil rights legislation of the
twentieth century.[49]

Congressman Adam Clayton Powell of New York avoided the vote on
the House bill. "Frankly, I was disheartened at the attitude of Adam Clayton Powell," Celler wrote in letters to at least a dozen constituents and civil
rights leaders that included Roy Wilkins of the NAACP, labor leader A. Phil-
lip Randolph, and the Rev. Gardner Taylor of Brooklyn, a youthful peer of
Martin Luther King Jr. "The day the civil rights bill came up on the floor of
the House, I found to my amazement that [Powell] left for Europe. Here was
a bill that meant a great deal to all of us. I warned him that consideration of
the bill was imminent. [Powell] said, 'of course I will be present.' He defaulted
on his promise."[50]

As the civil rights bill was debated in the House and Senate in 1956, people
had concerns that House Judiciary Committee chairman Celler was going to
punish Powell, a Democrat from Harlem, who declined to endorse Democratic presidential candidate Adlai Stevenson and instead threw his support
to Republican incumbent Dwight Eisenhower. In correspondence to multiple constituents, Celler explained, "I will not make any move against Adam
Clayton Powell unless every one of the members of the House, guilty of the
same political omission, is treated exactly as he is."

The passage of the law was a breakthrough because every year since 1945, civil rights legislation put to a congressional vote had failed.[51] Because the new law established a federal Civil Rights Commission and a division inside the Justice Department, the NAACP filed reports with the Justice Department documenting discrimination and harassment of black voters and civil rights activists in the South. Following passage of the law, the attorney general brought four lawsuits against local registrars for denying blacks the right to register and vote. By holding hearings and filing detailed reports, the Civil Rights Commission began educating all of America about the realities of southern racism and the need for political action.[52]

Southern legislators and state politicians made good on their vow to resist school desegregation and other forms of racial integration. On September 4 in Little Rock, Arkansas, the state militia blocked nine black students attempting to desegregate Central High School. Governor Orval Faubus called in the Arkansas National Guard to prevent desegregation in direct violation of the *Brown vs. Board of Education* decision.

On September 20, Faubus ordered Arkansas state troops out of Central High in response to a federal injunction. White demonstrators began rioting outside the high school and the black students withdrew for their safety. On September 25, President Eisenhower dispatched US troops to Little Rock to escort the nine black students to their classes.[53]

During the first Eisenhower term, Emanuel Celler sought justice for several constituents who had been smeared during the McCarthy-era Red Scare. As the Cold War deepened, Celler sympathized with Eisenhower's attempts to circumvent strict immigration laws so America could welcome refugees from places such as Hungary. Celler, the pro-Israel Zionist, anxiously watched Israelis invade Egypt as the proxy for England and France in the Suez Canal dispute.

Over decades, Celler was a committed civil rights advocate. He fought many losing legislative battles and experienced rare victories. But in 1957 he scored a significant victory in cowriting and guiding through Congress a civil rights bill that President Eisenhower eventually signed into law.

At first glance, the first civil rights law in eighty-plus years appeared toothless. It lacked enforcement power against voting rights violations in the South. Yet the subtle strength of the civil rights law was its infrastructure. It mandated a commission to hear complaints and a division within the Justice Department that could accept documented cases of abuses against blacks and other citizens.

Celler had an established reputation as an immigration advocate and an antimonopoly watchdog. With the 1957 civil rights law, he lay the foundation as a legislative civil rights leader. His record of achievements was far from finished.

11

Celler and the
1964 Civil Rights Act

In 1959, Emanuel Celler introduced another civil rights bill, and William McCulloch, R-Ohio, the ranking member of Celler's House Judiciary Committee, submitted a comparable bill. The committee rejected a hybrid Celler-McCulloch bill 18–13. During the compromise that followed, Celler's nondiscriminatory public accommodations proposal was deleted. Celler was an organization man loathe to strain party unity, wrote David Berman, author of a book about the 1960 civil rights act. Convinced the full Judiciary Committee that had ten southern members would never vote out a strong bill, Celler pushed a weaker bill and hoped once the draft reached the House floor, strengthening amendments—such as public accommodations—could be added.[1] The US Civil Rights Commission, the key element of the breakthrough 1957 Civil Rights Act, applied fact-finding pressure. A 668-page report released September 9, listed sixteen southern counties in which blacks were a majority of the residents, yet not a single African American was registered to vote.[2] On February 7, 1960, President Eisenhower sent a civil rights plan to Congress that promoted a modest approach that called for the attorney general (at that time William Rogers) to seek injunctions against state or local actions that precluded individuals from voting. If an injunction was obtained a court would determine if some "pattern or practice" of discrimination existed. If discrimination existed, the attorney general could appoint a referee to register the voter(s).[3]

The watered-down Celler-McCulloch House bill had to pass through Howard Smith's Rules Committee, where it faced purgatory; however, Celler was able to collect a majority of House votes in order to enact a rare discharge petition and propel the bill to the House floor. On March 10, McCulloch rose to speak in favor of the bill, which consisted of five titles: (I) would make willful obstruction of court orders in school desegregation cases a crime; (II) would make it a federal offense to cross any state line in an effort to avoid prosecution for bombing or burning any building; (III) required that voting rights records be preserved for three years and that courts have the jurisdiction to direct that these records be made available; (IV) promoted the desegregation of public schools and authorized the US attorney general to file lawsuits to enforce the act; and, (V), that in the event that military children attending public schools were unable to do so because their school closed to avoid desegregation, they would be educated at the expense of the federal government.[4]

Critics said the bill would unduly burden the federal courts. John V. Lindsay, a New York Republican, countered that the *Brown vs. Board of Education* created work for the courts, but would it be proper to accept segregation to save a few dollars? In that moment Celler offered amendments to strengthen the civil rights bill, such as ending racial discrimination federal contracting. A voice from the floor objected, contending that Celler's amendment was not germane and out of order. The chairman—Francis Walter, D-Pennsylvania—sustained the objection, leaving Celler flabbergasted. Additional Celler amendments—defended by McCulloch—were rejected by opponents.

Warren Magnuson, D-Michigan, rose to say: "We all have known for a long time that the Negro in the United States is a second-class citizen. We know that his company is shunned. We know that he is denied the same educational opportunities that the rest of us enjoy. We know that the color of his skin is an automatic handicap to his seeking and obtaining job opportunities equal to his ability and training . . . We know that the subtle, silent hand of racial discrimination surrounds him at every turn, blocks his natural human desire to enjoy life, liberty and the pursuit of happiness."[5] Southern congressmen advanced opposition that fell into five rhetorical categories: that (1) post-Reconstruction, they were able to devise a system in which both races could live peacefully and with mutual respect with "separate but equal" opportunities and facilities; (2) all problems were the doings of outsiders, including do-gooders, unscrupulous politicians, and communists; (3) northerners were simply ignorant of southern ways; (4) the civil rights bill was a low, shameless hustle by liberal northern Democrats and Republicans to attract black votes; and (5) if the bill passed, blood will run in the streets and "It won't be long now before the official slaughter of white people in the South begins," said Mendel Rivers, D-South Carolina.[6]

Debate and parliamentary moves continued until 295–124 approval of a partial House civil rights bill and then a 311–109 approval of the final bill. Those decisions ended a ten-day dispute. Moved to the Senate, an emasculated bill was approved 71–18 on April 8 and President Eisenhower signed the bill into law on May 6, 1960.

Celler, in an attempt to salvage something from a Pyrrhic victory, said blacks should be aware that although the measure was small, "sometimes a small key can open a large door." The 1960 Civil Rights Act, said NAACP lead attorney Thurgood Marshall, "isn't worth the paper it's written on."[7]

Beaten but unbowed, Celler pushed onward. He was the principal House author of a bill to abolish poll taxes in federal elections. Poll taxes were prohibitive fees that blacks—and some impoverished whites—were ordered to pay before they could vote. The tactic effectively disqualified potential black voters. Five southern states—Virginia, Alabama, Mississippi, Arkansas, and Texas—with substantial black populations enforced this practice. Other southern states, including North and South Carolina, Georgia, Florida, and Louisiana, did not enforce poll taxes, but still practiced other Jim Crow tactics that discouraged voting by black Americans. US representative John Lindsay, R-New York, asked Celler to strengthen his bill, and include access to vote in state and local elections too: "If we're going to have a Constitutional amendment, let's have a meaningful one."[8] Judiciary Committee chairman Celler however proceeded with the constitutional amendment as introduced.

The legislation passed the House 295–86 on August 27, 1962. It moved to the Senate and Spessard Holland, D-Florida, a conservative who opposed most civil rights proposals during his career, introduced the anti-poll tax amendment, thus splintering monolithic southern opposition.[9] Richard Russell, leader of that opposition, acknowledged that after successful attempts to block poll tax bills in the 1940s and 1950s, he and colleagues this time could not hold the line. "I believe the Negro has been imposed upon," Russell told *Newsweek* in August 1963. "He has been subjected to indignities. But we shouldn't upset the whole scheme of constitutional government and expect people to swallow laws governing their most intimate social relations. The tempo of change is the crux of the whole matter. Any realist knows that the 'separate but equal' doctrine is finished." State ratification began in November 1962 and on January 23, 1964, the law banning poll taxes in federal elections became the Twenty-Fourth Amendment of the US Constitution after South Dakota ratified it. Abolishing poll taxes was one of three constitutional amendments in which Celler served as the principal writer.

The other amendments granted voting rights to residents of the District of Columbia (23rd) and established a clear succession if the president is removed from office (25th).[10]

On February 28, seven weeks after the 88th Congress convened in 1963, President Kennedy asked Congress for legislation that would broaden existing laws to protect African Americans. JFK asked for minor changes in voting rights laws, modest assistance to school districts attempting voluntarily desegregation, and an extension of the commission that studied civil rights matters.[11] The president's tame suggestions were mindful of the House Democratic majority that included many pro-segregation white southerners. On April 4, Emanuel Celler introduced the president's request, H.R. 5444, in the House of Representatives.[12] Celler introduced the bill the day after the Rev. Martin Luther King Jr. and the Southern Christian Leadership Conference in Birmingham, Alabama, had begun daily sit-ins and demonstrations to protest discrimination at lunch counters and in public facilities. The nonviolent resistance was the first protracted demonstration to be televised, nationwide and live. In ten weeks, the Birmingham confrontation spread to seventy-five southern cities and resulted in 758 demonstrations and 10,000 arrests.[13]

On June 11, President Kennedy in a national TV and radio address, said that segregation was morally wrong and that it was "time to act in the Congress, in your state and local legislative body, and . . . in all of our daily lives."[14] On June 19, Kennedy sent his civil rights proposal to Congress;[15] US representative Howard W. Smith of Virginia called the legislation "nefarious." Smith, a banker, dairy farmer, and former judge in Alexandria, was an apologist for slavery, who cited the Greeks and Romans in its defense. Smith was also a committed opponent of civil rights. In response to the Civil Rights Act of 1957, of which Celler was the primary drafter, Smith said, "The Southern people have never accepted the colored race as a race of people who had equal intelligence and education and social attainments as the white people of the South."[16]

On June 30, as Celler was writing the main provisions of the administration's civil rights legislation, African American leaders met with the House Judiciary Committee chairman to ask him to attach a fair employment practices provision to President Kennedy's civil rights bill. The black leadership pressed for a mandatory cutoff of federal funds to federally assisted segregated programs, instead of the optional authority requested in Kennedy's measure. The Negroes' expanded legislative front was announced by Representative Adam Clayton Powell Jr., D.-New York, after a telephone exchange with half a dozen Negro leaders across the country.[17]

Celler worried aloud on an ABC Network Sunday TV news show about the marchers coming to Washington, DC, on August 28. "Your comment was something to the effect that the legislators are taking 'umbrage' at the forthcoming civil rights demonstration," wrote David Willmarth of Bowling Green, Ohio, in a letter in response to Celler's comments. "What I would like to ask you and the rest of your colleagues is 'just who elects you to office?' It would seem to me that as long as this mass demonstration remains orderly, these people have a constitutional right to come to Washington to impress upon the legislators their feelings. And particularly since this session of Congress has been so slow in meeting the problems of our country. It is about time someone put the legislators on notice."[18] Meanwhile, a "Southern white gentle woman" from Virginia Beach, who was a representative of the opponents, sent an August 27 telegram protesting the march and criticizing Celler's support of civil rights. "The cannibals are coming, hurrah, hurrah. Let's hope they camp on your back doorstep forever."[19] After his appearance on the ABC Sunday news show, Celler received a significant number of letters and telegrams from Americans with strongly worded opposition or support for the march.

At that time, the District of Columbia was a racially segregated town, under the thumb of Congress. Lawmakers routinely assigned the city's operating budget to a rabidly racist southern member of Congress so that person would not embarrass the chamber with racist ramblings about other pressing national legislation.[20] Interracial marriage was illegal in Virginia, including DC suburbs of Alexandria and Arlington. The march for jobs, peace, and freedom was expected to call attention to the stark gap in opportunities for blacks and whites. At that time eleven out of every twenty black citizens lived in poverty and middle-class and professional blacks were rare.[21]

Anticipating tens of thousands of black and white marchers, pundits, police, and news managers anticipated violence and chaos. The DC police force at that time was segregated. In a rare development, some white and black officers worked the march for the first time as partners.[22]

Benjamin Bradlee, a young reporter who later became executive editor of the *Washington Post*, was sent to the scene to cover rioting, but the expected violence did not materialize. Instead, 250,000 racially integrated marchers arrived peacefully at the National Mall. The *Post* barely mentioned the event. Student Nonviolent Coordinating Committee activist John Lewis gave a speech that Kennedy administration officials criticized as incendiary.

Martin Luther King Jr. spoke near the end of the rally. Speechwriter and adviser Clarence B. Jones convinced King to reference a "promissory note," a metaphor of America's shabby treatment of black citizens. The inspiration for the metaphor was funds the Rockefeller family provided to bail out young people arrested at demonstrations in Birmingham, Alabama. Civil rights leaders signed a promissory note to assure the Rockefellers that the borrowed money would be repaid. As he read from a prepared speech, King was goaded by gospel singer Mahalia Jackson, who sat at the preacher's back. "Tell them about the dream, Martin! Tell them about the dream!" she demanded. King dropped the prepared words and improvised much of the "I Have a Dream" speech.[23]

After the March on Washington in late August, the civil rights bill was reported out of Celler's House Judiciary Committee. In mid-September, Celler became the focal point of unrelenting pressure from longtime constituencies—black, white, union, and clergy—to strengthen the bill. Celler also believed that because of his seniority he could ultimately satisfy his base yet compromise with the conservative House members. Some colleagues had doubts. "Despite seniority based on forty years' service, intellect and his committee position," wrote Richard Bolling, D-Missouri, "Celler often finds himself in the awkward position of a chairman who presides over but does not command a majority of his committee."[24] Others were less charitable and said seventy-five-year-old Celler had grown out of touch with the changes on Capitol Hill.[25] What Celler did not notice was that his strategy ran counter to the pledge President Kennedy made to McCulloch in order to gain the Republican's support.[26] McCulloch and GOP Minority Leader Charles Halleck, R-Indiana, faced a Hobson's choice: support a bill too progressive to become law, or become the members who watered down the bill civil rights leaders wanted.[27] Yet the liberally amended bill was approved by Subcommittee No. 5, which recommended passage by the full Judiciary Committee.

On October 8 when the full House Judiciary Committee opened hearings on the subcommittee amendments, Celler backed down. Instead of presenting weakening amendments himself and disappoint his liberal constituents, he passed that unpleasant task to Representative Roland V. Libonati, D-Illinois, a longtime but low-profile committee member. Libonati on October 10 introduced a motion to reject the Subcommittee No. 5 amendments. His action drew condemnation back home in Chicago, including Representative William Dawson, D-Illinois, who harassed Libonati to change his vote.[28] Clay Risen, author of *Bill of the Century*, wrote that Libonati was Celler's "willing accomplice," although in time Libonati realized he was actually Celler's sacrificial lamb. The Chicago congressman watched Celler do an interview with CBS News. "So then I'm sitting down, just like you and me are sitting down, and I'm watching television and who do I see on the television but my chairman," Libonati told a *Time* magazine reporter. "And he's telling them up there in his district that he's for a strong bill, and that he doesn't have anything to do with any motion to cut the bill down. So when I hear that, I say to myself, 'Lib, where are we at here anyway?' And I think that if they're gonna get Republican votes anyway, and if the chairman says he doesn't have anything to do with my motion, then certain representations that were made to me is out the window."[29]

On October 21, Libonati rose and announced, "Mr. Chairman [Celler], I move to withdraw my amendment!" Confusion and shouting coursed through the meeting room. Libonati's motion was approved by a voice vote, and then Representative Arch Moore, R-West Virginia, moved to approve the unamended civil rights bill that faced certain death if it went to the House Rules Committee, where chairman Howard W. "Judge" Smith, R-Virginia, vowed to bottle it up forever.[30] Through the end of October, members of the Kennedy administration and bipartisan congressional leaders meet several times to repair and reassemble the civil rights bill.[31]

By early November, Celler was coaxed and coddled by the Robert F. Kennedy–led Justice Department to accept broad compromise on the civil rights bill with Judiciary Committee colleague William McCulloch, R-Ohio. Washington political columnists Rowland Evans and Robert Novak reported that details of the compromise were leaked to a black member of the Civil Rights Leadership Conference, who exploded in protest. However, after the member read the text, the leadership conference representative told Celler that if the compromise passed both houses of Congress and was signed by JFK, he would consider it a good bill, but would never say that out loud.[32] Meanwhile, Clarence Mitchell of the NAACP, and another member of that leadership conference, also got wind of the proposed compromise. Mitchell visited Celler's office to vigorously complain. Celler tried to calm Mitchell, but the congressman also hinted that Representative Charles Mathias Jr., R-Maryland, was trying to embarrass Democrats by holding out against the compromise. Indignant, Mitchell took his protest to the Civil Rights Leadership Conference and all of the members representing about fifty organizations agreed to fight Celler and the compromise.[33] "'Manny' Celler was stomped," wrote Evans and Novak. The columnists wondered whether the civil rights bill supporters were ready to take on the wily southern segregationists in Congress, who learned "the fine points of parliamentary procedure—about points of order and quorum calls and filibusters—before they learn to feed themselves."[34]

On November 20, the civil rights bill moved to the House Rules Committee, which was chaired by Smith. Two days later Kennedy traveled to Dallas where he was assassinated by gunman Lee Harvey Oswald. The nation was distraught and paralyzed with fear of the unknown.

Successor Lyndon B. Johnson, the Texan, wanted to assure northern and western liberal Democrats that he would be an acceptable president. Johnson appealed to Republican US senator Everett Dirksen of Illinois, and promised to make him a "hero in history" by supporting JFK's civil rights legislation. A Johnson strategy was to get help from midwestern Republicans who felt less threatened by blacks, unlike segregationist white Democrats who felt threatened by the substantial—and suppressed—black population in their states.[35]

Internationally, America was engaged in a cold war with the Soviet Union and its satellites. People lived daily with the threat of mutually assured destruction—nuclear bombs and missiles pointed at opposing sides, east and west—and now, the free world's leader was dead. It seemed that a meaningful civil rights law might die with him.

Skeptical that Rules Committee chairman Smith would release the civil rights bill for debate on the House floor, on December 9, Celler with other civil rights supporters filed a discharge petition. The rare parliamentary tactic meant that provided enough House members signed the petition, the bill would be forced out of the Rules Committee despite the committed segregationist's opposition.[36] Defeated, but unbowed, Smith in mid-January 1964 lectured Celler in dirge-like tones about his opposition to the tactics to liberate the civil rights bill from his committee.[37] Celler gave no quarter and attacked Howard Smith's bids to weaken the legislation.[38]

On January 23, 1964, Celler's poll tax elimination bill that had comfortably cleared the House in summer 1962 became the Twenty-Fourth Amendment of the US Constitution after South Dakota ratified the legislation.[39] Elimination of the poll tax was a building block in the movement for a comprehensive civil rights law. President Johnson asked that all 435 House members approve the bill "without a word or comma changed." That would be quite a feat considering the number of southern foes, northern advocates, and indifferent midwestern representatives.[40] Judiciary Committee chairman Celler was the floor manager of the bill. The Brooklyn Democrat had a stalwart Republican ally on the committee, William M. McCulloch of Ohio. Celler's adversary was Rules Committee chairman Howard W. "Judge" Smith of Virginia, a staunch segregationist. Smith proposed that "sex" be added to the bill, which bewildered many House members.

"Now I am very serious about this amendment," Smith, eighty-one, told colleagues. He read a letter "to show how some of the ladies feel about discrimination against them." Celler rose to oppose the amendment as unnecessary because of the "delightful accord" that prevailed in his household for fifty years. "I usually have the last two words," Celler, seventy-five, told Smith, "and those words are 'yes dear.'"[41] Both House leaders engaged in a tongue-in-cheek duel of henpecked witticism. Celler's tactics were familiar. Though often portrayed in press accounts as the angry elder of the House because of his determined stands advocating civil rights and open immigration, for decades Celler dueled with segregationists and xenophobes on the House floor. From lengthy experience, Celler learned to disguise his anger and use humor—the latter learned as a young man at home in Brooklyn from witty family repartee—as a means to get results. Nevertheless, eleven of the twelve of the time female representatives stood indignantly to challenge Smith and Celler's jocular moment. Had there been any doubt that "women were a second-class sex, the laughter would have proved it," said Martha Griffiths of Michigan. She demanded respect for the amendment on its merits, and not as a southern ploy to kill the civil rights bill.[42]

Griffiths's colleague Katherine St. George, a New York Republican, spoke up in support, noting that white women historically had been treated as chattel and they were not mentioned in the Constitution, yet, "We do not need special privilege. We outlast you. We outlive you. We nag you to death. So why should we want special privileges? I believe that we can hold our own. We are entitled to this little crumb of equality. The addition of this little, terrifying word 's-e-x,' will not hurt the legislation in any way."[43]

Smith's amendment stirred up a storm. Southern representatives claimed that without the amendment, black women would have more rights than white women. Other representatives were silent so as not to appear antiwoman or antiwhite. The Johnson administration, however, was able to find a female loyalist to oppose Smith's amendment. Edith Green of Oregon said she did "not believe this is the time or place for this amendment." For every slight to women, Green continued, "there has been ten times, maybe one hundred times, as much humiliation for the Negro woman, for the Negro man and the Negro child, yes, and for the Negro baby who was born into a world of discrimination."[44]

President Johnson opposed the slight modification to the civil rights bill; he counted on Celler to guide it through committee un-nicked. Nevertheless, the Smith amendment stayed and the revised bill was approved 168 133.

————— • —————

Two days later, February 10, the civil rights bill was put to the final vote of the full House. H.R. 7152, the omnibus Civil Rights Act of 1964, included ten titles that outlawed segregation in schools, public accommodations, and federally assisted programs. Another title outlawed racial and sexual discrimination in employment. The House approved the vote, 290–130. Celler nearly collapsed from joy over what he called the zenith of his forty-one years in Congress, saying, "I sort of feel like I climbed Mount Everest."[45] Colleagues and supporters

showered the chairman with thunderous applause. For the Johnson administration, he guided to passage a law that retained virtually all the elements of
the draft that President Kennedy had submitted the year before.[46] Smith, dean
of the Virginia delegation, who tried to kill the bill with a gender amendment,
outfoxed himself, said a Michigan representative. In addition to passage of a civil
rights bill, the federal government established an Equal Employment Opportunity Commission and US Civil Rights Commission to enforce its provisions.[47]

The Senate managed to bypass sending the civil rights bill to the chamber's
judiciary committee, chaired by segregationist James Eastland of Mississippi.
Nevertheless, intransigent southern Democratic senators unleashed a filibuster on the legislation. They were determined to talk the proposal to its death.
"We will resist to the bitter end," said Richard Russell, Georgia Democrat and
leader of the "Southern Bloc," "any measure or any movement, which would
have a tendency to bring about social equality and the intermingling and
amalgamation of the races in our (Southern) states."[48] The filibuster lasted
fifty-four days. In an impassioned speech, Senator Everett Dirksen of Illinois
convinced enough colleagues to end discussion of the bill and vote. The senate required sixty-seven of its one hundred members to get on board and
end the debate. On June 10, the Senate imposed cloture for the first time on
a civil rights measure, ending the southern filibuster 71–29.[49]

On June 19, the US Senate passed the civil rights bill by a 73–27 vote.[50] Senators Dirksen, Majority Leader Mike Mansfield, Republican Whip Thomas H.
Kuchel of California, and Vice President Hubert Humphrey were the leading
advocates. When LBJ signed the bill into law on July 2, photographs showed
a beaming Emanuel Celler at the president's left shoulder as Martin Luther
King Jr. leaned over, behind LBJ's back.[51] Unlike previous civil rights laws—
including the 1957 bill written by Celler and another by the congressman in
1960—the 1964 version had muscle. For example, employers could no longer
discriminate in hiring people based on their race, color, sex, nationality, or
religion.[52] Title VII of the new civil rights act prohibited discrimination in
employment on the basis of sex, sexual harassment in employment, and
retaliation in employment for making or otherwise participating in a complaint of sexual discrimination or harassment.

When interviewed years later by Lawrence Rubin for the American Jewish Committee, Celler acknowledged that the civil rights bill he championed
opened the door to ethnic confrontations, specifically between Negroes and
Jews in New York:

> Well yes, the act of 1964 providing for equal opportunities in employment—
> that there can be no discrimination in opportunities employment based on

race, color or creed or sex—that has resulted in extreme ethnicity, as you say, so that we have a sort of discrimination in reverse now in the sense that they're seeking to create in the education system in the New York Board of Education. The fact there must be the same number of Jews and Puerto Ricans and Negroes and whites in the education system as there is in proportion to their numbers in the general population. Well, Jews, having been more or less denied entrance into professions generally over the years gravitated to the education field. The result is that there are a great many Jews in the educational system supervised by the Board of Education of New York. Now, with this concept of equality—equal employment on race, Jews are now being ousted to make way for blacks and Puerto Ricans, even regardless of ability or merit, and in a certain sense Jews are now being ousted, and one might say, discriminated against. So, there's a glaring example of how the emphasis being upon ethnic considerations to a very unfair and evil extent based upon my own act.[53]

Still, a meaningful civil rights law represented a radical and scary reality. Once approved, some black citizens gingerly tested its effectiveness. For example, despite the law, the custom on Pennsylvania Railroad trains traveling south of Washington, DC, was for black passengers to move to the Jim Crow cars. George Starling was among the black railroad porters who were given manifests by white conductors of the black passengers who sat wherever they reserved their seat. At Washington, the North-South dividing line, those passengers were instructed to move. Starling covertly challenged segregationist customs now that a civil rights law was in effect. As trains pulled out of Baltimore en route to DC, the porter discreetly approached some black passengers and informed them they had a right to stay where they were. "Look, what I want to say to you is confidential, between you and me. If you don't think you can keep it confidential, let me know now, and I won't say any more. But it's to your benefit."

Starling knew he could not be accused of defying the conductor or inciting passengers and risk getting fired or physically harmed. Starling had some close calls with ignorant passengers ("What? What the hell you talkin' 'bout?" some passengers would say, forcing Starling to feign ignorance). Over a decade in the late 1960s and early '70s, other workers labored covertly to break down segregationist customs and, on the ground, enact the dramatic law granting black Americans full citizenship rights.[54]

Hours after Johnson signed the bill into law, Atlanta restaurant owner Lester Maddox famously not only refused to serve black customers, he chased them away with a gun as photographers recorded the act. Yet in the same city that day a black civil rights worker walked into the restaurant at the Henry

Grady Hotel and was served as if he had been patronizing them for years. That morning in Kansas City, Missouri, Eugene Young, a thirteen-year-old black boy, entered a barbershop in the Muehelbach Hotel and asked for a haircut. He handed Lloyd Soper $2 and hopped into a chair. Eugene left satisfied. The previous day, he was refused service, a tradition since 1915. "I didn't mind cutting that little boy's hair," said Sopher. A Department of Justice report monitoring interactions a month after the new civil rights law went into effect concluded, "The general picture is one of large-scale compliance."[55]

White southern Democratic members of Congress voted against the civil rights bill. The majority of white congressional Republicans supported the bill. The new law was inked five months before the presidential election and Lyndon Johnson's run as the Democratic candidate. GOP challenger Barry Goldwater of Arizona opposed the civil rights law. He said the public accommodations section violated people's right to do business with whomever they pleased.

Goldwater did not have a racist record; he had integrated the workforce at his family's Phoenix department store. Yet because of his civil rights stand Goldwater attracted near-unanimous support from white southerners. Many of these Dixiecrats converted to the GOP after 1968. With the party change, for the rest of the twentieth century they carried the stigma that the Republican Party was irredeemably hostile to blacks, even though most white Republicans had endorsed the civil rights act in the mid-1960s.[56]

Emanuel "Manny" Celler successfully ran a seven-year race in which the prize was civil rights for American Negroes. Celler's marathon began as writer of the 1957 Civil Rights Act, the first update in eight decades since the Civil Rights Act of 1875, a toothless law passed just before Reconstruction ended. Critics derided Celler's 1957 bill as weak, but as the civil rights movement gained momentum, the twentieth-century law was a good start after a half century of Jim Crow brutality. In 1960, just months before JFK broke barriers as the first Irish Catholic American elected president, the candidate tasked workhorse Celler to begin crafting another civil rights bill, with teeth. During that trek, Celler wrote two constitutional amendments, the Twenty-Fourth that abolished poll taxes, a tactic used in a handful of southern states to deny Negroes the vote, and the Twenty-Third that granted voting privileges for District of Columbia residents. At that time 70 percent of the capital's citizens were Negroes. The civil rights bill was supposed to die when JFK was murdered in the closing weeks of 1963, yet the southerner who succeeded JFK vowed to carry Kennedy's bill to the finish line. LBJ needed Celler to carry the bill safely through a thicket of southern obstructionists and indifferent midwesterners. Celler applied stamina, tenacity, and when necessary levity to get the bill through the House undiluted during a rare opportunity for advocates in the Senate to also approve a bill that LBJ signed into law five months before he—and the appointed president—was elected to the office. Celler was justifiably proud of the civil rights law. In another year, LBJ asked him again to shepherd a follow-up civil rights proposal.

As Emanuel Celler celebrated his seventy-fifth birthday in May 1963, his legislative productivity indicated that he was not slowing down. Civil rights activities expanded and moved fast on the streets. When President Kennedy unequivocally said it was time to treat Negroes as full citizens, it was Celler's job to guide the president's proposal through the judiciary committee. When JFK was assassinated that November, Celler's challenge was to carry on Kennedy's plan, because successor Lyndon B. Johnson insisted upon finishing the job. Resolute and crafty, Celler worked with adversaries and allies to get the transformative 1964 Civil Rights Act passed and moved to LBJ, who signed it into law.

The impact of the 1964 Civil Rights Act is evident fifty years later in twenty-first-century America. Citizens are not restricted—at least by law— on how they can travel, where they can eat, and what types of jobs they can work. The Civil Rights Act led to the future blossoming of the Sunbelt South. Instead of repressive racial customs that stunted economic growth and opportunity, southern states added jobs, professional sports teams (Atlanta Braves and Hawks, Miami Dolphins, New Orleans Saints, Houston Astros and Oilers) and significantly slowed—then reversed—a half century of black migration out of that region. Celler, godfather of civil rights legislation, would continue his work in 1965 and write another landmark bill that Johnson would sign into law. Also, after four decades of defeats, incremental victories, and inertia, Celler would score a landmark victory in immigration reform.

Hart-Celler Immigration Reform, 1965

For four decades Emanuel Celler advocated for immigrants in the United States and immigrants eager to come to America. Celler's legislative victories and defeats during the World War II and early Cold War eras were incremental. Then, actions in 1965 emboldened Celler to legislatively and dramatically reform American immigration policy. International conflicts such as Vietnam pressed the United States to radically reform its Eurocentric immigration policy. Surrogates and refugees in Asia—plus other continents—also required the attention of the global democratic superpower that was always there for Europe. On the domestic front, the black civil rights struggle applied its own pressure. As leader of the free world, American leaders could no longer exude moral authority yet still confer second-class citizenship upon its native-born blacks and browns. Cold War–influenced refugee crises pressed American presidents from Eisenhower to Kennedy and now Lyndon B. Johnson to use executive power in order to allow people into the United States who were not Northern European and white.

Two years before he was elected president, Senator John F. Kennedy in 1958 wrote the book *A Nation of Immigrants* in which he satirized Emma Lazurus's poem to express his view of US immigration policies: "Send me your tired, your poor . . . as long as they come from northern Europe, are not too tired or too poor or slightly ill, never stole a loaf of bread, never joined any questionable organizations, and can document their activities for the past two years."[1] A year later, Kennedy proposed a bill to eliminate much of the bias in the quota system and provide for the regular admission of refugees. His bill died in a Senate committee. After he was elected president in 1960, 1920s-style Eurocentric US immigration policy tormented Kennedy during a time of Cold War. From 1961 to 1962 in the multiracial, Afro-Latin Caribbean, the United States cut diplomatic relations with Cuba, then a failed US-instigated coup at the Bay of Pigs, and then a nuclear missile crisis—Russian missiles in Fidel Castro's Cuba positioned less than one hundred miles from US shores—ensued. The Kennedy administration circumvented the immigration quota and "paroled" 60,000 Cuban refugees, fourteen times the number of people from that nation admitted to the United States in the previous two years.

Meanwhile, 1.5 million Chinese fled the communist mainland for Hong Kong. The Kennedy administration absorbed a few thousand Chinese—again using the parole exception—and exceeded the puny existing Asian immigrant quota, one hundred people a year from eleven nations.[2]

Kennedy operated within a national origins immigration system that allocated 70 percent of all visas to three Northern European countries: England, Ireland, and Germany. Two percent of the visas were allocated to the Asian continent and 1 percent to the African continent.[3] Kennedy proposed phasing out the national origins program over a five-year period and replacing it with a system that was truly global. The president called the existing system "an embarrassment," out of synch with American ideals, and nettlesome in America's role as *the* freedom-loving, anticommunist world leader.

———— • ————

Celler called immigration policy an important site in the US Soviet "race for the minds of men." It is intolerable that we should continue to maintain our own Iron Curtain—against visitors and alien immigrants alike—while criticizing the Iron Curtain abroad." He recognized President Kennedy was eager to reform immigration.[4] Celler also gained two powerful allies to help him press for immigration reform, House colleague William McCulloch, an Ohio Republican and member of the Judiciary Committee, and US senator Philip Hart, a Michigan Democrat and member of that chamber's Judiciary Committee.

McCulloch was born in 1901 to Scottish Americans who had been abolitionists. He was raised in Holmes County, Ohio. McCulloch rode a bicycle to undergraduate classes at the College of Wooster. He earned his law degree from Ohio State University. When he moved to Jacksonville, Florida, in the 1920s to practice law, he witnessed Jim Crow in action. McCulloch returned to Piqua, Ohio, and cultivated a thriving law practice. He served in the Ohio House of Representatives and rose to Speaker in 1939. McCulloch was nicknamed "the red-headed lion." He enlisted—voluntarily at age forty-two—in the army during World War II and served two years in Europe as a captain.[5] Postwar, he worked with the Piqua NAACP. The city bus station voluntarily desegregated its lunch counter. McCulloch was in regular contact with NAACP activists Emerson and Viola Clemens, and their daughter Colleen socialized with Nancy and Ann McCulloch. McCulloch was a frugal man of simple tastes—red suspenders and pumpkin pie served with cold turkey gravy that he consumed at the Elks club. He stuffed his own campaign literature, maintained an office staff of one to two people, and every June returned from Washington to make the rounds in his seven-county congressional district.[6]

Like Celler, McCulloch was a bank director. Regarding civil rights, he led the way. "How can you oppose these clear mandates of the Constitution?" he would tell his mostly conservative constituents.[7]

In 1958, Michigan voters elected Philip Hart to the US Senate. He was a devout Catholic who served a state with a large ethnic working class. In addition to people of Southern European heritage who were Catholic or Jewish, there were Middle Eastern immigrants, notably the parents of Kemal Amen Kasem, better known as Casey Kasem of Detroit, who would grow up to become an iconic rock and roll and pop music impresario. Over decades, thousands of African Americans migrated from the Deep South to Michigan largely for the automotive industry jobs. When Hart discussed immigration, he often emphasized how the immigrant working class and their American children and grandchildren literally built the United States. Hart wanted to replace the national origins system with a policy that favored skilled labor and unified families separated by long waiting lists.[8]

Hart was a member of the Senate Judiciary Committee. That meant that he was in regular contact with House Judiciary chairman Celler, the veteran immigration reform advocate. Within his first term, Hart earned the nickname "Conscience of the Senate" because of his principled stances on labor issues and civil rights. In March 1962, Hart introduced Senate bill 3043, which proposed revising the national origins system Anglo-Saxon and Celtic bias by creating quotas based on post–World War II immigration. That meant issuing 250,000 quota visas per year. Twenty percent of those visas—50,000—was to be reserved for refugees. Also, 80,000 visas were to be divided among countries based on the proportion of their population to that of the world, with no country receiving more than 3,000 visas per year. The remaining 120,000 visas, Hart proposed, were to be issued to countries based on the proportion of their immigration to the United States over the previous fifteen years to the total of all immigrants to the United States for the same period. That time span would begin in 1948, the year Celler cowrote the Displaced Persons Act.[9]

Hart proposed pooling all unused quotas. There was a surplus of slots from desired countries such as England and those slots were to be divided among countries with backlogs of applicants. His bill also proposed setting aside 60 percent of all visas in each quota category and extending non-quota status to parents of US citizens and to people with special skills. The Western Hemisphere was to remain outside the quota system.

Hart's proposal did not call for abolishing national origins, but if it had been accepted, it would have significantly redefined the United States' definition of national origins. The revolutionary immigration reform bill died in committee. Eleven months later in February 1963, the senator reintroduced virtually the same proposal as S.747.[10]

In March–April 1963, Celler introduced H.R. 3926. It proposed eliminating national origins as the basis for immigration and replacing the law with a new policy that divided 250,000 annual visas into categories of family reunification, labor needs, refugees, and refugee resettlement. Celler's House resolution also proposed increasing executive power over immigration policy by granting the president the responsibility to recommend to the Congress the number of immigrants to be allocated in each of the four visa classes.[11]

As the Hart and Celler immigration reform proposals circulated in Congress, the Kennedy administration began articulating its views of immigration reform. The issue was tasked to President Kennedy's attorney general and younger brother Robert F. Kennedy. RFK in 1962 delegated the job to Norbert Schlei, an assistant attorney general in the Justice Department.

Schlei was concerned that Celler and Hart threatened to take the lead on immigration policy before the president made his ideas known. While conducting research to craft a plan for the Kennedy administration, Schlei concluded that despite forty years of opposition to national origins, few liberals had clear or concrete ideas of what an alternative immigration system would look like or how it would operate.[12]

Schlei's Justice Department responsibilities and work clashed with the 1962 agenda of Abba Schwartz in the State Department, which was responsible for consulates that reviewed visa applications. Schwartz of the Office of Security and Consular Affairs had two advantages Schlei lacked: a good working relationship with House Immigration Subcommittee chairman Francis Walter and the patronage of Eleanor Roosevelt, seventy-eight, the grand dame of US liberalism. Schwartz publicly opposed abolishing the national origins system because he believed that radical change was not possible as long as the conservative Walter chaired the immigration subcommittee. Schlei countered that the Kennedy administration should take a firm stand against national origins as a statement of principle. Schwartz responded that half a policy loaf was better than nothing.[13]

In May 1963, Schwartz's proposal to the White House recommended that the administration amend the existing refugee law and eliminate the ban on Asian immigration. He recommended that the Western Hemisphere maintain its non-quota status as a reaffirmation of the US "good neighbor" policy with Latin America. Schwartz also recommended redistributing unused quotas, but leaving the national origins system intact. His proposal in essence relaxed the quota but did not abolish it, unlike what Celler, administration officials, and others sought to do.[14]

Just days after Schwartz's White House recommendations Francis Walter, sixty-nine, the immigration subcommittee chairman and conservative restriction advocate, died from leukemia.[15] With Walter's death, Celler recognized an opportunity to liberalize immigration policy. Walter, a Pennsylvania Democrat and longtime chair of the House Immigration subcommittee, was the House cosponsor of the 1952 McCarran-Walter law that restored the isolationist spirit of 1924 Johnson-Reed National Origins immigration policy. Walter rolled back many of the tweaks Celler had made to US immigration law in the 1930s and 1940s in order for refugees to escape war-ravaged Europe. At a caucus of committee Democrats, Celler proposed enlarging the immigration subcommittee to seven members from five. US representative Michael A. Feighan balked. Based on seniority, the Ohio Democrat was in line to chair the subcommittee. Feighan believed Celler's proposal was a slap at him. Celler suspected that Feighan would follow Walter's conservative precedent and continue the national origins policy.[16] Other Democrats sided with Feighan, so Celler withdrew his suggestion, realizing he would lose in a vote of the full committee.

On July 23, 1963, President Kennedy issued his long-awaited immigration proposal. He followed Schlei's and the Justice Department's recommendation to abolish the national origins quota system over the course of five years. Kennedy also revealed what he expected to be his position on immigration during his 1964 reelection campaign, asserting that US immigration law needed to be revised "to permit families to be reunited, to welcome the persecuted and oppressed and to eliminate the discriminatory provisions which base admission upon national origin."[17] Main provisions of the Kennedy proposal included increasing the annual quota from 157,000 to 165,000; establishing a minimum quota of 200, from the existing 100; ending the discrimination against Asians by eliminating the barred Asia-Pacific Triangle immigration zone; ending the national origins quota system over the next five years and replace it with a first-come, first-served policy that would give priority to skilled immigrants and families of US citizens; continuing to exempt the Western Hemisphere—Latin America, the Caribbean, and Canada—from any quotas; expand the Fair Share Refugee Act and give the president the authority to reserve up to 20 percent of the annual quota for refugees, and establishing an immigration board with advisory and investigatory powers.

On the day Kennedy released his immigration reform proposal, Celler introduced a revision of his former immigration bill that now was in synch with the president's proposal.[18] The day after, Hart also introduced a revised bill that synchronized details with Kennedy's. The only difference was that the senator's plan retained the national origins element.[19]

After the president's death four months later, immigration reform authority Christine Anne Ziegler-McPherson wrote that Kennedy's lack of direct involvement in the immigration reform process emboldened others, notably Vice President Lyndon B. Johnson, to use JFK's death to lobby for support of the July proposal. As president, LBJ used Kennedy's legacy to press for more aggressive and far-reaching legislation than perhaps Kennedy would have supported.[20]

Immigration reform stayed on track. In January 1964, LBJ convened a high-profile meeting. That occasion revealed a longstanding feud between Celler and immigration subcommittee chairman Feighan.[21] Their animosity was rooted in mutual distrust. Initially, the Ohio legislator seemed friendly toward Celler's immigration reform proposals. Celler, however, was perturbed by Feighan's decision to activate a Joint Committee on Immigration and Nationality Policy. The committee, established in 1952, never functioned. Former chairman Francis Walter believed the committee would dilute his power base. Feighan asked that the committee's budget be increased to $160,000 from $20,000 in order to investigate alleged bribery and corruption in individual immigration cases. Feighan wanted an eight-fold increase in committee funding, yet his views on immigration were not known.[22] Skeptical,

Celler labeled Feighan an obstructionist. At one subcommittee meeting, Feighan bitterly criticized Celler. The elder from Brooklyn answered icily, "To what the gentleman from Ohio says, I give the thunder of my silence."[23]

Clashing personalities aside, in May 1964, chairman Feighan held hearings on Celler's bill. Celler testified that his document was really an "Administration Bill" because it reflected the vision of immigration policy put forth by the "late, lamented, and martyred President Kennedy."[24] During the summer and fall, President Johnson campaigned for election in November. Immigration reform was not a campaign issue; civil rights and cold war politics maintained a higher profile.

Democrat LBJ crushed Republican US senator Barry Goldwater in a landslide. A week before his inauguration, President-elect Johnson on January 13, 1965, sent his immigration reform proposal to Congress. The document reflected the outlines of Celler's House bills, and Hart's Senate bills. Johnson's proposal reiterated JFK's emphasis on skilled labor and family reunification. LBJ's proposal recommended that no more than 10 percent of total immigration come from any one country.[25]

Johnson's plan also recommended eliminating discrimination against independent nations in the Western Hemisphere—particularly former European colonies in the Caribbean—but giving them non-quota status; giving non-quota status to the parents of citizens and lesser preference to the parents of resident aliens; eliminating the requirement that immigrants entering on an employment preference visa be required to find work prior to emigrating; giving a preference to low-skilled workers in industries that have labor shortages; and eliminating technical restrictions that had kept the United States from taking its "fair" share of refugees.

In February, Senate hearings began. Philip Hart became preoccupied with an antitrust case and ceded leadership of his immigration reform bill to Edward M. Kennedy, the late president's brother and junior senator from Massachusetts.[26]

As the Senate hearings carried on for months, in the House, Feighan in May introduced his counterproposal to the Celler bill reviewed the previous year. Feighan called national origins quotas "a myth" and also said the so-called policy had not been a barrier to immigration in the United States.[27]

Other critics weighed in. Myra C. Hacker of the New Jersey Coalition of Patriotic Societies told the Senate subcommittee, "Are we prepared to embrace so great a horde of the world's unfortunates? At the very least, the hidden mathematics of the bill should be made clear to the public so that they may tell their congressmen how they feel about providing jobs, schools, homes, security against want, citizen education and a brotherly welcome . . . for an indeterminately enormous number of aliens from underprivileged lands."

"Whatever may be our benevolent intent toward many people," Hacker continued, "the bill fails to give due consideration to the economic needs, the cultural traditions, and the public sentiment of the citizens of the United States."[28]

Hacker's critique clashed with the perspective of Hiram Fong, a Pacific Islander of Chinese descent, World War II Army Air Corps major, a Republican, and the first Asian American US senator from the five-year-old fiftieth state, Hawaii. New civil rights laws, said the senator, loosened the grip of racial discrimination and cast a spotlight on the national origins system, which had promoted theories of ethnic superiority that contradicted "America's ideal of the equality of all men without regard to race, color, creed, or national origin."[29]

Subcommittee chairman Feighan challenged reformers' assertions that eliminating national origins would not dramatically increase immigration. His counteroffer was to impose a worldwide quota that granted preferences for family reunification. Unlike the Kennedy-Johnson-Celler plans, Feighan proposed ending the national origins system immediately instead of phasing it out over five years.

However, Feighan held firm to hemispheric quotas.[30] Feighan's stand was a new tactic on the part of immigration restriction advocates, wrote immigration reform expert Christina Anne Ziegler-McPherson in *Making Modern Immigration*. They abandoned the fight to maintain individual national quotas in favor of a worldwide numerical limit that maintained a restrictive immigration policy. The Johnson administration, like the one before it, opposed Western Hemisphere quotas, fearing they would interfere with foreign policy. A prominent example was the Cold War–related refugee situation with Cuba.

Celler and Feighan continued to feud. Celler resisted the subcommittee chairman's efforts to introduce amendments to his immigration bill, and Celler informed the Johnson administration that he would not allow an amended bill to leave the House Judiciary Committee. He expected any debated immigration legislation to bear the name of Emanuel Celler, not Michael Feighan.

Feighan was unable to compromise with Celler or the Johnson administration. In June 1965, Feighan introduced H.R. 8662.[31] His bill proposed immediate repeal of the national origins quota system and an end to limits on immigration from Asian countries; an annual quota of 225,000 immigrants from countries outside of the Western Hemisphere for a total worldwide limit of 325,000 visas per year; an annual limit of 20,000 people per year from any single country; seven new preference categories for spouses, children, and parents of US citizens without limit; professionals and persons with skills in demand (as determined by the secretary of labor); spouses, children, and parents of resident aliens; married children of US citizens; siblings of US citizens, and persons fleeing communist oppression; presidential authority to use up to 50 percent of unallocated quotas for emergencies and refugees, and new flexibility and authority that would allow the secretary of labor to regulate labor markets for the protection of US workers.

Feighan's introduction of H.R. 8662 represented his last stand in a two-year battle with Celler over control of immigration policy. The subcommittee chairman and Celler reached an understanding in mid-June. Feighan suddenly agreed to support Celler's bill. The Ohio Democrat also agreed to withdraw his name from Celler's bill.[32]

At the time of this agreement those legislators and administration officials were way ahead of the American people on the immigration issue, according to a Harris poll taken in May. The sample of 1,110 respondents reported that the public opposed easing the immigration law by a 2-to-1 margin, 58 percent to 24 percent. Eighteen percent of the respondents polled were unsure.[33] Celler's H.R. 2580 was voted out of the immigration subcommittee 8–0 in July, and the Judiciary Committee voted 27–4 to send the bill to the full House on August 3.

On that day, President Johnson said:

> This bill does not signify that the floodgates are open. But it does say, without doubts, that the national origins procedure, which has since 1924 shamefully governed immigration in this country, will be forever abandoned. Now the country of a man's birth does not need to disbar him from our society. Walt Whitman once sang his American saga in these words: "These states are the amplest poem; here is not merely a nation but a teeming nation of nations." This new immigration bill sings the same kind of melody.

There was some debate and an amendment to limit immigration from Latin America but that proposal was defeated on a 218–189 vote. The House passed the intact bill 318–95 on August 25.

The Senate's immigration subcommittee voted 6–2 to pass Philip Hart's bill with an amendment that included the Western Hemisphere in the overall quota. LBJ quietly dropped his objection to limits on immigration in the Western Hemisphere. The full Senate passed the immigration bill 76–18. Most of the minority opposition came from southern Democrats who objected on racial grounds to ending the national origins system.[34]

Senator Sam Ervin of North Carolina was among the opponents. He argued that it was impossible not to discriminate and that it was therefore all right to favor "groups who historically had the greatest influence in building the nation," and to put all the earth's peoples on the same basis as prospective immigrants to the United States "was to discriminate against the people who had first settled and shaped the country."[35]

Proponents sought to assure critics that a new law would not overwhelm the United States with immigrants. "With the end of discrimination due to place of birth," Celler told colleagues during the House debate, "there will be shifts in countries other than those of northern and western Europe. Immigrants from Asia and Africa will have to compete to qualify in order to get in, quantitatively and qualitatively, which itself will hold the numbers down. There will not be, comparatively, many Asians or Africans entering this country . . . Since the people of Africa and Asia have very few relatives here, comparatively few could emigrate from those countries because they have no families in the U.S."

"First, our cities will not be flooded with a million immigrants annually," Edward M. Kennedy said to critics. "Under the proposed bill, the present level of immigration remains substantially the same . . . Secondly, the ethnic mix of the country will not be upset . . . Contrary to charges in some quarters, [Senate bill 500] will not inundate America with immigrants from any one country or area, or the most populated and economically deprived nations of Africa and Asia."[36] His brother, Senator Robert Kennedy, D-New York, predicted an immigrant increase of "at most 50,000 a year."[37]

Celler and the Kennedys, leaders of the liberal wing who made persuasive moral arguments for ending national origins discrimination, accidentally misled conservative critics about a future immigrant explosion in America. Mae Ngai, author of *Impossible Subjects*, explained that Celler and company had a poor grasp of Western Hemisphere immigration that was dominated by Mexico. Abolishing race and nationality restrictions won the moral arguments; however, in setting quota for all continents, the unintended consequence was a coming explosion in Mexican, Central American and, residually, Caribbean immigration. The problem, said Ngai, was while the 1924 and 1952 National Origins laws restricted immigration mostly by ethnicity and race, both laws' proponents did not restrict Western Hemisphere immigration, composed largely of people of color from Latin America and the then Euro-colonized West Indies. Politicians and officials at the State Department said they were exercising a "good neighbor" policy.

Actually, the United States imposed its will over the hemisphere: Its western farmers needed cheap labor from Mexico, and Caribbean people were seasonal fruit pickers in Florida, upstate New York, and New England. The Monroe Doctrine was still in force, so the United States invaded "neighbors" whenever it felt the need to protect its economic and strategic interests. On April 28, two months after Senate hearings on immigration began, the United States entered Western Hemisphere neighbor the Dominican Republic. Marines were sent to the Caribbean island to protect Americans trapped in a civil war between US-backed government forces opposed to rebel troops loyal to former president Juan Bosch. In a month, the Organization of American States agreed to provide a peacekeeping force in order to enforce a truce. American forces—20,000 marines at its peak—withdrew.[38]

With the House and Senate bills approved, the next step was to reconcile a few significant differences in a conference committee. Celler said he would accept the Senate version of the bill and he did not think a conference was necessary. The congressman attempted to avoid a protracted fight that could kill the reform he had sought for four decades. Feighan, the House immigration subcommittee chairman, insisted on a conference and represented House members in negotiations. The legislation that emerged was almost identical to the Senate bill except for a few tweaks. The conferees agreed to allow 10,200 refugees and expanded the definition of "refugee" to include victims of natural disasters. The compromise bill established a fifteen-member Select Commission on Western Hemisphere Immigration that consisted of five House members, five Senate members, and five members appointed by the president.[39] On September 30, Celler read the conference report into the *Congressional Record.* That same day the House of Representatives voted 320–69 to accept the compromise bill. On October 3, 1965, in front of the Statue of Liberty in New York Harbor, President Johnson signed the Immigration and Nationality Act into law. "It does repair a very deep and painful flaw in the fabric of American justice," said Johnson. "It corrects a cruel and enduring wrong in the conduct of the American nation. Speaker [John] McCormack and Congressman Celler almost 40 years ago first pointed that out in their maiden speeches to Congress, and this measure that we will sign today will really make us truer to ourselves both as a country and as a people. It will strengthen us in one hundred unseen ways."[40] The president acknowledged Celler a second time, plus additional players in the successful law: "In the final days of consideration, this bill had no more able champion than the present attorney general, Nicholas Katzenbach, who, with New York's own 'Manny' Celler, and Senator Ted Kennedy of Massachusetts, and Congressman Feighan of Ohio, and Senator Mansfield and Senator Dirksen constituting the leadership of the Senate, and Senator Javits, helped to guide this bill to passage, along with the help of the members sitting in front of me today."[41]

The new law was a moral rejection of the 1924 immigration law that had whitened and ethnically cleansed America for four decades.[42] Celler and company, however, could not have foreseen world events. India, once a vast British colony in Asia, was home to many English-speaking technocrats with democratic values who wanted to emigrate.[43] Advocates and critics alike also underestimated immigration from newly independent Caribbean nations where individuals used to be counted under the generous British quota.

The Hart-Celler Immigration and Nationality Act of 1965 created the conditions for the dramatic increase in immigration and ethno-racial diversity in the United States in the first decades of the twenty-first century. Most famously, the 1965 immigration act ended the longstanding policy of restricting entry based upon ethno-racial criteria that had been established in the 1920s, replacing it with a system that judged immigrants on the basis of their relationships to US citizens and their ability to contribute to their adopted nation's economy and society.

Emanuel Celler was the person primarily responsible for the dramatic change in immigration policy. Philip Hart shared the credit for the breakthrough law, but the senator's involvement was minimal, even though he introduced the Senate version of the bill.[44]

In order to pursue his other passion—labor issues—Hart handed off his immigration bill to another junior senator, Edward Kennedy of Massachusetts, and he served as the Senate floor manager whose actions complemented those of House advocate Celler. Over decades, Celler took advantage of changing political and social contexts—the plight of World War II refugees, and then of Cold War and postcolonial peoples—that largely shaped the contours of the 1965 Immigration and Nationality Act, which emerged as one of the most significant pieces of legislation passed in the twentieth century.[45]

13

Voting Rights Act, 1965

The unrelenting force of civil rights clashes propelled Emanuel Celler into the voting rights campaign. In January 1965 President Johnson met with civil rights leaders and informed them he would push for a law protecting voting rights after Congress passed an education bill and Medicare. The proposed voting rights bill was carved out quietly by administration and Senate leaders. Civil rights leaders however were frustrated with the wait because in the South black activists and protestors faced increasing violence.[1] On March 7, Alabama state troopers violently attacked peaceful civil rights marchers as they crossed the Edmund Pettus Bridge in Selma, Alabama, en route to the state capital in Montgomery. The black-and-white news footage of mostly black and white men and women collapsing to the pavement under the force of horseback-mounted troopers and other lawmen on foot beating the fallen with clubs became known as "Bloody Sunday." Among the badly beaten was John Lewis, a college-age native Alabaman and organizer/leader among the Student Nonviolent Coordinating Committee.[2] Many outraged Americans put pressure on Congress and the president to pass a bill protecting the right to vote for all Americans.[3]

Eight days later on March 15, in a televised speech to a joint session of Congress, Johnson delivered a stirring, historic speech calling on Congress to pass a voting rights bill. He appropriated the language of Negro leaders and said the nation "must overcome the crippling legacy of bigotry and injustice. And, we shall overcome."[4] With the exception of members of Congress representing southern states, the entire House chamber stood and cheered, interrupting the president with thirty-nine ovations.[5] Celler stood and applauded with his hands over head of his five-foot, two-inch frame. Martin Luther King Jr., who watched the president's speech from a hotel room in Selma, Alabama, at the time ground zero of the voting rights struggle, wept. A King aide said that was the first time he ever saw the civil rights leader cry.[6]

As Johnson stepped down from the dais, congressional leaders walked toward him to greet him. At the front of the crowd was a septuagenarian committee chairman. "That was a great speech, Mr. President," said Emanuel Celler. "I'm going to start hearings on this bill tomorrow." Johnson jabbed Celler in the chest and said, "Start them tonight."[7]

On March 17, LBJ sent a voting rights proposal to Congress. The next day, Celler introduced the administration bill, H.R. 6400. Johnson did not want the bill, potent because of lightning-fast news developments, to lose momentum. As the Selma march made front-page news throughout the nation, the Voting Rights Act was before Congress. In the House Judiciary Committee, Celler rallied his colleagues: "Recent events in Alabama, involving murder, savage brutality, and violence by local police, state troopers and posses, have so aroused the nation as to make action by this Congress necessary and speedy . . . the climate of public opinion throughout the nation has changed so much because of the Alabama outrages, as to make assured the passage of this solid bill—a bill that would have been inconceivable a year ago."[8]

Celler also said that people preventing blacks from voting "must be smashed and banished" and that any obstruction of the bill's passage was "inexcusable."[9] However, obstruction did occur in the House. Celler and his House Judiciary Committee reported a revised H.R. 6400 bill on June 1, but the congressman endured a month's delay in bringing the bill to the floor. His nemesis during the Civil Rights Act clash the previous year, Representative Howard W. Smith, D-Virginia and chair of the Rules Committee, held the voting rights bill hostage. In response, Celler initiated proceedings to have the bill discharged. On June 24, the Rules Committee began hearings. Celler received crucial help from Rules Committee member, Representative Richard Bolling, D-Missouri. Bolling made a motion to send the bill to the floor under an open rule that passed the Rules Committee by an 11–4 vote.[10] The motion authorized ten hours of debate and gave the minority Republican Party the chance to offer a substitute bill. GOP members proposed a substitute bill, H.R. 7896, but the House rejected that bill by a 215–165 on July 9. The House then considered fourteen amendments to Celler-introduced H.R. 6400, but approved three amendments that made no consequential changes to the bill.

US representative Hale Boggs, D-Louisiana, House Majority Whip, who had opposed the 1964 Civil Rights Act, said, "I shall support this bill, because I believe the fundamental right to vote must be a part of this great experiment in human progress under freedom which is America." The House passed the voting rights bill 333–85.[11]

————————•————————

In the Senate, broad, bipartisan support for voting rights was signaled by sixty-six senators who were eager to sign as sponsors of an administration-backed bill that had been discretely negotiated by Senate leaders. When introduced on March 18, forty-six Democrats and twenty Republicans signed on as sponsors. Voting rights legislation was likely to pass on the floor if an acceptable bill was reported from the committee. Minutes after the bill was introduced, Senate Majority Leader Mike Mansfield, D-Montana, and Minority Leader Everett Dirksen, R-Illinois, made a motion that the bill be referred to the Judiciary Committee with instructions to report back no later than April 9. The Senate agreed to the motion by a 67–13 vote. Such instructions to the Judiciary Committee were necessary and noteworthy because its chairman, Senator James O. Eastland, a Mississippi Democrat, had never voluntarily reported a civil rights bill, and in 1964, the Senate voted to bypass his committee when it considered that landmark bill.[12]

Unlike the House version of the voting rights bill, the Senate bill, S. 1564, did not ban poll taxes for state and local elections. The Twenty-Fourth Amendment—Emanuel Celler's legislation—that outlawed poll taxes in all *federal elections* became law on January 23, 1964. A bill reported by the Senate Judiciary Committee included a complete ban on poll taxes; however, the Johnson administration and many senators did not believe a ban on poll taxes for state and local elections would withstand a constitutional challenge.[13] When the bill went to the floor, Mansfield and Dirksen deleted the provision and substituted a provision authorizing federal courts to determine if poll taxes were racially discriminatory.[14] On May 11, the Senate by a 49–45 vote defeated a floor amendment by Edward M. Kennedy to restore the Judiciary Committee bill's ban.

A filibuster against the voting rights bill lasted twenty-four days. Southern senators expressed their belief that the bill was unconstitutional and punitive to their region. Philip A. Hart, the bill's floor manager, initiated a petition for a cloture motion, the only procedure by which the Senate can vote to place a time limit on consideration of a bill and thereby overcome a filibuster. That petition was signed by twenty-nine Democrats and nine Republicans. After four days the Senate achieved cloture by a 70–30 vote on May 24. Bill S. 1564 passed the Senate 77–19 on May 26.[15] The bill also passed in the House July 9 after five weeks of debate. On August 6, President Johnson signed the Voting Rights Act.

"Today we strike away at the last major shackle of those fierce and ancient bonds," said the thirty-sixth president that afternoon. "Today the Negro story and the American story fuse and blend.

"This act flows from a clear and simple wrong. Millions of Americans are denied the right to vote because of their color. This law will ensure them the right to vote. The wrong is one in which no American, in his heart can justify. The right is one in which no American, true to our principles, can deny."[16]

He wasn't named, yet Celler's impact—speed and results—was referenced in Johnson's two-thousand-word speech: "Last March with the outrage of Selma still fresh, I came down to the Capitol one evening and asked the Congress and the people for swift and sweeping action to guarantee to every man and woman the right to vote. In less than 48 hours I sent the Voting Rights Act of 1965 to the Congress. In little more than four months, the Congress with overwhelming majorities enacted one of the most monumental laws in the entire history of American freedom." (Johnson tasked Celler to begin hearings the day after the speech and the congressman was the House floor manager of the Voting Rights Act.)

During the remaining four months of 1965, the impact of the voting rights law was dramatic. Only four of thirteen southern and border states had less than 50 percent of its black citizens registered to vote. By 1968, nearly 60 percent of African Americans in Mississippi had registered as voters.[17] As for voting rights legislation singling out the South, a 1966 voting rights challenge was filed in the North—Kings County, Brooklyn, New York—and the federal courts ruled in 1968 that white politicians engaged in racial gerrymandering in predominantly black Central Brooklyn. Five congressional districts cut up a compact, contiguous neighborhood that was 80 percent black and Puerto Rican.[18] The case resulted in the election of the first black woman to Congress, Shirley Chisholm.[19]

As with the milestone Civil Rights Act the previous year, 1964, Emanuel Celler was a floor leader who carried major legislation like a football over the goal line. The voting rights bill endured a rocky road in the Senate. The initial Senate draft did not include a ban on poll taxes that included state and local elections, ironic because the previous year the Twenty-Fourth Amendment to the US Constitution was initiated by Celler and banned poll taxes in federal elections. The state and local poll tax ban was restored in the Senate version, with a lot of help from Edward M. Kennedy, Celler's young, passionate ally who collaborated on immigration reform. Once again, Celler had to protect the bill from suffocation by a formidable adversary, segregationist and Rules Committee chairman Howard "Judge" Smith. The revised bill survived the House.

Within a decade after the Voting Rights Act became law in August 1965, former Confederate states began electing the first black officials since Reconstruction ended in 1877. Andrew Young, a lieutenant of Martin Luther King Jr., was elected to Congress from Georgia's mostly white Fifth District in 1972 and served three terms before serving as UN secretary and later Atlanta mayor. John Lewis, the young man who was beaten unconscious in Selma, was elected to represent an Atlanta-area congressional district.[20] In Texas, Barbara Jordan followed Shirley Chisholm as the second black woman elected to Congress in 1972. Previously, Jordan was elected to the Texas state senate in 1966 after two unsuccessful attempts.[21]

Within a generation, black members of Congress were elected in Virginia, North Carolina, Florida, Alabama, Louisiana, and Mississippi.[22] The first elected black mayor in the South, Charles Evers of Fayette, Mississippi, was the brother of civil rights martyr Medgar Evers. Big city mayors and governors were elected too, notably Douglas Wilder of Virginia, the grandson of slaves. In Alabama, eight black mayors representing a combined 61,000 constituents were elected by 1974. By 2007, African American politicians served fifty-three municipalities and a combined 800,000 constituents. By the 1970s in Mississippi, black elected officials began to win local and state elections. By the twenty-first century, this state with a nearly 40 percent black population consistently ranked first or second in the number of African American elected officials.

The federal enforcement provision of the Voting Rights Act was renewed multiple times by the Congress and Republican and Democratic presidents, however in the twenty-first century Alabama challenged the practice in lawsuit *Shelby County vs. Holder*. (Eric Holder was the first African American attorney general, serving in the administration of the first African American president, Barack H. Obama.) The US Supreme Court ruled 5–4 in favor of the plaintiffs, with the majority opinion concluding that the nation made so much progress, federal oversight, particularly of southern states that historically denied blacks their voting rights, was no longer necessary.

"Voting discrimination still exists; no one doubts that," said the June 25, 2013, majority opinion. "The question is whether the Act's extraordinary measures, including its disparate treatment of the states, continue to satisfy constitutional requirements."[23]

Alabama was among seven southern states previously required to obtain approval from the federal government before they could make changes in their election laws. The South was not exclusively singled out. Alaska and

Arizona, which had substantial Latino or indigenous citizens, were monitored as well, and parts of six states that included New York and California previously needed pre-clearance too. Post *Shelby County vs. Holder*, there were skirmishes over alleged voter suppression, dubious photo ID demands, and racial gerrymandering.

At the end of 1965, Celler, seventy-seven, an unwavering advocate of civil and human rights for forty-two years of public service, emerged as leader and champion of three milestone laws: twentieth-century civil rights, voting rights, and immigration reform.

14

———— ⋅ ————

Congressional Bulldog, 1967–1971

On November 9, 1966, Celler received a letter from President Lyndon B. Johnson congratulating him on his reelection to a twenty-second term: "The speaker described the 89th as the most dedicated Congress he has seen in 38 years," wrote LBJ. "I join him in looking forward to an even greater 90th Congress." The congratulatory words obscured a constitutional crisis that would involve—and haunt—Celler. That month, Celler's New York colleague Adam Clayton Powell Jr. was reelected to an eleventh term. Powell received 74 percent of the votes from his mostly Harlem district and Powell recorded the eighth-highest margin of victory of any member of Congress in the United States.[1]

Popular at home, Powell was at the peak of his powers. From his father, he took over as senior pastor of Abyssinian Baptist Church, and the namesake the pulpit of the largest congregation in America. He was a political demagogue, wrote Thomas A. Johnson of the *New York Times*; a congressional rebel; a civil rights leader three decades before Martin Luther King Jr. and the 1955 Montgomery bus boycott; a wheeler-dealer; a rabble-rouser; a grandstander; a fugitive; a playboy, and the most effective chairman of the House Committee on Education and Labor ever, despite his high absentee rate in Congress.[2]

Powell was the self-described "bad nigger" who battled with segregationist southern Democrats and hostile northern Republicans and often won legislative battles because he was a rare black man who wielded the power of the gavel. Yet late in 1966, Powell's foes saw an opening to crush him. The congressman from Harlem was vulnerable because one of his constituents won a $211,500 defamation judgment. Powell called Esther James a "bag lady" who had collaborated with crooked police officers in his Twenty-Second Congressional District. In spring 1963, three years after making the baseless charge on a late-night local news show, Powell was found in contempt of court and was subject to arrest in New York except on Sundays when he preached at Abyssinian. (Warrants were not served on Sundays.)[3] Powell spent a lot of time in exile on the Bahamian island Bimini, sixty miles off the Florida coast.

Powell's foes said that, by itself, constituted grounds for his expulsion from Congress. In January 1967, Democratic leaders John McCormack, Richard Bolling, and Morris Udall countered critics with a "two-rocket" plan: to strip Powell of his chairmanship and seniority and to seat him anyway in the 90th Congress because his constituents had overwhelmingly reelected him. House Speaker McCormack of Massachusetts did not want the hostile southern Democrats to dispense Powell's punishment. Udall was tasked because the Arizona Democrat, with few blacks in his district, did not have to worry about reprisals from African Americans.[4]

On January 9, 1967, Congress swiftly adopted Udall's motion to strip Powell of his Education and Labor chairmanship. The next motion, whether to unseat the Harlem Democrat, was in the hands of Congressman Lionel Van Deerlin of California, a former TV journalist from San Diego. At first, Van Deerlin was oblivious to what was at stake in considering the expulsion of Powell from Congress, but he quickly recognized the seriousness of the matter. Van Deerlin received phone calls from Powell supporters who threatened him with bodily harm. Meanwhile, an Alabama House member called seeking to confirm that there were rumors that Van Deerlin would withdraw the motion to remove Powell. Van Deerling assured the southern Democrat that he had not changed his mind.[5]

On the day of the vote, Celler warned colleagues that to refuse Powell his seat would mean much more than punishing the man; it would be an attack on the Constitution. In defending Powell, Celler swallowed his pride, since he had battled Powell over the appropriate use of federal antipoverty funds. In response, Powell of Harlem taunted him about impoverished Bedford-Stuyvesant, the black and Puerto Rican ghetto within the elder congressman's district. Celler resented those attacks on his honor and integrity.[6]

Van Deerlin presented his motion to deny Powell seating in Congress until after an inquiry. The motion passed overwhelmingly, 364 to 64. McCormack's "two-rocket" plan to demote Powell but allow him to retain his seat failed; other members of Congress disregarded the House speaker's authority. One hundred sixty years had passed since the last time Congress had denied a duly elected representative his seat. Powell, furious, assembled a team of defense lawyers.

House leaders called upon Powell's New York delegation colleague Celler to mediate the constitutional dilemma. McCormack chose Celler to lead the select committee that investigated Powell's fitness to return to Congress. McCormack needed someone he could trust, not a southern Democrat or a northern Republican. Celler was a forty-four-year veteran of the House who revered the chamber's traditions and maintained a deep respect for Congress. He called the lopsided House vote against Powell the actions of a "kangaroo court," a travesty that ignored recognized standards of law of justice. Powell, said Celler in a 1970 interview, was "a bone in the throat of Congress," difficult to extricate:

> Powell in the beginning was a very credible member of the House and, as chairman of the Committee on Education and Labor, guided through the House some very salutary bills. But his private life involved considerable and excessive drinking and carousing with the opposite sex and taking unwarranted vacations, and I imagine he became intoxicated with his own growing reputation. He exploited his reputation, all of which was exacerbated by excessive drinking and his leading a life of a wastrel.[7]

Furthermore, the committee chairman (Celler) had to be immune from potential charges of racism. Celler, a proven civil rights champion, was the man for that tough job.[8] "As a good soldier, I am willing to take on the task," Celler said. Someone wished him well. Celler winced, then said, "I'm entitled to commiserations, not congratulations."[9]

Celler's nine-member select committee consisted of five Democrats—including lone southerner Claude Pepper of Florida and only black representative John Conyers of Detroit—and four Republicans. Celler established a weighty tone for the hearings. His aides sat at both ends of the table in the spacious House Judiciary Committee conference room. Committee member Andrew Jacobs Jr., D-Indiana, said Celler evoked Winston Churchill because his discourse was always formal.[10]

The Celler committee steered between the need to satisfy the public outcry for action against Powell and the need to devise a punishment that would not lay the groundwork for a court challenge. If the House followed the committee's carefully crafted plan, Celler said, Powell would have no right of appeal "except to the Lord Almighty."[11]

Celler's style attracted the spotlight of the *New York Times*. On February 24, he was the newspaper's "Man in the News." Under the headline "Congressional bulldog: Emanuel Celler." The article began, "Most men count their time in Congress by terms. Not Emanuel Celler of Brooklyn. He keeps time there on a grander scale, by epochs. He went to the House in the money boom of the 1920s. He has remained there—all imperturbably—through the Depression and New Deal . . . Once he stared at a conservative opponent in the House and said gently, 'we can give you the answer, but we cannot give you understanding.'"[12] The embattled Powell perceived Celler as an enemy despite the New York colleague's neutral, even sympathetic leadership of the special committee.[13]

The bipartisan committee's decision was shaded by the dissenting yet polarized votes of two Democrats. Conyers, the young black member from the North, rejected seating Powell because he believed the denial of seniority was too stiff a penalty. Pepper, the white liberal and the committee's lone Democrat from the South, held a grudge against Powell. Although Pepper was an FDR-style New Dealer, he had broken ranks with the president and declined to support the Fair Employment Practices Committee (FEPC), established in 1941 to prevent discrimination against African Americans in defense and government jobs. Pepper was sure he could not get support for the legislation in Jim Crow–era Florida. During a New York visit, Powell had denounced Pepper's stance. The verbal clash received prominent press play and may—or may not—have cost Pepper a shot at a US Senate seat. Two decades later, Pepper had not forgotten his beef with Powell.[14]

Despite the dissent, the Celler committee recommendation was to seat Powell, yet strip him of his seniority. Days before the vote, Republican Tom Curtis of Missouri waged a vocal campaign to banish Powell. Curtis lobbied a fellow midwestern Republican, Gerald Ford of Michigan, who was in the House leadership. Curtis believed he had public opinion on his side: A Lou Harris poll indicated that 54 percent of Americans favored Powell's expulsion.

Decision day was March 1, 1967. Curtis arrived in the House chamber bearing a copy of the Ten Commandments. The House narrowly defeated the Celler committee's Powell report that recommended a fine and stripping of seniority by 222–201. It marked the first time the House had ignored the recommendation of a bipartisan committee. Then the representatives voted on Curtis's resolution to expel Powell from Congress. That measure passed easily, 248 to 176.

Celler grimaced. After four decades, he thought he knew the institution. The combination of prejudice and irrational behavior strangled reason. Claude Pepper fooled Celler as the only select committee member to vote for Powell's expulsion.[15] The last time Congress had denied a duly elected member his seat was in 1919 when Socialist Victor L. Berger of Milwaukee was rebuffed because of an ongoing legal battle related to his antiwar positions.[16] Four decades later, the most powerful black politician and arguably Congress's most prolific legislator was barred from his "house."

Powell followed the news of his expulsion while in Bimini. The day after the votes, newspaper editorials posited that Congress had overstepped its bounds. "Despite the enormity of Mr. Powell's offenses," said the *Washington Post*, "we think the outcome was emotional, vindictive, and foolish." A *New York World-Journal Tribune* editorial said that although Powell "may be politically finished, his case is not. It is a major piece of unfinished business that will haunt the House."[17]

Indeed, it did. The vindictive actions of most House members enraged Powell's Harlem constituents. Republicans encouraged jazz bandleader and registered Republican Lionel Hampton, then civil rights figure James Meredith, to run for the vacated seat. Both men declined. A woman elder from Abyssinian Baptist Church agreed to run, but she campaigned passively. Since Powell faced arrest in New York for contempt of court, he traveled from Bimini to Miami where his lawyers had him sign the papers to place his name on the ballot. That April, Powell won the special election in New York with 86 percent of the votes.

Celler, meanwhile, vowed to fight for the right to seat Powell, but there was no congressman present to fight. Powell was determined to reclaim his seat on *his* terms. Because Congress had unconstitutionally blocked him from his House seat, he vowed to take his battle to the courts.

When he arrived in Washington, Powell was about to throw another bomb, and this time, hold Congress hostage too.[18] Voting to exclude Powell set up the very clash between Congress and the courts that the Celler committee had tried to avoid. After staying away fifteen months, Powell returned to Harlem in March 1968.[19] His lawyers managed to get the Esther James libel judgment reduced from $1 million to $50,000. Still, Powell was a fugitive in New York. His lawyers worked out a deal for the exiled congressman. Powell would go to the judge's home, where he would be greeted by a marshal who would arrest him then immediately release him on the condition that the congressman would appear at future court dates. That deal averted a public spectacle and possible mayhem. Powell enjoyed a celebrated return to his turf on March 22. Word spread among constituents at well-known gathering places from 125th to 145th streets.

On April 4, Powell was on the road, traveling from Florida to Durham, North Carolina, to deliver a talk at Duke University. While unpacking at the hotel he became tired and experienced chest pains. Students who had waited for thirty minutes learned that Powell had suffered a mild seizure and had to be hospitalized. That same day, the Rev. Dr. Martin Luther King Jr. was slain as he stood on a motel balcony in Memphis. Powell had been a critic of King even as he recognized that the thirty-nine-year-old possessed extraordinary gifts. Powell checked out of the hospital and returned to Bimini. King's assassination, along with his own illness, made Powell fearful and anxious about a conspiracy to kill black leaders.[20]

Weeks later in the primary election Powell won easily, but it was a deceptive victory. Turnout was low (11,052 votes) and the 60 to 40 percent margin of victory was slim compared to his previous landslides. One reason for the lower voter turnout was that many families had left the district. In a few years the US Census would reveal the black population center of New York City had shifted from Manhattan's Harlem to Brooklyn.[21]

In January 1969, Adam Clayton Powell Jr. walked into the well of the House of Representatives and raised his hand to take the oath as a member of the 91st Congress. In order to be readmitted, he had to accept a $25,000 fine and the loss of twenty-two years of seniority. Weeks later, the US Supreme Court ruled that Congress had acted unconstitutionally in 1967 in denying Powell his seat. The decision was anticlimactic for Powell, yet he was satisfied that the court's rebuke prompted wails of protest inside the House.[22] Washington insiders believed the high court would prevent a confrontation with the legislative branch. But the court's judgment served as vindication for Powell.

———— • ————

Stella B. Baar Celler, the congressman's wife, died in New York Hospital on Monday, March 21, 1966, at age seventy-five. Mrs. Celler wore an electric pacemaker to keep her heart pumping during her final days, said family members. The congressman's wife endured years of excruciating arthritis yet entered her wheelchair and traveled to the House Gallery to encourage her husband when he spoke "in behalf of some unpopular cause like civil rights—early," said Rabbi Eugene M. Sack, who delivered the eulogy. Sack continued, "No man we have ever met had so loyal, loving and devoted a wife. It is no accident that the leaders of our city and state and the President and his wife have come to pay their last respects."[23]

President Lyndon B. Johnson and the First Lady ("Lady Bird" Johnson) flew into New York unexpectedly and in secrecy. About fifty persons aboard the presidential jet plane included New York representatives, members of the House Judiciary Committee, Attorney General Nicholas Katzenbach, Postmaster General Lawrence F. O'Brien, and FBI director J. Edgar Hoover. Journalists traveling in the presidential entourage were not told until the doors closed on their chartered plane that they were traveling to New York. Johnson told the assembled press that he had special affection for the Cellers. Emanuel, seventy-seven, at that time was among five House members still remaining from 1931, when Johnson arrived in Washington from Texas as a congressional secretary.[24]

Mrs. Celler's funeral was a thirty-minute ceremony held in the main sanctuary of Congregation Beth Elohim in Brooklyn's Park Slope. About seven hundred people were in the temple and two hundred onlookers waited outside. Her passing ended a fifty-one-year marriage that began June 30, 1914. Mrs. Celler was active in Jewish philanthropies and charities in Brooklyn and Washington, DC. She cared for daughter Judith who had special needs—cerebral palsy—throughout her life. In order to spend time with his family, Congressman Celler commuted to Brooklyn on weekends. While there, he and his wife often took in nights at the opera. Judith survived her mother.[25] With Stella's passing, the congressman spent more time in Washington, splitting time between a large, comfortable office in the Rayburn Building and his room at the Mayflower Hotel.[26]

For most of the 1960s, New York City was a seven-newspaper town. The *New York Times*, *New York Daily News*, and the *New York Post* were the leaders, followed by the *Herald Tribune*, *Journal-American*, *World-Telegram & Sun*, and the *New York Mirror*. In 1962, a 114-day strike by the typesetters union seriously wounded the *Herald Tribune*, the Hearst-owned *Journal American*, and the Scripps Howard-owned *World-Telegram & Sun*.[27] The Hearst-owned *Daily Mirror*, a tabloid launched in 1924, died from financial strangulation in October 1963.[28]

In 1966, the typesetters struck again and knocked out three newspapers. *Herald Tribune* owner John Hay Whitney shut down his New York paper and sold half of his prosperous overseas publishing enterprise, the *Paris Herald Tribune*, to the Washington Post Company (the

Paris edition was valued at $250 million, according to a 1964 estimate). Whitney's next move was to merge the three weakest newspapers into one, renamed the *World Journal Tribune*. "The widget," as its journalists called that combined newspaper, lasted eight months from September 12, 1966, until May 5, 1967.[29]

O. Roy Chalk, publisher of Spanish-language daily *El Diario*, appealed to Emanuel Celler to step in and use his influence to revive the *World Journal Tribune*. Chalk's first appeal letter was dated May 17. He and Celler exchanged more letters June 1, 2, and 7 and July 31.[30] Maybe Chalk believed Celler was sympathetic because a decade before in 1965, the congressman witnessed the loss of his hometown newspaper, the *Brooklyn Eagle*, in 1955. It even missed the opportunity to cover the Dodgers' remarkable World Series championship season that fall.

The attempt to save the *World Journal Tribune* was doomed. Local television and radio news had emerged as co-equal competitors to newspapers. Meanwhile, general interest picture magazines such as *Life* and *Look* were in rapid decline, not because of declining readership but because TV advertising reached consumers more efficiently.

Later in 1967, the *New York Times* bought a 33 percent share of the healthy *Herald Tribune*, and renamed the overseas daily the *International Herald Tribune*, which thrived into the twenty-first century.[31] Post-1967, three papers primarily served New York City—the broadsheet *New York Times*, and tabloids the *New York Daily News*, and *New York Post*. Although the *New York Herald Tribune* has died, its legacy lived on. Former Sunday supplement magazine *New York* continued as a weekly, and about a dozen writers continued to produce "New Journalism," narrative nonfiction that read like novels. The writers dazzled readers for decades with books and screenplays that became Hollywood movies. Tom Wolfe, Nora Ephron, and Jimmy Breslin were among that stable of *Herald Tribune* expatriates.[32]

Celler the civil rights sympathizer and others endured the "long, hot summer" of 1967. On July 23 in Detroit, a police vice squad raid on an after-hours club escalated into widespread violence. A celebration for two returning Vietnam vets was interrupted and 80 people were arrested. An angry mob hurled objects at police. A week of rioting resulted in 43 deaths, 473 injuries, 7,200 arrests, and an estimated $40 to $80 billion in property damage that included 2,500 stores vandalized or torched.[33] Also that month, 26 people—24 of them blacks—died during rioting in Newark. The flashpoint was the arrest and beating of a black cab driver over a minor traffic infraction. Over two days, and the event caused at least $15 million in property damage.

———————•———————

Demographic change had a political impact on Celler. He represented one of the five gerrymandered congressional districts that grotesquely subdivided Bedford-Stuyvesant. Forty percent of that neighborhood's residents lived in Celler's district. During the 1961 census redistricting, 70,000 residents from the Rockaway section of Queens were added to Celler's district to ensure that the political boundaries would not end up predominantly black.[34] In 1966, Andrew W. Cooper, a brewery executive and political activist, alleged a cozy collaboration between local Democratic and Republican political machines. He sued New York State. Cooper's voting rights lawsuit advanced to the US Supreme Court and in 1967 the justices concurred that the 80 percent black and Puerto Rican ghetto needed to be immediately redrawn.

When the New York legislature recast the boundaries, Celler's congressional district was merged with Representative Edna Flannery Kelly's district. In July 1949, she was appointed to fill a vacancy caused by the death of Andrew L. Somers. Kelly became the first Democratic woman to represent New York City in Congress. A month shy of her forty-third birthday, Kelly was the widow of Edward Kelly, a New York City court judge appointed by Governor Herbert Lehman. Ed Kelly died eight months later in an automobile accident. Edna, who had studied history and economics at Hunter College, entered politics and worked her way through the ranks by reviving a political club's women's auxiliary and then serving as a research director for the New York State legislature. By 1944, Kelly had advanced to co-leader of the Eighteenth Assembly District in Brooklyn, where Celler happened to live.[35]

During ten terms in Congress Edna Kelly built a reputation as a foreign affairs expert and Cold Warrior. Associates said she had innumerable contacts that were not available to the State Department. Kelly was credited with successfully introducing resolutions that deplored religious persecution in Eastern Europe and throughout the 1950s and 1960s from her perch on the House Foreign Affairs subcommittee/Europe, Kelly urged the United States to play an aggressive role in mediating Arab-Israeli peace accords via the United Nations.[36]

By 1968, congressional district realignments in Brooklyn forced a spring primary contest between incumbents Kelly and Celler. Kelly was mounting the first primary challenge against the seventy-nine-year-old representative since 1923 when Celler entered the House. Celler prevailed because Kelly, affected by dilution of her power base, received 32 percent of votes and lost by

8,500 ballots. President Johnson offered Kelly (1906–1997) the position of US treasurer, but she declined the offer.[37] Meanwhile, the newly drawn congressional district was claimed by Shirley Chisholm, the first black woman elected to Congress, and the second African American to represent New York.[38]

The next May 6, Emanuel Celler celebrated his eightieth birthday. Several New York newspapers took measure of the octogenarian's achievements. The *Long Island Press* Washington correspondent Richard Seelmeyer wrote, "Celler has written and guided to passage more bills than any other man. His impact on American laws, some believe, has been greater than any man since the Constitution was written. Forty percent of all bills that pass through Congress do so via Celler's committee."[39]

A few weeks later the *New York Daily News* featured Celler prominently in a Sunday magazine four-photo spread and article titled "Mainly for seniors." Celler told reporter Jack Leahy, "When I first came to Congress, I was not a happy man. I was impatient with Washington ways and Washington ideas. I seemed to be climbing a greased pole whenever I tried to get things done."[40]

Celler recalled his days as a thirty-something freshman who inherited a congressional district of "aliens" and was facing mostly hostile and anti-immigrant House colleagues.

Celler did reveal a political desire he had resisted acting upon: "I did consider running for the Senate some years ago. But at the time, Herbert Lehman was in office and I don't think the voters would have permitted the state to have two Jewish senators." Lehman, FDR's successor as governor of the Empire State during most of the 1930s, served as US senator from New York from 1949 to 1956. "That," Celler explained, "was my simple, pragmatic reason for staying put." Celler said he was disappointed that Lehman did not run again because he was certain the senator would have been reelected, based on Lehman's sense of conviction and sincerity.[41]

Emanuel Celler was among the primary advocates of a fair housing law that would prohibit discrimination on the basis of the race. President Johnson had proposed fair housing legislation to the majority Democratic Congress in 1966. On January 17 of that year, Judiciary Committee chairman Celler introduced the legislation. The bill was referred to Subcommittee No. 5, which Celler chaired and had jurisdiction over civil rights matters.[42]

The fair housing bill made it out of the subcommittee and became part of a larger bill to protect civil rights workers who were being beaten and intimidated in the South. Celler anticipated that his subcommittee would become deadlocked over the fair housing title, so he convinced the members to report the larger bill that included Fair Housing Title IV without recommendation.[43] Celler had another reason to be worried about safe passage of the bill. Constituents in his overwhelmingly Jewish Crown Heights district opposed blacks moving into their neighborhoods, said LBJ aide Joseph Califano.[44]

The bill moved to the Senate, whose members were confronted by real estate agents and their trade association. That industry contended that homeowners should be able to sell to whomever they chose. Clarence Mitchell of the NAACP and Leadership Conference of Civil Rights was among the leading advocates for the fair housing legislation.

By June 24, Celler met with McCulloch, his Republican colleague on the House Judiciary Committee, Senator Charles "Mac" Mathias Jr., R-Maryland, and the attorney general to reach a compromise and save the bill. Their solution was to exempt sales of owner-occupied homes and rentals of small owner-occupied duplexes and triplexes. The fair housing bill proceeded on a slow, bumpy path. On June 28, a motion to report the bill out was defeated. The next day, June 29, the Celler-led Judiciary Committee reported the bill to the full House. Debate began on the House floor July 25 and the members worked through seventy-seven amendments.

On August 9, the bill passed by a bipartisan vote of 259–157 that included 183 Democrats and 76 Republicans among the "yeas."[45]

The bill moved to the Senate, where it was filibustered. The bill stalled and lawmakers turned their attention to other pending legislation. On August 16, 1967, the House by a 326–93 vote passed H.R. 2516, a trimmed-down civil rights bill. That summer there were civil disturbances in one hundred US cities, most famously Newark and Detroit. Racially motivated housing discrimination was among the flashpoints of the violence and destruction. Congress was compelled to act. In fall 1967, Senate Majority Leader Mike Mansfield, D-Montana, called up the House bill intended to protect civil rights workers. Senator Walter Mondale, D-Minnesota, asked Senator Edward M. Brooke, R-Massachusetts (and the lone African American in that chamber), to join him in offering a fair housing bill as an amendment to the civil rights bill. Senate debate began in January 1968.

For weeks, southern senators filibustered. On February 18, Mansfield forced a cloture vote in order to end debate. His motion failed 55–37. Within that vote, Dirksen's GOP colleagues were divided 18–18. Three days later on February 21, Mansfield moved to kill the fair housing amendment in order to break the gridlock and keep the rest of the Senate legislative agenda moving. However, Mansfield's motion failed 58–34, which surprised some civil rights advocates.[46] Attorney General Ramsey Clark called Dirksen. The senator told him, "I'm trying to plow through a compromise that will be fair to you and everybody else." A year before, Dirksen said he favored a civil rights bill but was unequivocally against open housing proposals. Now the senator suggested he was flexible. "It depends on how all-inclusive you make it," he told Clark, "on what you excluded. For instance, if it did not apply to an individual; I have a house, and you want to buy, and I don't want to sell it to you. That's one situation. When it's handled with brokers and agents—they operate under a license of the state—it's a different picture."[47]

On February 28, Dirksen introduced a substitute bill that was a patchwork of old bills, odd amendments, and new language pasted at negotiating sessions. Dirksen said America changed since his strenuous opposition in 1966 to open housing. He repeated a saying of his that the only persons who did not change their minds were in insane asylums or cemeteries.

Dirksen changed his mind but he faced difficulty getting a half-dozen GOP colleagues to change their votes. They were annoyed and angry with Dirksen because they made commitments that they were now being asked to break. On March 1, Mansfield scheduled another cloture vote. The 59–35 count was still short of the two-thirds of ayes needed for approval. Three days later, Mansfield tried again. Several senators hid in the cloakroom and had to be persuaded by colleagues to come out and vote. The count this time was 65–32, just enough to impose cloture.[48]

So the Celler-introduced H.R. 2516 returned to the House to achieve concurrence with the Senate amendments. The next step was debate in House Rules Committee, chaired by Representative William Colmer, D-Mississippi, a segregationist. He deferred action on the bill—twice—until mid-April 1968. Members feared that the bill would die in the Rules Committee.[49] On April 4, Martin Luther King Jr. was assassinated in Memphis, Tennessee, gunned down by sniper James Earl Ray. Most Americans reacted with shock and grief. Elsewhere, another series of civil disturbances followed, this time within blocks of the US Capitol. Martin Luther King's April 9 memorial service broke H.R. 2516 free. House members insisted on action from its Rules Committee. Chairman Colmer of Mississippi resisted; however, Republican John Anderson of Illinois changed his vote and the bill was reported to pass out of the committee and move to the floor.[50]

On April 10, the House debated the Civil Rights Act of 1968 for one hour and the chamber then passed the bill 250–71. The next day, LBJ signed the bill into law. Fair housing became Title VIII of the Civil Rights Act of 1968. Celler, godfather of civil rights legislation, according to fair housing advocate Gary Rhoades, watched his fair housing bill over more than a year evolve from consideration to near death, to resurrection, to another near strangulation, to recovery and to a third civil rights law.[51]

On March 1–3, 1969, Lyn Shepard of the *Christian Science Monitor* conducted a Question & Answer profile of the congressional bulldog. During the years 1967 and 1968, Celler's Judiciary Committee reviewed 9,304 bills and resolutions introduced by members of Congress. Such a workload meant that Chairman Celler's committee reviewed nearly 40 percent of all legislation.[52] Bills that became laws included the Civil Rights Act of 1964 that ended seventy years of legal, American apartheid, followed by the 1965 Voting Rights Act that reaffirmed African Americans' right to vote, promised by the post–Civil War Fourteenth Amendment, but nullified largely in the South through Jim Crow laws, lynching, and other acts of domestic terrorism. Civil rights crusader Celler had tangled repeatedly with southern colleagues who disagreed with his views, yet a number of them paid grudging tribute to his talents. Virginia Democrat Howard W. Smith, grand strategist of "massive resistance" against desegregation and integration, proclaimed Celler one of the ablest members of the House, largely because "he does his homework."[53] Celler framed and argued his positions forcefully and persuasively, even as his gruff exterior also contained a collegial lawmaker who could disarm adversaries with an aphorism or a pithy literary quote. For relaxation, Celler sketched portraits of friends. To unwind he also played piano (he had one in his congressional office or apartment at the Mayflower Hotel).[54] What legislation made him the proudest? the reporter asked. His answer was three hundred public laws that bear his name. They included immigration legislation for displaced persons. In economic areas, he emphasized the Celler-Kefauver Act of 1950 that prohibited companies from merging with distributors and suppliers if the acts impeded competition.

"I am principal House author of three constitutional amendments," said Celler, "the 23rd [presidential voting rights for residents of the District of Columbia], 24th [abolished poll tax in federal elections] and 25th [succession to the presidency]."[55] Celler was, indeed, a square-jawed congressional bulldog. Rather than chase, he was better at holding his ground and battling until he gained the upper hand. Celler had a bulldog's stamina, grip, and resolve. On civil rights matters, Celler wore down his opponents. He carried the 1957 civil rights bill to President Eisenhower. During that hot time of civil rights flashpoints—*Brown vs. Board of Education*, Emmett Till's murder, the Montgomery bus boycott, and the Little Rock Nine high school desegregation—the 1957 law had baby teeth that grew bigger and sharper during the seven years before Celler carried a new civil rights bill through Congress, initiated by JFK and followed up on and signed into law by LBJ.

Celler's Judiciary Committee leadership aided his writing of the Twenty-Third Amendment that abolished poll taxes, an insidious tactic by southern whites to take voting rights away from black citizens. The Brooklyn congressman's action created law that assisted the Civil Rights and Voting Rights Acts of 1964 and 1965 that emphatically declared that African Americans and other racial minorities were to be treated—at least by law—as first-class American citizens.

Celler's bulldog tenacity and integrity made him the credible go-to man to tackle a messy case, the investigation of the unconstitutional removal of Powell. Celler was expected to punish a flamboyant House leader and correct the unjust removal of a legally elected official. Celler's peers rejected his sage advice, and unlike many of his colleagues, he emerged unscathed.

15

Old-World Liberal Celler
Is Upset, 1972–1973

Celler was a pioneer regarding women's rights in the Congress. In the 1930s, a coalition of women's organizations praised Celler for ending the ban on wives working in government if their husbands were also federal employees. Also, during World War II Celler lobbied for the acceptance of women doctors into the Medical Reserve Corps, but the congressman's request was rejected by the secretary of the navy.

Nearly four decades later, however, the twenty-five-term congressman was perceived as an archvillain of young, emerging professional women and the National Organization for Women (NOW) because of his unequivocal opposition to the Equal Rights Amendment (ERA). The ERA proposal had been bottled up in his Judiciary Committee for twenty years.[1] Yet on July 20, 1970, Representative Martha Griffiths, D-Michigan, collected enough signatures for a rare discharge petition, bypassing the committee and Chairman Celler, who had strong labor ties. At an August 10 House hearing, Griffiths pleaded, "Give us a chance to show you that those so-called protective laws to aid women—however well intentioned—have become in fact restraints, which keep wife, abandoned wife, and widow alike from supporting her family."[2] The ERA, Celler answered, would set America back. "What we are being asked to do is vote on a constitutional amendment, the consequences of which are unexamined, its meaning non-defined, and its risks uncalculated. Ever since Adam gave up his rib to make a woman, throughout the ages we have learned that physical, emotional, psychological and sociological differences dare not be disregarded. The adoption of a blunderbuss amendment would erase existing protective female legislation with the most disasterous consequences."[3]

Congresswoman Bella Abzug of New York said her colleague Celler held "quaint" views about the opposite sex: "He said women were not present at The Last Supper. I told him we may not have been at the last one, but you can be damn sure we will be at the next one."[4]

The amendment was approved 352–15 in the House in 1971 and on March 22 of that year, the Senate approved the ERA 84–8 without amendments. The ERA was submitted to the states for ratification and was approved by thirty-five states but fell short of the minimum thirty-eight states needed to be ratified as a constitutional amendment.[5]

Another stance that ran counter to modern conventional wisdom and distanced Celler from young, liberal, and urban constituents was his support of the Vietnam War and his opposition of giving the right to vote to eighteen-year-olds. Heartland America had turned against that conflict by the early 1970s. In liberal Brooklyn, New York, Celler's constituents were either stridently against the war, or were indifferent. Furthermore, the congressman had opposed the bill to lower the voting age to eighteen from twenty-one. For generations, teenagers had been eligible to be drafted for military service and to fight—and die—in wars, yet they were not eligible to elect their leaders. In 1942—World War II—members of Congress cosponsored a bill to lower the voting age to eighteen. At that time, half the US Marine Corps consisted of men under twenty-one. Teenagers made up a quarter of the army; a third of the navy.[6]

That proposal did not go far. When Celler resumed chairmanship of the Judiciary Committee in the 1950s, he was committed to tamping down the youth-vote idea. The liberal challenged legislators' old-enough-to-fight-in-wars, then old-enough-to-vote mantra in 1954:

Voting is as different as chalk is from cheese.

When the draft age was lowered from 21 to 18 years of age, the generals told us that this was a necessary move because young men under 21 were more easily molded into good soldiers than were their elders who had grown to maturity. Young men under 21 are more pliable and more amenable to indoctrination.

Instant and unquestioning obedience may be the most desirable from soldiers on the battlefield, but in a voter such obedience would be most undesirable. Self-interested groups and corrupt politicians would find such obedience a fertile playground.[7]

Celler continued to resist but he reluctantly released the bill from his committee. Members of Congress—not adolescents through a national, grass-roots
movement—relentlessly pressed the youth vote proposal.[8] The bill passed
the Senate unanimously, then passed overwhelmingly in the House. President Richard M. Nixon signed it into law on July 5, 1971. Out of the four he
guided, the Twenty-Sixth Amendment that lowered the minimum voting
age to eighteen was Celler's reluctant amendment.[9]

Celler frequently bottled up other controversial bills, such as abortion
reform and proposals for amnesty for Vietnam War resisters, by refusing to
refer them to a subcommittee or to hold hearings. He helped thwart efforts to
adopt a constitutional amendment that would allow prayer in public schools.
Celler held hearings on various prayer bills in 1964 and brought in constitutional lawyers who testified against the legislation.[10] Celler took these
defensive actions on proposals he feared would weaken the Bill of Rights.
He was also criticized for failing to seek larger appropriations and a larger
staff to handle the committee's workload. In the 92nd Congress (January
1971-1973) more than 5,000 bills and resolutions were referred to Celler's
House Judiciary Committee to be handled by a 36-member staff. Meanwhile,
the Senate Judiciary Committee, with far fewer bills to consider, employed
204 staff, nearly six times more.[11]

In his final years in the House, Celler led hearings on six major conglomerates and opposed both the Equal Rights Amendment and an amendment
to prohibit busing for school desegregation.[12]

Celler, meanwhile, remained a powerful senior legislator in what he and
others considered a safe district. A widower, he spent most of his time in
Washington and returned to his Brooklyn home at 9 West Plaza Street on
weekends to see his adult daughters and grandchildren. Playful away from
the Capitol, Celler entertained the children with handkerchief puppets, dis-
appearing coins, and match tricks.[13]

Against that backdrop of issues—equal rights, Vietnam, and voting privileges for teenagers—thirty-year-old Elizabeth Holtzman, a lawyer young
enough to have been Celler's granddaughter, rose up to challenge her elder.
She decided to go after the incumbent in November 1970. While visiting
her parents, their neighbor Pearl Marcus, who had just voted, said wearily,
"I can't believe that man [Celler] is still on the ballot. He's been there far too
long and he's way too old."[14]

Holtzman appeared to be very smart but she was no match for the wise,
wily congressman. She graduated from Harvard Law School in 1965 then
worked for the civil rights movement in Georgia before returning to New
York to practice law and work two years for first-term liberal Republican
mayor John Lindsay, a former colleague of Celler's, in the House.[15]

Holtzman then became involved in party politics as a Democratic state committee member and a district leader. Still, she recognized a formidable opponent in Celler. She tested her idea to run on Edward N. Costikyan, respected lawyer and former chairman of the New York County (Manhattan) Democratic Committee. Expressionless, he listened to the pitch, then broke into a smile. "I think you can do it," he told Holtzman.

Holtzman's law firm colleagues were less enthusiastic about her plan. They gave Holtzman a choice: continue working for the firm or resign and run against Celler. She chose the latter, a blessing in disguise because Holtzman could campaign full-time for the congressional seat.[16]

Holtzman's adventure promised to be rugged. Eighty-three-year-old Celler let it be known that he was preparing to run for his twenty-sixth term in the House. With $36,000—$4,000 of it borrowed—Holtzman ran a low-budget grass-roots campaign in Brooklyn with an army of unpaid volunteers, who handed out leaflets as the challenger spoke to community groups.[17] "We had no money for television or radio; we had one mailing, one ad in a New York newspaper and no more than four or five people on the payroll," Holtzman told a wire service reporter in July 1972. "But we handed out physically over 200,000 pieces of literature."

As crowds wrapped around theaters waiting to watch the blockbuster movie *The Godfather*, Holtzman volunteers engaged people in line and distributed literature. They applied the same tactic outside supermarkets and subways.[18] Celler did not take Holtzman's challenge seriously. He described her as "a toothpick trying to topple the Washington Monument." Celler also called her a "non-entity" whose chances of winning "are about as good as they have been in any year ending in two, four, six, eight or zero." If Celler sounded dismissive, Meade Esposito, Kings County Democratic leader and boss of Brooklyn, was coarsely sexist, calling Holtzman "a young broad," who had "all kinds of young girls running around for her. Indians, freaking squaws."[19]

Holtzman said Celler was beholden to special interests because he consistently approved an antiballistic missile defense system that benefited New York engineering firm Fishbach and Moore in which the congressman owned stock. Furthermore, said challenger Holtzman, Celler engaged in "double dooring," a way of getting around a congressional rule that barred sitting House members from having legal clients.[20]

Double dooring meant two doors in the law office that opened into the same conference room. If clients arrived to discuss matters that involved the federal government, they were escorted to the door that did not list Celler.

Celler told the *Washington Post* that his New York law practice posed no conflict of interest because he never worked on cases that involved the federal government. The separate door, he said, provided a firewall.[21]

Clients with business that did not involve the federal government were escorted to the door that listed Celler as a partner. Celler eloquently, and if not persuasively, explained why he believed members of Congress should not have to give up outside income-producing activities:

> The average length of a congressman's tenure is eight years. If he is going to divest himself of his calling as a farmer or a banker or a lawyer, what is going to happen to him when he is defeated or resigns? He is bereft, he no longer has his profession, he no longer has his job, he no longer has his wealth, he is like a rudderless ship on a sea without a shore.[22]

Celler continued to brush off criticism regarding his extracurricular law firm connection by cavalierly assuming that his constituents knew what he did and were capable of judging him. Celler who only a few years before bristled at Powell's ability to live on edges of what was legal but ethically dubious, apparently failed to see the irony of his defense. That extra law firm activity earned him a scolding from the *New York Times* editorial board, which endorsed Holtzman, the upstart candidate, instead of the dean of the House.[23]

Holtzman's tenacity dug under the skin of the elder congressional leader. She accused the incumbent of neglecting his district. In the Brownsville neighborhood "some areas look bombed out," said Holtzman, "and the rubble in the streets looks like Berlin after the war. He [Celler] was never a major spokesman for getting housing in that district or any district." She also ran as an antiwar candidate and criticized Celler because he supported the Vietnam War effort. Holtzman's campaign sent primary voters a Jack Anderson column that reported some of Celler's top donors were Vietnam War contractors. Presidential candidate Senator George McGovern, D-South Dakota, was on the primary ballot and he too was antiwar. Both campaigns worked together. A few days before the June primary, Celler described his opponent as "irritating as a hangnail, which nail I am going to cut off."[24]

Three days before the primary, six men believed to be intoxicated kicked and damaged posters outside Holtzman's campaign office during the early evening. When a campaign aide came outside to complain a fracas ensued and campaign workers were assaulted, including campaign manager Mike

Churchill, who was rushed to an emergency room and treated for minor injuries.[25] The Holtzman camp did not find out the rowdy men's identities. The attack had no impact on the campaign, said Holtzman in a 2018 interview. Nevertheless, the candidate was filled with moral indignation.

Back in Brooklyn, June primary turnout was light. About 35,000 eligible Sixteenth Congressional District voters cast ballots. The Holtzman camp used a clever and respectful ploy to persuade voters to retire their congressman. They didn't say that eighty-four-year-old Celler was "old"; he was too "tired" to do the job. "Darling, I'm 84," said a woman voter with a Yiddish accent. "If Celler feels anything like I do, he has no business being in Congress."[26]

Furthermore, Robert E. O'Donnell, a third candidate, took 4,433 votes, or 12.5 percent of the ballots cast. Holtzman said O'Donnell was sent by the Celler-backed Brooklyn Democratic machine to siphon Irish votes from her. During the last congressional redistricting, Brooklyn lost a seat, after which Celler defeated Edna Kelly. Maybe O'Donnell's double-digit share of votes hurt Celler instead since Irish American voters were annoyed that he had snatched the musical chair from a favorite daughter.[27]

Celler lost to Holtzman by 562 votes and also by an ultra-slim margin, 44 percent to 43.5 percent. The upset stung and stunned the eighty-four-year-old incumbent. He asked for a recount. It reaffirmed Holtzman's vapor-thin win. Her vote count increased from 562 to 609 votes.[28]

When asked by reporters, Celler suggested that he would not campaign for the new Democratic candidate. Through the summer, Celler considered running for his old seat as the Liberal Party candidate. That ballot listed him, but he did not campaign. By the fall, Celler stepped aside.[29]

Celler's primary defeat was arguably the most surprising upset of a congressional incumbent in American political history, followed only by House Speaker Joe Martin, a Massachusetts Republican, who lost to Margaret Heckler in 1966, and the 2014 loss of House Majority Leader Eric Cantor of Virginia to Dave Brat, an economics professor and Tea Party candidate.[30] The November general election in 1972 was a *fait accompli* for Holtzman. The Republicans did not field a competitive opponent in the Democrat-centric district.

—————— • ——————

About a week after the Celler-Holtzman primary battle and upset in June, police arrested a handful of men who burglarized Democratic National headquarters in Washington, DC's Watergate complex. The burglars were linked to President Nixon's reelection campaign.[31]

That November, incumbent Nixon demolished Democrat George McGovern. He won 61 percent of the popular vote and forty-nine of fifty states in the electoral college.

Holtzman replaced longtime chairman Celler as a junior member of the House Judiciary Committee. Peter W. Rodino Jr., a New Jersey Democrat, ascended to replace Celler as chairman. Rodino, elected to the House in 1948, was a product of the notorious Essex County Democratic political machine yet managed to steer clear of personal scandal. The son of immigrants was a fierce advocate of Italian causes and was at the forefront of civil rights battles in the House. Celler and Rodino were chummy colleagues and his rise to the top was welcome.[32]

Soon, Rodino had reason—for the first time in US history—to apply the eight-year-old constitutional amendment that Celler had coauthored with Senator Birch Bayh of Indiana. When Vice President Spiro Agnew resigned in 1973 amid a corruption scandal, the Twenty-Fifth Amendment defined the proper succession to the vice presidency.[33] Nixon appointed US representative Gerald R. Ford of Michigan to succeed Agnew. The amendment also provided guidance on who would succeed the president if the commander-in-chief was unable to perform or vacated the seat. The year 1974 would provide the test.

Holtzman, the young—and at the time, rare, woman newcomer—assumed a back-bencher role. In the early months of 1973 the Judiciary Committee was in the spotlight. The Watergate story ripened. It turned out to be much more than a "third-rate burglary," as a Nixon supporter had claimed. It was a corruption scandal traceable to the attorney general, then the president. But once thrust into the game, Holtzman emerged as a star of the Nixon impeachment hearings. For the first time, women's voices and votes were in the committee room.[34] Celler, who had commanded the room like Winston Churchill, watched from the sidelines.

———————

For the previous twenty-two years as either chairman or as ranking minority member of the House Judiciary Committee, Celler had reigned as one of the most powerful men in America—a man who served with nine presidents. Celler, "Last of the Victorians," according to United Press International correspondent Arnold Sawislak, authored or cosponsored four amendments to the US Constitution and in 1957 sponsored the first Civil Rights Act since Reconstruction, and then he pressed passage of the civil rights amendments of 1960, 1964, 1965, 1968, and 1970.[35]

The "Star Spangled Banner" that Americans customarily sing at sporting events became a tradition for four decades because Celler sponsored the House measure to officially make the song America's national anthem.[36] Celler had served longer in the House than anyone except former representative Carl Vinson of Georgia, who served fifty years and two months.

Although Celler's advanced age became an effective primary election issue, the record showed that his greatest legislative accomplishments—immigration reform, civil and voting rights—occurred during the mid-1960s when he was in his late seventies. Celler demonstrated he had the necessary physical stamina and institutional memory to complete lasting works for the American people.

Inside the Judiciary Committee, Celler never hesitated to use his considerable power to advance some bills and kill others by scorn, apathy, suffocation, or the prospect of long hearings. All in all, Celler had a hand in the enactment of some four hundred laws. His signature triumph was abolition of national origin quotas for immigrants in 1965.

Emanuel Celler's legislative record was that of a New Deal liberal and champion of civil rights. Yet in 1972, in many ways he had far more in common with rural conservatives of his own generation than with the emerging, younger breed of urban liberals. Some of Celler's opinions did outlive their time. His stubborn opposition to the Equal Rights Amendment made him an archvillain of feminists and lent great irony to the octogenarian's primary defeat by a thirty-year-old woman lawyer.[37]

Yet Celler, despite his age, was not ready to retire from public service. In late 1972, he became a member of Washington-based Weisman, Celler, Speth, Modin, and Wertheimer. Celler retained his fifty-year District of Columbia residence at the Mayflower Hotel.[38]

On December 18, Celler received the president's medal from B'nai B'rith at a Washington luncheon in his honor. One hundred members attended. For forty-five minutes the former congressman recalled his long career: President Franklin D. Roosevelt was "adroit, voluble, smiling . . . but when I went to see him I was never quite sure he was interested in my business because we spent so little time on it."[39]

Furthermore, Celler told the audience that a national crisis liberated him and made him find his purpose: "You remember the WPA and PWA, the various other acts which pulled us out of the valley of depression. I voted as the other members did in those days. I wasn't voting to remedy the new and difficult onslaught of economic distress. I had come from a little bit of world where economic distress it seemed always had been a part of life. What I had known, what I had seen in Brownsville, on Pitkin Avenue, Brooklyn, the markets of Brooklyn had become the generalized, commonplace experience of the whole nation. The panic of the [Great] Depression loosened my inhibitions against being different. For the first time in ten years I could be myself. I realized there were things I cared about most passionately. One, establish a homeland for Jews in Palestine, another for independence of India, another for equitable immigration laws, another for civil rights and judicial reform and still another, economic freedom, meaning of course antitrust. These all I have realized must have a common theme—the equality of opportunity for all people without regard to race, color, religion or national origin. Equal opportunity, I realized, means independence in the fullest sense."[40]

Specifically, Celler recalled the 1924 Johnson-Reed Immigration act that had repulsed him as a freshman legislator. He came from the "district of aliens" and opposed the bill strongly. He fought to defeat the bill and lost, "and I learned my first big lesson," said Celler, "Passion more than logic controls the minds of men." Forty-one years later in 1965, Celler cosponsored the bill that repealed the 1924 law: "Patience is bitter," he told the audience, "but it bears rich fruit."[41]

16

Post-Congressional Life,
1973-1981

Emanuel Celler praised Lyndon Baines Johnson, sixty-five, who died January 22, 1973, in San Antonio, Texas, nine months after he had suffered a heart attack the previous April.[1]

"I felt very close to him," Celler wrote in a January 29 letter to widow Claudia Alta "Lady Bird" Johnson. "We worked together with determination on important pieces of legislation . . . he was a great and good man and he will be sorely missed in the councils of D.C."[2]

Celler's civil rights bills in the late 1950s became law largely because Senate Majority Leader Johnson's deal making averted legislation-killing filibusters by southern segregationists. In 1964, President Johnson pressed Celler to guide a transformative civil rights bill unscathed through the Congress and Celler answered the challenge. LBJ in 1965 signed into law Celler's signature accomplishment, immigration reform, in front of the Statue of Liberty in the congressman's home state.

Celler wrapped up fifty years of service when the 92nd Congress adjourned in January 1973. Successor Elizabeth Holtzman in a February 6, 1973, letter to Celler's law firm expressed appreciation for the gracious cooperation of (Miss) Manny White from Celler's staff regarding cases pending in the district. Holtzman said she looked forward to thanking her personally.[3]

In 1974, Celler, eighty-five, was named New York City mayor Abe Beame's unsalaried congressional adviser. "I'm a lobbyist," the former congressman told a *New York Times* reporter. Beame was elected in November 1973, succeeding two-term mayor John V. Lindsay, Celler's former Republican colleague in the House during the 1960s. Celler's law firm Weisman, Celler, Spett, Modlin, and Wertheimer represented paying customers that included the National Football League Players Association, the Seafarers Union, and the American Society of Composers, Authors and Publishers (ASCAP).[4] Celler continued to live in the same room in the Mayflower Hotel, which was built in 1922, the year before he arrived in Washington.[5]

By the summer, Celler and his partners opened a new New York law office that occupied an entire floor at 425 Park Avenue.[6] President Nixon appointed Celler to a special commission to study US district courts, an appointment that would take the octogenarian all over the country to examine whether to redraw circuit court lines. The former lawmaker was considering a professorship at Brooklyn Law School (which was not offered or accepted, said school officials in 2018) and a raft of lecture offers. Celler was looking forward to the establishment of a new law school in New York—Touro College of Brooklyn—that was supposed to bear his name.[7]

"The former representative has a Bloody Mary at lunch and at dinner, smokes at least seven cigars a day and walks 1½ miles each Saturday. When asked the secret of his longevity, he looked toward Mary Doherty, his secretary for more than 40 years and says with a grin, 'Mary says novenas for me, and lights candles. That helps!'"[8]

Celler was an avid opera-goer. However, he considered the Metropolitan Opera House, located on Broadway at West 39th Street in Manhattan, a monstrosity. When groups formed to save the building from demolition in 1967, Celler protested: "Why the sudden urge? Is it publicity? Some of them probably think Puccini is a name for spaghetti and that Richard Wagner was a baseball player."[9]

As he aged, a thin ring of white hair encircled Celler's tanned dome. He was bandy legged and slope shouldered (or stooped), the latter condition a reminder of osteomyelitis that knocked him out of action for several months in 1941.[10] In private moments, Celler's blue eyes twinkled as he spun yarns with pungent phrases for adult audiences or when he shaped linen napkins into rabbits to entertain his grandchildren.

———————

A political scandal that simmered for two years boiled over inside the Executive Branch. On March 1, 1974, a grand jury indicted seven former White House staff members for conspiring to obstruct an investigation of the 1972

Watergate break-in. H. R. Haldeman, John Ehrlichman, John Mitchell, and Robert Mardian were convicted. Kenneth Parkinson was acquitted, and Gordon Strachan was tried separately. Watergate-related charges were dropped against Charles Colson because he pleaded guilty to crimes in connection with a break-in at the office of Daniel Ellsberg.[11] Ellsberg was the psychiatrist who had leaked the Pentagon Papers to the *New York Times*.

On July 24, the US Supreme Court, in a unanimous decision, demanded that President Nixon turn over audiotapes subpoenaed by special prosecutor Leon Jaworski in April. The case was the first time the high court had deliberated over a legal action in which a president was accused of criminal misconduct. The White House answered that the president would comply with the order.[12] Three days later, the House Judiciary Committee that Celler had chaired about two years earlier approved two Articles of Impeachment against Nixon, one charging him with obstructing justice and the second accusing him of repeatedly violating his oath of office. Three days later on July 30 the committee recommended a third Article of Impeachment, unconstitutional defiance of committee subpoenas.[13]

On August 5, what remained of the president's support in Congress had evaporated. As Nixon was about to release all of the subpoenaed tapes, he distributed three transcripts of a June 23, 1972, conversation with former chief of staff Haldeman.

Six days after the Watergate break-in, Nixon had ordered a halt to an FBI investigation of the case. The president conceded that in his earlier statements he had failed to include this information and thus had been guilty of "a serious act of omission."[14] On August 8 in a nationally televised speech, President Nixon announced his resignation, effective at noon the following day. Nixon bid his Washington staff farewell, and at 12:03 p.m., August 9, as he promised, he was en route to California.

Nixon's resignation was the first substantial test of the Bayh-Celler Twenty-Fifth Amendment. The legislation was proposed July 6, 1965. "Manny Celler played a critical role in the passage of the 25th Amendment as chairman of the House Judiciary Committee," said Bayh, ninety, in a June 2018 statement. "His wisdom and experience and his patience and knowledge of the legislative process eventually led us to a unanimous conference report—a result that appeared highly unlikely after a meeting of the conferees in which the senior Republican on his committee expressed opposition to the Senate provisions on the time period for required action. Working quietly behind the scenes with his Republican colleagues, he helped fashion a compromise that was acceptable to all and within 30 minutes, the two of us had agreed on what we would present to our conferees. That agreement sealed the deal and led to a unanimous, bipartisan amendment." The Bayh-Celler Twenty-Fifth Amendment was ratified by the states February 10, 1967.[15]

Unlike earlier presidential crises—Woodrow Wilson's paralyzing stroke in 1919, and FDR's heart attack that rendered him gravely ill in 1945 yet still in charge—where there was no written succession plan and both men were hidden from the American people, the Bayh-Celler constitutional amendment made it clear: Vice President Gerald Ford succeeded the president, who had relieved himself of his duties.

Ford was sworn in that August afternoon by Chief Justice Warren Burger.

Six years later, the Bayh-Celler Twenty-Fifth Amendment was applied again. On March 30, 1981, President Ronald Reagan, seventy, and in office for seventy days, was shot by John Hinckley Jr. Reagan was rushed to the hospital, where he was treated for a possible collapsed lung and then went into surgery. During the crisis Secretary of State Alexander Haig declared repeatedly, and inaccurately, that he was in charge of the federal government. Vice President George H. W. Bush was on a plane over Texas. Haig was in Washington briefing reporters: "Constitutionally gentlemen, you have the president, the vice president and the secretary of state in that order, and should the president decide he wants to transfer the helm to the vice president, he will do so. As of now, I am in control here at the White House."[16]

Haig forgot that the House Speaker, then the Senate's president pro tempore, and then the secretary of state formed the line of succession spelled out in the Twenty-Fifth Amendment.[17] Reagan survived the serious wounds and soon resumed his duties as commander-in-chief. Haig's *faux pas* dashed his future presidential ambitions.

Celler's ninetieth birthday was on May 6, 1978. Invited to a luncheon in Celler's honor, Supreme Court justice William O. Douglas sent regrets and praise: "You are, without doubt, one of our greatest living Americans. Your long public career demonstrates your profound understanding of the basic values of humanity and of human freedom, and your total dedication to these values. As chairman of the judicial committee of the House, you were a staunch defender of individual freedom and justice and of economic freedom. In difficult times, you opposed the assault on human dignity. You were a fearless and effective foe of monopoly and a formidable advocate of equal opportunity for all. You worked tirelessly to open the doors of our nation to the oppressed people of the world who sought refuge, freedom and opportunity in this country."[18]

At his advanced age, Celler's saltiness and alertness were evident in a September 1978 interview with the *Washington Post*. "I still have my marbles," he said, "but I still have qualms . . . I often repeat this story: the three qualms of old age. The first is lapse of memory. And . . . really . . . I can't remember the other two."[19]

On January 15, 1981, Celler died at his home in Brooklyn. The cause of his death at ninety-two was pneumonia.[20] Funeral services were held Sunday, January 18, at Campbell Funeral Home at Madison Avenue and 81st Street in Manhattan. Celler was survived by his daughter Jane Wertheimer of Scarsdale, New York, two granddaughters, and two great-grandchildren. Two weeks later on February 3, 1981, Peter Rodino, Celler's House Judiciary Committee successor, read into the *Congressional Record*:

"Let me list those laws and amendments so that we can appreciate the true measure of this man: The Civil Rights Act of 1957; the Civil Rights Act of 1960; the Civil Rights Act of 1964; the Voting Rights Act of 1965; the Fair Housing Act of 1968; the constitutional amendment allowing the citizens of the District of Columbia to vote in Presidential elections, the constitutional amendment outlawing poll taxes in Federal elections; the constitutional amendment on Presidential disability and succession; and the constitutional amendment lowering the voting age to 18.

"Mr. Speaker, as you will recall, after passage of the 1964 act, the House, in a rare tribute, gave Manny Celler a standing ovation. Those were exciting years. The issues were difficult and passions high. Through it all, Manny Celler was a fierce and untiring leader in causes he knew were just and right. It was my privilege to serve at his side. During those many years, during those many battles, Manny Celler generously referred to me as 'my right hand.' It is an appellation I am proud of and one I will cherish all my years.

"Because he was such a truculent and tenacious advocate for just causes, with a manner sometimes gruff, it could be forgotten that he was a gentle man, a master of words and wit and humor that was, as often not, directed at himself. His supply of jokes was inexhaustible. For this, those of us less facile were grateful, for he generously tolerated our plagiarizing his humor for our own purposes."[21]

Celler had kept two battered pocket-size notebooks: a black-covered appointment diary dated 1935, and a brown-covered notebook that at one time kept telephone numbers but later was used to store carefully transcribed *bon mots* for use during speaking engagements. A few sheets of notepaper headlined "House of Representatives" were folded into the notebook pages.[22]

Here's some of what they contained:

Your ancestors came over on the Mayflower—Mine came over when they had stricter immigration laws.

Irish immigrant writes back home. "Great country, not only am I pulling down a Protestant Church, but I'm being paid to do it."

Brandeis: "I am sorry that I was born a Jew." This caused consternation. Then he said, "If I had a choice, I would have chosen to be a Jew."

As a lad of 15, father refused to allow [me] to go to burlesque. The more he objected, the more desirous I became. Finally, I got together some cents [from] doing odd chores and went to a burlesque show. There was something I should have never seen—my father.

When people asked how he had navigated life in the House, the elder answered: "To be a successful Congressman, one must have the friendliness of a child, the enthusiasm of a teenager, the assurance of a college boy, the diplomacy of a wayward husband, the curiosity of a cat and the good humor of an idiot."

Celler's successor in Congress, Elizabeth Holtzman, served four terms in the House from 1973 to 1981. In addition to her role on the House Judiciary Committee during Watergate, she later earned a reputation as a Nazi hunter. She joined a delegation in Paraguay to search for Josef Mengele, "the Angel of Death." She also urged that Austrian president Kurt Waldheim—a former United Nations secretary general—be barred from the United States after his Nazi ties became known.

Holtzman ran for the US Senate in 1980. In the Democratic primary she beat better-known rivals Bess Myerson (the first Jewish Miss America) and former mayor John Lindsay. Holtzman lost the general election by 81,000 votes to Alfonse M. D'Amato, an obscure Republican county supervisor from Long Island. Jacob Javits, the liberal Republican D'Amato had beaten in the primary, decided to run as a third-party Liberal candidate that November. Javits's decision very likely took votes away from Holtzman. In November 1981, she was elected Kings County (Brooklyn) district attorney and made history as New York City's first female district attorney. Holtzman served from 1981 to 1989, and then was elected comptroller (chief city financial officer) in 1989.[23]

In 1984, thirty-five years after Emanuel Celler's strongly worded letter to the State Department, the United States resumed full diplomatic relations with the Vatican. The United States had cut off relations a century before during the post–Civil War. That lack of communication became a hardship during World War II when the pope tried to assist in moving refugees to safety.[24] In December 2014, the United States, led by the administration of

President Barack Obama, resumed diplomatic relations with Cuba after a fifty-two-year freeze. Pope Francis brokered the deal with both nations during eighteen months of negotiations.[25]

Celler was also remembered—briefly—in the 2014 Broadway play *All the Way* about 1964, Lyndon B. Johnson, Martin Luther King Jr., and the Civil Rights Act. Lead actor Bryan Cranston, who played LBJ, also played Celler for two character lines. The play opened March 6 and closed June 29 at the Neil Simon Theatre on West 52nd Street.[26] *All the Way* was also a 2016 HBO movie, also starring Bryan Cranston. Celler was not among the characters; however, Ken Jenkins was cast as Howard "Judge" Smith, Celler's fiercest adversary regarding the Civil Rights and Voting Rights bills.[27]

———— • ————

"I think I accomplished a lot," Emanuel Celler said after he was toppled from his House seat, the only elected political job he had held in fifty years of government service. The luck of seniority gave Celler, a liberal from New York, jurisdiction over the decisive House Judiciary Committee dominated by southern Democrats who had stymied civil rights legislation for decades. Celler had maintained a burning desire to advocate for the underdogs of society since his childhood in Brooklyn at the dawn of the twentieth century when muckraking journalists and social reformers championed fair employment, consumer and worker safety, and regulation of monopolies.

Tenacity and stamina were Celler's dual strengths. He despised ethnicity-based immigration restrictions when he entered politics in the 1920s because he represented a community of aliens, Jews, Irish, Italians, Slavs, and Negroes. Though beaten, Celler did not give up the immigration fight. He chipped away and won small concessions. Then history forced more dramatic changes. World War II pressured America to tinker with its immigration policy and accept some refugees escaping war and persecution

A cold war ideological struggle in the 1950s and 1960s between the democratic United States and its Western allies versus the communist Soviet Union and its satellites compelled presidents Truman, Eisenhower, Kennedy, and Johnson to declare that foreigners who yearned to become Americans should not be limited to Northern Europe. Emerging superpowers such as India and the strategically significant new nation Israel could either embrace Western values or reject them if America held on to an isolationist policy. Fortunately, the United States did not.

In the 1960s, Celler was well into his seventies when he made decisive legislative pushes for immigration reform and civil rights. He displayed remarkable mental and physical stamina in order to finish both crusades. He also knew how to balance his bulldog-like toughness with humor and charm to work with adversaries and allies. Emanuel Celler is among the most transformative American political leaders of the twentieth century. His influence lives on in the twenty-first century in an America that is a dynamic demographic mosaic.

Acknowledgments

When I published the Andrew W. Cooper biography *City Son* in 2012 a colleague said it was apparent that twenty hands were involved in the making of the book. I embraced that compliment. It's foolish for an author to believe they can write a good book by themselves. Contributions big and small from colleagues, friends, professionals, and students guide the writer to the finish line.

That said with completion of the Emanuel Celler biography, thanks, librarians, at the Franklin D. Roosevelt Presidential Library in Hyde Park, New York, and to librarian John Hill of the John F. Kennedy Presidential Library and Museum in Boston. To the staff at the Morgan State University Earl Richardson Library in November 2017, where I found breakthrough documents by Bernard Lemelin, a Canadian professor who wrote a laser-sharp 1994 journal article about Celler's legislative work from 1945 to 1952, plus other documents, including a journal article about the 2017 national anthem controversy involving NFL quarterback Colin Kaepernick that referenced Celler's work in the 1930s in order to make the "Star-Spangled Banner" the official US anthem.

Thank you to the librarians at Hampton University, where I taught from 2005 to 2017. Timothy Woodard found bound copies of the *Congressional Record* and then he contacted librarian colleague Alan Zoellner at the College of William and Mary in Williamsburg to research my questions about testy exchanges between Celler and Joe McCarthy (facts say the Celler-McCarthy showdown was indirect, direct confrontation was between Celler's ally US senator Herbert Lehman of New York and the senator from Wisconsin). Donzella Maupin, head of the Hampton University archives located inside the campus museum, found 1906 correspondence between President Teddy

Roosevelt and H. B. Frissell, the former Hampton Institute's second president. The evidence answered a nagging question in chapter 2. In 2016 Johnny Cook of Hampton University Harvey Library staff showed me how to operate the key card printer in order to print out Celler's scholarly journal articles and Ann Hardy-Lemasters showed me how to operate the change machines in order to pay for copies.

Thanks to librarians and support staff at Old Dominion University, Christopher Newport University, Norfolk State University, University of Texas-Austin, Brooklyn Public Library Brooklyn Room director; Princeton University Library Reading Room official (John Day Company papers); Library of Congress; Fran Williams, alumni relations, Columbia Law School; Sabrina Sondhi, special collections librarian, Columbia Law School; Virginia (yes, that's her first name) at Library of Virginia archive and reference. Also thanks to librarians at Towson University, Baltimore County, who provided 1926 *New York Times* microfilm, and Reference and Instructional Services librarian Sabine Lanteri of the University of Delaware Library who over a weekend emailed details from a rare 1940 book written by Celler and provided additional details I needed to meet a peer review deadline.

Judith Lowney, a Federal Trade Commission librarian, and Janice M. Herd of the Library of Congress cheerfully assisted a colleague and me in pointing to clues in order to find Celler's antitrust work. A University of Texas-Austin assistant pointed me to Celler papers inside their library and at the University of Virginia.

Colleague-friends assisted, encouraged, and hosted me. To Drew Berry, for hosting me at his Maryland home when I needed to save airfare and drive from Virginia instead for a necessary 2013 research trip to New York. To Angela Dodson and Mike Days of New Jersey for also hosting me on that fateful trip.

Todd S. Burroughs taught me the value of an author having a great lead researcher. After tracking down the obscure book *My Promised Land* by Ari Shavit, Burroughs called with excitement. Via a random amazon.com search—a fourth-grade move by a PhD, he said—on July 10, Burroughs found a Celler document about criminal justice, and then, a documentary about Jews and the Holocaust, starring Celler! Burroughs, who said research commitments prevented him from helping me officially, like he did with the Cooper biography, nevertheless still managed to find time to make calls and appointments to march on Washington the next week and probe the halls of the FTC and Library of Congress.

Cheryl Devall, an indispensable reader/editor of the *City Son* manuscript, returned in summer 2014 to read chapters and edit with passion. She magnificently sharpened and polished my prose. Flabby sentences became muscular, weak verbs became strong, the right words replaced indecisive words. Thanks also to Annette Walker and Barbara Linde for reading and critiquing rough initial drafts.

Hampton University colleagues Lynn Waltz and Michael DiBari generously agreed during winter break 2017–2018 to read and give feedback on final drafts. DiBari also lent me the Bain News Agency coffee table book he reviewed for the American Journalism Historians Association. Its clues led to photos of Celler and his family taken by that agency in the 1920s.

Another Hampton colleague, Mavis Carr, edited a new chapter and rewrote part of the final chapter during her spring break.

Thank you to students at Hampton University, Deniqua Washington and Winnie M. Dortch, both who did Honors College credit projects as research assistants. So did fall 2014 Honors College research assistants Amber Bentley (photo permissions) and Caleb Jackson (research; i.e., congressional facts). Sydney Bland, Joseph Gaither, Arriana McLymore, and Nyaa Ferary were the fall 2015/spring 2016 Honors College student researchers. Spring 2016 researcher Brianna Oates joined them in spring 2016 and continued through fall 2016.

I moved on to Morgan State University and I am grateful to the fall 2017 communication research class students who accepted and completed my assignments to find details in the campus library in order to tie up loose ends on a few dozen chapter notes: Simone Benson, Penelope Blackwell, James Bullock, Kierra Clanagan, Simone Ferguson, Lexus Faison, Bianca Lumpkin, Jazmin McMillan, Aaron Rayfield, Bi'ja Thatch, and Kyle Thomas; also, Blanca Assie, Alia Knight-Kemp, and Noah Haney from the spring 2018 communication research class. Assie was an especially thorough and enthusiastic researcher, and Knight-Kemp deserves an honorable mention.

Thanks to DeWayne Wickham, dean of the Morgan State University School of Global Journalism and Communication, and Jacqueline Jones, assistant dean and multimedia journalism chair, for granting me fall and spring course reductions in order for me to finish the research and writing of this biography. Also, thanks to Vestina "Teena" Lingham, an administrative assistant at Morgan, who unsolicited, assisted me in printing out half of the final, marked-up, approved peer review manuscript.

Other people assisted me in ways large and small that always matter. There was the staff of the National Archives in Washington. I visited in October 2017, received my research card, and was briefed on the sources available to assist my work. Donald Luzzatto, *Virginian-Pilot* (Norfolk) editorial page editor, published three of my op-eds, about Celler's leading role in guiding the 1964 civil rights bill to law, another op-ed about the 1965 Voting Rights Act, the other major legislation that Celler staged-managed into law, and the fiftieth anniversary in September 2015 of Hart-Celler immigration reform.

Thanks to Douglas C. Lyons and Dee DePass, co-coordinators of the National Association of Black Journalists Authors Showcase, for inviting me several times to moderate author sessions and allowing me to talk about research and the writing of the Celler biography. Kudos to David Carter of the Montauk Club in Brooklyn, for finding census data that identified Ernest and Josephine Mueller; to Kip Branch, for lending, then giving me a copy of the 2014 Clare Boothe Luce biography. Special thanks to Celler granddaughters Jill Rifkin and Sue Serphos for looking up and sharing Celler family photos.

A hearty thank-you to Craig Gill, editor of University Press of Mississippi, for enthusiastically signing me up for the second book, and keeping faith in me through the six-year adventure, and to agent Regina Brooks of Brooklyn-based Serendipity Lit for sticking with an academic press author/ biographer. And finally, to Claudia Cox Dawkins for devil's advocate advice and also for printing out the first half of the final, marked-up and approved peer review, and also for giving me permission—within reason—to lapse into the writer's trances that block out everything else.

Notes

CHAPTER 1: EARLY LIFE, 1888–1906

1. Richard Hofstadter and Beatrice Hofstadter, *Great Issues in American History: From Reconstruction to the Present Day, 1864–1981* (New York: Vintage, 1982), 177–78.

2. Jackson Lears, *Rebirth of a Nation: The Making of Modern America* (New York: HarperCollins, 2009), 93, 94–95.

3. Ibid., 107–8.

4. Ibid., 52, 57.

5. Ibid., 93–94.

6. Lerone Bennett, *Before the Mayflower: A History of Black America* (New York: Penguin Books, 1984), 529, 534.

7. Mueller was among the Germans who fled after protests for political freedom by middle-class liberals, radical demands by the working class, and crackdowns by the conservative ruling classes. The exiles were known as "48ers" in some accounts. In his 1970 oral history, Celler said his maternal grandparents were from Mannheim, 432 kilometers (259 miles) from Hanover, the latter location that Ernest Mueller told US Census officials.

Celler also said Mueller traveled with Carl Schurz, the future US senator and *New York Post* editor. Celler says the year was 1840. Schurz's bio says he participated in the 1848 revolution and emigrated to the United States in 1852.

Robert W. Lougee, *Midcentury Revolution, 1848: Society and Revolution in France and Germany* (Lexington, MA: D. C. Heath and Company, 1972). Also, Friedrich Engels and Leonard Krieger, editors, *The German Revolutions: The Peasant War in Germany and Germany, Revolution and Counterrevolution* (Chicago: University of Chicago Press, 1967).

8. Emanuel Celler did not identify his immigrant grandfather by name in his 1953 autobiography. In fall 2013, two database sources identified Celler's grandfather. His first name was Ernest of Hanover, Bavaria, and his last name matched the confirmed maiden name of his daughter, Josephine Mueller, who was Emanuel's mother. Sources: 1870 US Census data identified an Ernest Mueller, thirty-seven, who had a nineteen-year-old daughter, Josephine, and 1900 US Census records reported that Josephine (Mueller) Celler, forty-one, lived in Brooklyn.

Also, siblings Mortimer was born in 1880, Lillian was born in 1882, and Jessie was born in 1889. Source: archives.com/1900 US Census.

Emanuel Celler, *You Never Leave Brooklyn* (New York: John Day Co., 1953), 26. Henry Celler, forty-eight, was born in Manhattan; however, his parents were German immigrants. Many thanks to David Carter of Brooklyn's Montauk Club, who successfully searched for Ernest Mueller after a friendly email exchange.

Gabriel Furman and Paul Royster, "Notes Geographical and Historical, Relating to the Town of Brooklyn," digitalcommons.uni.edu, 2006.

9. Michael Barone, *The New Americans: How the Melting Pot Can Work Again* (Washington, DC: Regenery, 2001).

10. Ibid.

11. Celler, *You Never Leave Brooklyn*.

12. Siblings Mortimer M., Jessie, and Lillian (Lily) were identified in the 1900, 1910, and 1920 US Censuses. Lillian married Joseph Marsch on May 28, 1901. Mortimer married a woman named Addie according to the 1920 census. Ancestry.com.

13. Irving Werstein, *The Blizzard of 1888* (New York: Thomas Y. Crowell Company, 1960), 5–6, 41, 67.

14. Ibid., 68–70. As the snow piled up, Conkling closed his Wall Street law office that afternoon and then hailed a cab. The driver demanded $50 to take the former senator to 25th Street and Madison Square. Conkling balked. He decided to walk the 2.5 miles. He slipped into a snowdrift and was buried to armpits. Conkling struggled to break free. He collapsed shortly after arriving at the New York Club. A month later, Conkling, fifty-nine, died from mastoiditis and pneumonia.

15. Ibid., 72–73.

16. Lears, *Rebirth of a Nation*, 150, 152, 175.

17. Arthur M. Schlesinger Jr., *The Almanac of American History* (New York: G. P. Putnam's Sons, 1983), 366.

18. Carla L. Peterson, *Black Gotham: A Family History of African Americans in Nineteenth-Century New York City* (New Haven, CT: Yale University Press, 2011), 286.

19. Ibid.

20. Marc Linder and Lawrence S. Zacharias, *Of Cabbages and Kings County: Agriculture and the Foundation of Modern Brooklyn* (Iowa City: University of Iowa Press, 1999), 2.

21. Ibid., 4.

22. "New Name: Avenue Becomes a Boulevard," *New York Times*, October 22, 1987. Also, "The Caning of Senator Charles Sumner, May 22, 1856," Senate Historical Office.

23. Denis Tilden Lynch, *"Boss" Tweed: The Story of a Grim Generation* (New York: Boni and Liveright, 1927), 381–82, 384, 386, 398–401, 416–17.

24. Maurice Carroll, "Emanuel Celler, Former Brooklyn Congressman, Dies at 92," *New York Times*, January 16, 1981, 16.

25. Lears, *Rebirth of a Nation*, 186–89.

26. Celler, *You Never Leave Brooklyn*, 47–48.

27. Ibid., 23.

28. Ibid.

29. Carroll, "Emanuel Celler."

30. Dodger ballparks, 1862–present, losangeles.dodgers.mlb.com. Retrieved December 30, 2017. "Skully Central: All about the Street Bottlecap Game," streetplay.com. Retrieved December 30, 2017.

31. Celler, *You Never Leave Brooklyn*, 30.

32. Ibid.

33. Ibid., 46.

34. Tony Long, "An Invention to Beat the Heat, Humidity," Wired.com, July 17, 2009.

35. Doris Kearns Goodwin, *The Bully Pulpit: Theodore Roosevelt, William Howard Taft, and the Golden Age of Journalism* (New York: Simon & Schuster, 2013), 386, 399.

36. Celler, *You Never Leave Brooklyn*, 33.

37. Emanuel Celler Collection, Brooklyn Public Library, Oral History Memoir, June 24, 1970, American Jewish Committee, 5.

38. Ibid.

39. Celler, *You Never Leave Brooklyn*, 32.

40. Ibid., 40–41.

41. Ibid.

42. Ben Wattenberg, *The First Measured Century*, PBS. Retrieved December 30, 2017.

43. Bennett, *Before the Mayflower*, 303.

44. Lears, *Rebirth of a Nation*, 127.

45. Ibid., 128.

46. Ibid., 129–30.

47. Ibid., 130.

48. Ibid., 123 (blacks tried to reinvent themselves, even as white supremacist counter-revolutionaries sought to shut them down); 127–28 (re-adjusters and terror in Louisiana and Virginia); 129 (make white supremacy legal, disenfranchise blacks with laws instead of guns); Michael Barone, "The Many Faces of America," *Wall Street Journal*, September 21–22, 2013. This is an excerpt from Barone's book, *Shaping Our Nation: How Surges of Migration Transformed America and Its Politics* (New York: Crown Forum, 2013). In 1892 the immigration station opens on Ellis Island in New York Harbor. For most of the mid- to late 1800s, European immigrants came from Ireland and Germany. During the 1890s surge, the immigrants came largely from eastern and southern Europe. They were Poles, Jews, Czechs, Slovaks, Serbs, and southern Italians from Sicily. The newcomers spoke languages that were further from English than German or even Irish Gaelic. Their customs were perceived as odd or exotic. In response, American elites launched aggressive Americanization programs.

49. MacLean, *Behind the Mask of Chivalry: The Making of the Second Ku Klux Klan* (New York: Oxford University Press, 1994), 23.

CHAPTER 2: COLUMBIA UNIVERSITY, YOUNG LAWYER, 1906–1921

1. Kathleen Dalton, *Theodore Roosevelt: A Strenuous Life* (New York: Alfred A. Knopf, 2002), 330–32.

2. "Samuel Grabfelder Dead. Was One of the Founders of Hospitals in Louisville and Denver," *New York Times*, April 19, 1920. Samuel Grabfelder, distiller, was a well-off philanthropist (National Jewish Hospitals, University of Denver Libraries).

3. Celler, *You Never Leave Brooklyn*, 28–30.

4. Ibid.

5. Ibid., 28–29, 34.

6. forgotten-ny.com/2007/12/withering-myrtle-the-last-days-of-the-myrtle avenue-el.

7. E. R. Thomas, "Future of the Motor Car Makes Outlook Bright," *New York Times*, October 16, 1910, 2.

8. US Census 1900 via archives.com. (Mortimer Celler, twenty-six, was born in 1880; Lillian, twenty-four, was born in 1882; and Jessie, seventeen, was born in 1889, one year after Emanuel, eighteen.) Mother Josephine Mueller Celler was about forty-eight when she died in 1907 (she was listed as age forty-eight in the 1900 census).

9. Celler, *You Never Leave Brooklyn*, 34.

10. Ibid., 44.

11. Barone, *The New Americans*, 257.

12. Ronald Takaki, *A Different Mirror: A History of Multicultural America* (Boston: Little, Brown, 1994), 248. A matter of national honor. By 1920, women were 46 percent of the Japanese population in Hawaii and 35 percent in California (ibid., 247).

13. Ellis Cose, *A Nation of Strangers: Prejudice, Politics, and the Populating of America* (New York: William Morrow & Co., 1992), 64–65.

14. Ibid., 66, Gentleman's agreement, Japan, and Deidre Moloney, *National Insecurities: Immigrants and U.S. Deportation Policy Since 1882* (Chapel Hill: University of North Carolina Press, 2012), 39, 114, 135.

15. Schlesinger, *Almanac of American History*, 416.

16. Julius Goebel, *A History of the School of Law, Columbia University* (New York: Columbia University Press, 1955), 231.

17. Columbia Law School annual catalog, 11th series, number 6, 1911–12.

18. Goebel, *A History of the School of Law*, 218.

19. Ibid.

20. Celler, *You Never Leave Brooklyn*, 46.

21. Goebel, *A History of the School of Law*, 474.

22. Dave Von Drehle, *Triangle: The Fire That Changed America* (New York: Atlantic Monthly Press, 2003), 18–19.

23. Tyler Anbinder, *City of Dreams: The 400-Year History of Immigrant New York* (New York: Houghton Mifflin Harcourt, 2016), 438–40.

24. Officials at Columbia Law School explained that the program then was a two-year LLB. Today, the program is a three-year Juris Doctorate.

25. Celler Oral History Memoir, William E. Wiener Oral History Library of the American Jewish Committee, Lawrence Rubin (interviewer), June 24, 1970, 11.

26. John Milton Cooper, *Woodrow Wilson: A Biography* (New York: Alfred A. Knopf, 2009), 146.

27. Ibid., 135.

28. Dalton, *Theodore Roosevelt*, 406.

29. Celler, *You Never Leave Brooklyn*, 25, 49.

30. Ibid., 58.

31. Frederick Binders and David Reimer, *All the Nations Under Heaven: An Ethnic and Racial History of New York City* (New York: Columbia University Press, 1996), 152. During next three years of World War I less than 1 million come, including only 110,000 in 1918. Postwar immigration grows to 800,000, but the United States shuts the door.

32. Celler Collection, Brooklyn Public Library, Oral History Memoir, American Jewish Committee, 9. Celler, *You Never Leave Brooklyn*, 49.

33. Celler, *You Never Leave Brooklyn*, 50.

34. Ibid., 141.

35. Philip Napoli, "The Peopling of New York, Brooklyn Jews," Macaulay Honors College Seminar 2 at Brooklyn College, 2013. Jill Rifkin (granddaughter) in discussion with the author, January 7, 2014. Celler Collection, Brooklyn Public Library, American Jewish Committee, 9 (Jane B. Celler birth). American Jewish Committee, 10 (synagogue members).

36. Binders and Reimer, *All the Nations Under Heaven*, 152.

37. Lears, *Rebirth of a Nation*, 102–3.

38. Ibid.

39. National Archives, archives.gov/education/lessons/volstead-act / . . . The law becomes effective January 16, 1920.

40. Charles McCormick, *Seeing Reds: Federal Surveillance of Radicals in the Pittsburgh Mill District* (Pittsburgh: University of Pittsburgh Press, 1997), 27–45.

41. Schlesinger, *Almanac of American History*, 438.

42. Celler, *You Never Leave Brooklyn*, 52.

43. John Kennedy Library, Boston, White House Staff file No. JFKWHSFL08-003-030, RE: daughter Judith Celler and her disability.

44. Patrick J. Hayes, *The Making of Modern Immigration* (Santa Barbara, CA: ABC-CLIO, 2012), 186. https://publisher.abc-clio.com/9780313392030/.

45. Moloney, *National Insecurities*, 38, 75.

CHAPTER 3: ELECTED TO CONGRESS, 1922–1923

1. Kurt F. Stone, *The Jews of Capitol Hill: A Compendium of Jewish Congressional Members* (Lanham, MD: Scarecrow Press, 2011).

2. "Thirteen Legion Men Won; List of Those Elected to the New Congress Is Compiled," *New York Times*, November 8, 1920, 5.

3. Ibid.

4. Michael Lerner, *Dry Manhattan: Prohibition in New York City* (Cambridge, MA: Harvard University Press, 2007).

5. Ibid.

6. Ken Burns and Lynn Novick, *Prohibition*, PBS.org/kenburns/prohibition/. Retrieved December 30, 2017.

7. Ibid.

8. Ibid.

9. Celler, *You Never Leave Brooklyn*, 60.

10. Ibid., 60–61.

11. Matthew Lifflander, *The Impeachment of Governor Sulzer: A Story of American Politics* (Albany: SUNY Press, 2012).

12. "Celler Raps Volk's Campaign Methods, Candidate Stirs Colored Meeting with Attack on Opponent," *Brooklyn Eagle*, November 2, 1922, 4.

13. "Henry Suydam Resigns; Quits State Department to Become Brooklyn Eagle Correspondent," *New York Times*, February 15, 1922, 22. Henry W. Suydam was a longtime *Brooklyn Eagle* Washington correspondent (archives.gov).

14. Henry Suydam, "Republican Rallies in East New York Apathetic," *Brooklyn Eagle*, November 4, 1922, 5; Candidates for Congress, state legislature, and judgeships, 3.

15. "Old Brooklynites Hear of Days of 1861, Emanuel Celler Lauds Brooklyn for Civil War Patriotism," *Brooklyn Eagle*, November 3, 1922, 14.

16. "Rep. Volk Calls for Investigations," *New York Times*, January 5, 1921: Volk asks Congress for "dry" inquiry; cites killing of "Monk" Eastman in demanding investigation of enforcement. Charges a graft scandal. Attack on "self-constituted agencies" resented by Anti-Saloon League counsel. Charges widespread "collecting." Text of Volk resolution. Also: four journal pages.

17. Feldberg, *Blessings of Freedom*, ch. 9, 74–75.

18. Celler, *You Never Leave Brooklyn*, 62.

19. ourcampaigns.com (Randy Parker, 2002).

20. Henry Suydam, "GOP Keeps Slim Grip on Congress, Holds State Senate by One Vote; Harding Silent on National Defeat," *Brooklyn Eagle*, November 8, 1922, 1.

21. Moloney, *National Insecurities*, 38 and 75.

22. Ibid., 145.

23. Takaki, *A Different Mirror*, 29.

24. Ibid., 305.

25. Ibid., 305–6.

26. Ibid., 307–8.

27. Ibid., 308.

28. Ibid., 309–310.

29. Francis Russell, *The Shadow of Blooming Grove: Warren G. Harding in His Times* (New York: McGraw-Hill, 1968), 591–92. (Harding was the first US president born after the Civil War. His election "was at a moment when 20th century America was inevitably, and belatedly taking form," said the author.)

30. Cooper, *Woodrow Wilson*, 595–96.

31. Ibid., 535.

32. E. Digby Baltzell, *The Protestant Establishment*, 105–8.

33. Ibid., 204–6.

34. Ibid.

35. Ibid.

CHAPTER 4: PASSION, EMOTION, FEAR, AND HATE, 1924–1927

1. Celler, *You Never Leave Brooklyn*, 135–36.

2. Peter Duffy, "The Congressman Who Spied for Russia," *Politico* magazine, October 6, 2014; Joseph E. Persico, "The Kremlin Connection," *New York Times*, January 3, 1999.

3. Roger Daniels, *Guarding the Golden Door*, 55: Congressman Albert Johnson (R-Wash., served from 1913 to 1933; defeated for reelection in November 1932) and Senator David Reed (R-Pa., served from 1922 to 1935) were the two main architects of the act. In the wake of intense lobbying, the act passed with strong congressional support. There were nine dissenting votes in the Senate and a handful of opponents in the House, the most vigorous of whom was freshman Brooklyn representative Emanuel Celler. Over the succeeding four decades, Celler made the repeal of the act his personal crusade.

4. Moloney, *National Insecurities*, 14.

5. Christina Anne Ziegler-McPherson, "Emanuel Celler/Immigration and Nationality Act of 1965," in *The Making of Modern Immigration: An Encyclopedia of People and Ideas*, ed. Patrick J. Hayes (Santa Barbara, CA: ABC-CLIO, 2012).

6. Ziegler-McPherson, "Emanuel Celler," 187.

7. Moloney, *National Insecurities*, 4–6, 22.

8. Baltzell, *The Protestant Establishment*, 204–6.

9. Michael Barone, *The New Americans: How the Melting Pot Can Work Again* (Washington, DC: Regnery, 2001), 126–33.

10. Celler, *You Never Leave Brooklyn*, 4.

11. Ibid., 5.

12. Hayes, *Making of Modern Immigration*, 187.

13. Jonathan Peter Spiro, *Defending the Master Race: Conservation, Eugenics and the Legacy of Madison Grant* (Burlington: University of Vermont Press, 2009), 225.

14. Spiro, *Defending the Master Race*, 231–32.

15. Ibid.

16. Spiro, "Defending the Master Race," 225–26, 229; "La Guardia Is Dead; City Pays Homage to 3-Time Mayor," *New York Times*, September 21, 1947, 1. RE: LaGuardia's dual heritage: LaGuardia (1882–9/1947) Mother Irene Coen was Jewish and practiced faith. Father was Achille Luigi Carlo La Guardia.

17. Franz Boas. Biography.com. A&E Television Networks. Retrieved April 29, 2015.

18. Celler, *You Never Leave Brooklyn*, 79–80.

19. Ibid., 81.

20. "Hunkies" were Carpatho-Rusyn Americans, aka Ruthenians, immigrants from the borders of Ukraine, Slovakia, and Poland. Source: Paul Robert Magocsi, everyculture.com. "Bulls" were a nonsensical term for Irishmen. Source: University of Hull, UK. Representative Tincher of Kansas represented a rural district in the southwest corner of that state. Source: esirc.emporia.edu.

21. Celler, *You Never Leave Brooklyn*, 80–81.

22. Randall Chase, "Inventor of Kevlar Was a Pioneer, Saved Lives," Associated Press, via the *Virginian-Pilot*, June 21, 2014.

23. Celler, *You Never Leave Brooklyn*, 83.

24. Alan Stoskopf, *Race and Membership in American History: The Eugenics Movement* (Alexandria, VA: National Science Foundation, 2002), 230. US representative Meyer Jacobstein was a Columbia University grad and economics professor. *Global Immigration: The Debate in Congress*, Facing History and Ourselves, retrieved December 31, 2017.

25. Gary Gerstle, *American Crucible: Race and Nation in the Twentieth Century* (Princeton, NJ: Princeton University Press, 2001), 117.

26. Celler, *You Never Leave Brooklyn*, 187–88.

27. Spiro, *Defending the Master Race*, 224–25.

28. Ibid., 226, "Nordic myth," Boas. Lothrop Stoddard (1883–1950) was author of *The Rising Tide of Color against White World Supremacy*. James P. Lubinskas, "American Renaissance, January 2000," *Occidental Quarterly* (March 29, 2010). A colleague of Celler, Representative Charles Anthony Mooney, D-Ohio, also invoked Boas to counteract the "Nordicologists."

29. Spiro, *Defending the Master Race*, 231, anti-immigration passes. Lazarus's sonnet, "The New Colossus," appeared on the bronze plaque at the pedestal of the Statue of Liberty since 1903.

30. Ziegler-McPherson, "Emanuel Celler," 186–87.

31. Ibid., 187.

32. Schlesinger, *Almanac of American History*, 445. Of 28.9 million votes, Coolidge's share was 15.725 million. Coolidge's challenger was affiliated with the House of Morgan.

33. Paul Lombardo, University of Virginia, *Eugenics Laws against Race Mixing*. Dolan DNA Learning Center, retrieved December 31, 2017.

34. MacLean, *Behind the Mask of Chivalry*, xi, xii–xiii, xv–xvi, 80–81, 84, 87, 89, 91, 92, 97.

35. *Fatal Flood*, American Experience/PBS (2001), Ku Klux Klan: Oklahoma's governor in September 1923 placed the state under martial law in order to quell rising Klan terrorism.

36. Schlesinger, *Almanac of American History*, 446.

37. Celler, *You Never Leave Brooklyn*, 234–35.

38. Ibid., 138–39.

39. Ibid., 137. Campbell, Martin, and Fabos, "Media & Culture," 8th edition, 390.

40. Celler, *You Never Leave Brooklyn*, 137.

41. A. Scott Berg, "1920s, V.F.'s First Century," *Vanity Fair*, October 2013, 236–38.

42. Celler, *You Never Leave Brooklyn*, 21.

43. Emanuel Celler Oral History Memoir, William E. Wiener Oral History Library of the American Jewish Committee, June 24, 1970, 1. Lawrence Rubin, interviewer.

Chapter 5: Celler Asserts Self, Chips at Immigration, 1930s

1. Joseph Connor, "National Anthem No Stranger to Perilous Fights," *American Heritage* magazine, February 2017. Jennifer Rosenberg, *The Star-Spangled Banner*, about.com.

2. Rosenberg, *The Star-Spangled Banner*.

3. Celler's H.R. 47 to H.R. 14, January 30, 1930.

4. Marc Leepson, *The Flag: An American Biography* (New York: St. Martin's Press, 2006), 68; Marc Leepson, *What So Proudly We Hailed: Francis Scott Key, A Life* (New York: St. Martin's Press, 2014), 60, 468; Lynn Sherr, *America the Beautiful: The Stirring True Story behind Our Nation's Favorite Song* (New York: Public Affairs, 2001), 80, 82.

5. Celler, *You Never Leave Brooklyn*, 141, 144.

6. Ibid.,141–42, 144. 33 percent (1909); 48 percent by 1928, 54 percent by 1930s.

7. "Old Money from the Brooklyn National Bank of New York," 13292, antiquemoney.com, retrieved December 31, 2017.

8. Celler, *You Never Leave Brooklyn*, 135–36.

9. "U.S. Government Cannot Intervene on Behalf of Minorities in Europe," *Jewish Daily Bulletin*, April 10, 1928. JTA.org: The Global Jewish News Source. Retrieved December 31, 2017.

10. Schlesinger, *Almanac of American History*, 451.

11. Charles C. Marshall, "An Open Letter to the Honorable Alfred E. Smith," *Atlantic*, April 1927. Retrieved December 31, 2017.

12. James Cannon Jr. pbs.org/kenburns/prohibition. Retrieved December 31, 2017.

13. Schlesinger, *Almanac of American History*, 451.

14. Ibid., 448–49.

15. *The History of American Technology: The Automobile Industry, 1910–1919*, web.bryant.edu. Retrieved December 31, 2017.

16. Schlesinger, *Almanac of American History*, 452–53.

17. Rexford G. Tugwell, *FDR: Architect of an Era* (New York: Macmillan, 1967), 98–99.

18. Schlesinger, *Almanac of American History*, 454.

19. Ibid., 456.

20. Ibid.,451.

21. "The Immigration Act of 1924 [The Johnson-Reed Act]," US Department of State, Office of the Historian, retrieved January 1, 2018. Ziegler-McPherson, "Emanuel Celler," 188.

22. Hayes, *Making of Modern Immigration*, 185–204.

23. "FBI in Society: The Nationwide Chilling Effect," *Harvard Crimson*, November 15, 1971, thecrimson.com.

24. Celler, *You Never Leave Brooklyn*, 138. James Landis was FTC commissioner from 1933 to 1934.

25. Schlesinger, *Almanac of American History*, 455, 457.

26. Ibid., 456.

27. "For the Record: Depression Legislation; A Chance to Be Himself," *Washington Post*, January 11, 1973. Remarks by Celler before B'nai B'rith President's Medal Luncheon, December 17, 1972.

28. Ibid.

29. Schlesinger, *Almanac of American History*, 457, Empire State Building. Cohen, *Nothing to Fear*, 49.

30. Tugwell, *FDR: Architect of an Era*, 82–83.

31. Jean Edward Smith, *FDR* (New York: Random House, 2007), 374.

32. Cohen, *Nothing to Fear*, 14.

33. Smith, *FDR*, 287.

34. Jonathan Lockwood Huie, "Dream This Day," retrieved January 2, 2018 (FDR took office); quotetab.com/quotes/by-emanuel-celler.

35. Cohen, *Nothing to Fear*, 13.

36. Jonathan Alter, *The Defining Moment: FDR's Hundred Days and the Triumph of Hope* (New York: Simon & Schuster, 2006), 277.

37. Celler, *You Never Leave Brooklyn*, 204, 205.

38. Richard Baldoz, *The Third Asiatic Invasion: Migration and Empire in Filipino America, 1898–1946* (New York: New York University Press, 2011). Richard Baldoz, "The Nativist Origins of Philippines Independence," Truthout.org, April 1, 2014.

39. "Asks Medal for Peary Aid: Celler also Favors $1,700 Pension for Matthew A. Henson," *New York Times*, October 29, 1926. Paul McCardell, "Matthew A. Henson," *Baltimore Sun*, February 4, 2007, http://www.baltimoresun.com/features/bal-blackhistory-henson-story.html.

40. Smith, *FDR*, 398–402.

41. "Mr. Celler on the Lynchings," *New York Times*, October 12, 1926, 26.

42. Billie Holiday and Abel Meeropol, "Strange Fruit," 1937; originated from a 1937 poem by a schoolteacher.

43. Amy Wood, "Fear Tactics: A History of Domestic Terrorism," *Backstory*, NPR, April 13, 2014. "Seen and Believed" segment with historian Wood. Celler, *You Never Leave Brooklyn*, 93–112.

44. Lang, *Fury*, 1936, Imdb.com.

45. Smith, *FDR*, 398–402; antilynching legislation defeated. Since 1933, 83 blacks—roughly 17 a year—had been put to death in the South (398). Robert Wagner's bill did not make lynching a federal crime. The bill was initially introduced in 1934. In 1937 the bill had a fighting chance (399). In April, the bill passed 277–120. The bill went to the Senate in January 1938, was filibustered, then Wagner withdrew the bill. The bill was reintroduced in 1940, when it passed the House, but was not taken up in the Senate. "Then the war came" (401).

46. Wilkerson, *Warmth of Other Suns*, 9.

47. Bennett, *Before the Mayflower*.

48. Burns and Novick, "Prohibition."

49. Thomas D. Grant, *Stormtroopers and Crisis in the Nazi Movement* (New York: Routledge, 2004), 2–3, 9, 16; RE: Hitler's rise.

50. Alan Bullock, *Hitler: A Study in Tyranny* (New York: Harper & Brothers, 1952), 229–41.

CHAPTER 6: WORLD WAR II, FDR, AND JEWISH REFUGEES

1. Hofstadter and Hofstadter, *Great Issues in American History*, 358–62. Also see Schlesinger, *Almanac of American History*, 470.

2. Schlesinger, *Almanac of American History*, 472; RE: 1936 presidential election; history-place.com.

3. Emanuel Celler letter, August 1, 1935, to President FDR regarding protest meeting in New York, July 31, 1935, where the congressman spoke; Franklin D. Roosevelt Presidential Library, Hyde Park, New York, PPF 2748. https://www.bklynlibrary.org/blog/2013/02/22/nazism-1930s-brooklyn.

4. "The Nazi Party: The Nazi Olympics [1936]," Jewish Virtual Library, A Project of American-Israeli Cooperative Enterprise, retrieved January 2, 2018. www.jewishvirtuallibrary.org/the-nazi-olympics-august-1936.

5. Celler, *You Never Leave Brooklyn*, 238.

6. Hofstadter and Hofstadter, *Great Issues in American History*, 375.

7. historyplace.com; World War II timeline.

8. Ziegler-McPherson, "Emanuel Celler," 189; Celler and Dickstein bills, 1938.

9. Luca Castanga, *A Bridge across the Ocean: The United States and the Holy See* (Washington, DC: Catholic University of America Press, 2014), 161. Emanuel Celler letter to Secretary of State Cordell Hull, Eleanor Roosevelt Papers, The George Washington University, Washington, DC.

10. Ibid. US-Vatican relations resumed in 1984, three years after Celler's death, to full, formal diplomatic relations between the United States and the Holy See.

11. Ibid.

12. Schlesinger, *Almanac of American History*, 479–80.

13. Doris Kearns Goodwin, *No Ordinary Time: Franklin and Eleanor Roosevelt: The Home Front in World War II* (New York: Simon & Schuster, 1994), 62–64.

14. Ibid., 69–70.

15. Ibid., 210–15.

16. Celler, *The Draft and You*, xiii–xv.

17. Ibid., 69, 71.

18. Ibid., 10.

19. Celler Oral History Memoir, American Jewish Committee, 20, MacDonald white paper. Benny Morris, *Righteous Victims: A History of Zionist-Arab Conflict, 1881–1998* (New York: Knopf, 2011).

20. Celler Oral History Memoir, American Jewish Committee, 19–20, rabbi's visit. Celler answered that he did not know the name of the visitor, however he did remember that the visit occurred on a Tuesday.

21. Ami Isseroff, *The Encyclopedia and Dictionary of Zionism and Israel* (Zionism & Israel Information Center, 2005), zionism-israel.com.

22. Celler Oral History Memoir, American Jewish Committee, page 21; RE: blocked at many doors. jewishvirtuallibrary.org.

23. William J. vanden Heuvel, "In Praise of Wendell Willkie, a 'Womanizer,'" *New York Times*, December19, 1987. Paul Glastris, "Roosevelt, Churchill, and . . . Willkie?" washingtonmonthly.com, July/August 2005 (review of Charles Peters's "Five Days in Philadelphia").

24. Kearns Goodwin, *No Ordinary Time*, 255.

25. Ibid., 188–89.

26. Schlesinger, *Almanac of American History*, 483.

27. Celler, *You Never Leave Brooklyn*, 239.

28. Ibid.

29. Ibid. Dr. Linder in 1932, a William Linder was president of the County of Kings Medical Society; http://www.msck.org/msck-practice.htm. In October 1961, Celler, seventy-three, was hospitalized for several days. JFK Library, file JFKWHCNF-0452, White House Central Name file, Celler.

30. Fleming, *The New Dealer's War*, 137.

31. Schlesinger, *Almanac of American History*, 484.

32. Fleming, *The New Dealer's War*, 137, ch. 6, note 4; Roland Young, *Congressional Politics in the Second World War* (New York, 1956), 169.

33. *The War*, Ken Burns, Civil Rights/Japanese Americans/Minorities, pbs.org. http://www.pbs.org/thewar/at_home_civil_rights_japanese_american.htm.

34. Ibid.

35. Schlesinger, *Almanac of American History*, 487. Eighty-eight percent for war effort; Columbia.edu (Labor history/The Brooklyn Navy Yard and war preparation), 22,600 workers.

36. Kearns Goodwin, *No Ordinary Time*, 316. *New York Times*, February 10, 1942, and January 27, 1942.

37. Celler Oral History Memoir, American Jewish Committee, 20–21.

38. "Report on the Acquiescence of FDR Government in the Murder of the Jews," January 13, 1944, JewishVirtualLibrary.org.

39. Celler, *You Never Leave Brooklyn*, 117.

40. Ibid., 117.

41. Ibid., 119.

42. Ibid., 118.

43. Samuel Merlin and Peter Bersohn, *Who Shall Live and Who Shall Die*, documentary. The congressman had four speaking parts that cover about five minutes of the eighty-four-minute film. Celler said that State Department officials charmed New York delegation colleague Sol Bloom but did not deliver on promises to help the refugees.

44. Merlin and Bersohn, *Who Shall Live and Who Shall Die*. Both men of the Emergency Committee to Save the Jewish People of Europe told their stories to the producers. Another key speaker was Nahum Goldman, cofounder in 1936 with reform rabbi Steven Wise of the World Jewish Congress.

45. John Pehle, executive director; Josiah DuBois, general counsel; Ira Hirshman, Turkey-based representative; James Mann, England-based representative, and Roswell McClelland, Switzerland-based representative, *Who Shall Live and Who Shall Die*. War Refugee Board officials who spoke on camera.

Chapter 7: Post–World War II, Truman, and the State of Israel

1. Sylvia Jukes Morris, *Price of Fame: The Honorable Clare Boothe Luce* (New York: Random House, 2014), 58.

2. Ibid., 83.

3. Ibid., 38, 55. Moloney, *National Insecurities*, 201–2.

4. Morris, *Price of Fame*, 38, n 21.

5. Bayard Rustin, "Interracial Primer: How You Can Help Relieve Tension Between Negroes and Whites," Fellowship of Reconciliation, 1944, 14. Retrieved January 2, 2018. Worthpoint.com/worthopedia/bayard-rustin-pamphlet-interracial-1818209501.

6. Timothy Thurber, *Republicans and Race: The GOP's Frayed Relationship with African Americans, 1945–1974* (Lawrence: University Press of Kansas, 2013), 28.

7. *Congressional Record*, April 23, 1952, 4,320. David Brinkley, *Washington Goes to War* (New York: Alfred A. Knopf, 1988), 83, 224, 247.

8. Robert L. Allen, *The Port Chicago Mutiny* (Berkeley, CA: Heyday Books, 2006), 67, 68. "Blast Death Toll Now 377; 1,000 Injured!" *San Francisco Chronicle*, July 19, 1944.

9. Bennett, *Before the Mayflower*, 572.

10. "Rep. Emanuel Celler Lauds Reversal of WAC Sentences," *Baltimore Afro-American* and Associated Negro Press, April 14, 1945, 6.

11. Patrick S. Washburn, *The African American Newspaper: Voice of Freedom* (Evanston, IL: Northwestern University Press, 2006), 225.

12. Schlesinger, *Almanac of American History*, 499.

13. David Pietrusza, *1948: Harry Truman's Improbable Victory and the Year That Transformed America* (New York: Diversion Books, 2018), 9–10.

14. James T. Patterson, *Grand Expectations: The United States, 1945–1974* (New York: Oxford University Press, 1996), 115–18.

15. Schlesinger, *Almanac of American History*, 501, 514, 514.

16. Ibid., 499, 522–32.

17. Cheryl Shanks, contributor, *Anti-Immigration in the United States*, ed. Kathleen Arnold, 241–42 (Santa Barbara, CA: Greenwood Press, 2011).

18. Ibid.

19. Ibid.

20. Celler, *You Never Leave Brooklyn*, 23–24.

21. Ibid., 203–4.

22. Ibid., 204–5.

23. Editors, "Aryan People," *Encyclopedia Britannica*, December 7, 2017.

24. Rebecca Raber, "What They Learned," Neilay Shah, August 11, 2014, retrieved January 2, 2018. https://blogs.haverford.edu/haverblog/2014/08/11/what-they-learned-neilay-shah-14/.

25. Celler Oral History Memoir, American Jewish Committee, 24–25. McCullough's *Truman* referenced a New York congressional delegation.

26. Celler Oral History Memoir, American Jewish Committee, 24; Schlesinger, *Almanac of American History*, 502.

27. Pietrusza, *Harry Truman's Improbable Victory*, 109–12.

28. McCullough, *Truman*, 597.

29. Patterson, *Grand Expectations*, 152.

30. Pietrusza, *Harry Truman's Improbable Victory*, 112.

31. Celler scorecard of Jewish Palestine vote. "From Haven to Home: 350 Years of Jewish Life in America," Library of Congress (Celler Papers, 183A). Retrieved January 2, 2018.

32. Pietrusza, *Harry Truman's Improbable Victory*, 108.

33. Ibid., 113.

34. McCullough, *Truman*, 611.

35. Ibid., 609.

36. Richard D. McKinzie, oral history interview with Edwin M. Wright, July 26, 1974, Harry S. Truman Presidential Library and Museum, transcript pages 37, 38, 126.

37. McCullough, *Truman*, 617–18.

38. Ibid.

39. Displaced persons, refugees, and 75 percent of American Jews have Eastern Europe heritage. http://mobile.myjewishlearning.com/history/Modern_History/1914–1948 /American_Jewry_Between_the_Wars/emanuel_celler.shtml.

40. McCullough, *Truman*, 619.

41. Celler Oral History Memoir, American Jewish Committee, 28.

42. *World Almanac*, 2007 edition, Nations-Israel, 786.

CHAPTER 8: ANTITRUST, COLD WAR, INCREMENTAL IMMIGRATION

1. McCullough, *Truman*, 586–89.

2. John Hersey, *Hiroshima* (New York: Alfred A. Knopf, 1963), 3–5, 24–26.

3. Jonathan W. White, *Emancipation, the Union Army, and the Re-Election of Abraham Lincoln* (Baton Rouge: Louisiana State University Press, 2014). Jack Waugh, *Re-electing Lincoln: The Battle for the 1864 Presidency* (New York: Da Capo Press, 2009).

4. In February, Truman proposed civil rights reforms to Congress. Nine days after Thurmond declared his Dixiecrat candidacy, Truman signed an executive order that desegregated the military and he also called for an end to racial discrimination in federal employment. Schlesinger, *Almanac of American History*, 517, 519.

5. A "Split with Party Denied; Seeks Democratic Convention Post," *New York Times*, March 7, 1948, 32.

6. Pietrusza, *Harry Truman's Improbable Victory*, 406.

7. "Popular and Electoral Vote for President, 1789–2008," *The World Almanac and Book of Facts* (New York: World Almanac Books, 2011), 523.

8. Joseph Bruce Gorman, *Kefauver: A Political Biography* (New York: Oxford University Press, 1971), 35, 47–49.

9. Celler, *You Never Leave Brooklyn*, 98.

10. Celler Papers, Library of Congress, Box Numbers 39, 43. Subcommittee investigates insurance industry; frequent subcommittee hearings, *Facts on File*, fofweb.com. The antitrust subcommittee Celler created in 1949 averaged fourteen hearings or reports per Congress from 1955 to 1962. From 1963 to 1970, activity slowed to five hearings per Congress, but civil rights activity grew (fofweb.com). Werner Sichel, "Conglomerates: Size and Monopoly Control," *St. John's Law Review* 44, no. 5 (2012): 358–59.

11. Celler Collection, Library of Congress, Box 39, FTC correspondence folder: US business and GNP/GDP grew 10- and 3-fold, respectively, between 1918–1953, however the FTC struggled to maintain adequate staff to regulate the growth explosion. Eisenhower and a majority GOP House proposed cutting FTC by 18.2 percent. In the last months of the 1952

Truman term, the FTC was to get $300,000 plus $150,000 from a Democrat-controlled Congress to support Celler's anti-merger amendment. Gorman, *Kefauver*, 68, 354, 377n, 383n.

12. Kai Bird, *The Chairman: John J. McCloy—The Making of the American Establishment* (New York: Simon & Schuster, 1992), 400. "Seven-billion-dollar Chase Manhattan bank merger set," American Banker. Walter Isaacson and Evan Thomas, *The Wise Men: Six Friends and the World They Made* (New York: Simon & Schuster, 1986), 23, 571, 599.

13. Bird, *The Chairman*, 402.

14. Ibid.

15. David George Surdam, *The Big Leagues Go to Washington: Congress and Sports Anti-Trust, 1951–1989* (Chicago: University of Illinois Press, 2015). Celler Papers, Library of Congress, Box No. 240, April 17, 1958, July 24, 1958.

16. Nathaniel Grow, "In Defense of Baseball's Antitrust Exemption," *American Law Journal* 49, no. 2 (2012): 211–73.

17. James McGovern, *To the Yalu: From the Chinese Invasion of Korea to MacArthur's Dismissal* (New York: William Morrow & Company, 1972), 38–47. Celler, *You Never Leave Brooklyn*, 248, 249.

18. McGovern, *To the Yalu*, 525.

19. Ibid., 526.

20. Ibid., 38–47.

21. Schlesinger, *Almanac of American History*, 527–528; Hofstadter and Hofstadter, *Great Issues in American History*, 424–26; "Celler Seeks Immigration Policy Shift," *Washington Post*, February 23, 1951.

22. *Congressional Record*, A3632, "American Forum of the Air," June 10, 1951.

23. McCullough, *Truman*, 714, 864–65.

24. Emanuel Celler papers, Library of Congress, Box 23, *Brooklyn Eagle*, June 10, 1951, correspondence, clippings folder.

25. Emanuel Celler, "1,300,000 Turn Desert into Nation," *Brooklyn Eagle*, June 10, 1951, 1, 6.

26. Celler, *You Never Leave Brooklyn*, 123.

27. Library of Congress, Emanuel Celler Collection, *Brooklyn Eagle*, June 13, 1951, correspondence, clippings, p. 30.

28. Library of Congress, Emanuel Celler Collection, *Brooklyn Eagle*, June 14, 1951, correspondence, clippings, p. 30.

29. Library of Congress, Emanuel Celler Collection, *Brooklyn Eagle*, June 15, 1951, correspondence, clippings, page unknown.

30. Shavit, *My Promised Land*, 160.

31. Ibid.

32. Ibid., 161.

33. Celler, *You Never Leave Brooklyn*, 128.

34. Cose, *A Nation of Strangers*, 91–92. "Should Congress Enact the Celler Displaced Persons Bill?" *Brooklyn Eagle*, July 25, 1949, 19. *Brooklyn Eagle*, April 12, 1949, 12.

35. Cose, *A Nation of Strangers*, 91–92.

36. Ibid., 96, 98.

37. McCullough, *Truman*, 770–71. Two days before his fifth year in office as president, on April 9, 1950, Truman drafted a statement he would announce in April 1952: he would not seek reelection to a third term. In 1947, a GOP majority passed the Twenty-Second Amendment, limiting the presidency to two terms. The constitutional amendment became law in 1951 and would not constraint Truman. However, Truman decided that eight years of service was enough.

38. Gorman, *Kefavuer.*

39. Gary Gerstle, *American Crucible: Race and the Nation in the Twentieth Century* (Princeton, NJ: Princeton University Press, 2002), 257.

40. Cose, *A Nation of Strangers*, 96–98.

41. Ibid., 96–98.

42. Gerstle, *American Crucible*, 257.

43. Ibid., 257. Cose, *A Nation of Strangers*, 96–98.

44. Gjelten, *A Nation of Nations*, 99–102.

45. *Congressional Record*, 1951, vol. 97, 1495; Bernard Lemelin, "Emanuel Celler of Brooklyn: Leading Advocate of Liberal Immigration Policy, 1945–52," *Canadian Review of American Studies* 24, no. 1 (Winter 1994): 9.

46. Lemelin, "Emanuel Celler," 9.

47. Ibid., 10. "Liberalize," Emanuel Celler Papers, 1951.

48. *Congressional Record*, 1952, vol. 98, 8217, Lemelin, "Emanuel Celler," 10.

49. Gjelten, *A Nation of Nations*, 92.

50. Cose, *A Nation of Strangers*, 97.

51. Shanks, contributor, *Anti-Immigration in the United States*, ed. Arnold, 241–42.

52. Emanuel Celler Papers, "Mary Liroff," 1949, Lemelin, "Emanuel Celler," 12.

53. Lemelin, "Emanuel Celler," 12, L20.

54. *Congressional Record*, 1952, vol. 98, 4316, Lemelin, "Emanuel Celler," 13.

55. Schlesinger, *Almanac of American History*, 529.

56. Gorman, *Kefauver*, 112–16, 134–35.

57. Ibid., 139.

58. FJC.gov, Federal Judiciary Center.

59. Murrey Marder, "Celler Squeezed out of His Seat on Alien 'Watchdog' Group," *Washington Post*, January 27, 1953, 13. "Whom Shall We Welcome, Report," President's Commission on Immigration and Naturalization, 1953, Boston Public Library.

Chapter 9: You Never Leave Brooklyn, Early 1950s

1. Celler, *You Never Leave Brooklyn*, 176–85.

2. *The House on Carroll Street*, 1988, imdb.com.

3. Schlesinger, *Almanac of American History*, 528.

4. Sam Roberts, "Soviet Spy in Congress Still Has His Street," *New York Times*, May 23, 2013, A29.

5. Ibid.

6. Sam Tanehaus, "Mud Wrestling: The 1950 Senate Race in California Pitted Helen Gahagan Douglas against Richard Milhous Nixon. It Wasn't Pretty," *New York Times*, February 1, 1998

7. "Mud Wrestling," review of Sam Tanenhaus's "Tricky Dick and the Pink Lady," by Greg Mitchell, *New York Times*, February 1, 1998.

8. McCullough, *Truman*, 765.

9. Emanuel Celler Papers, Library of Congress, Box 21, Internal Security, HUAC folder: "The McCarthy balance sheet," by Frederick Woltman, Scripps Howard, Washington, DC, *New York World-Telegram*, July 12, 1954.

10. Emanuel Celler Papers, Library of Congress, Box 21, Folder 9. *American Legion* magazine, March 1954.

11. McCullough, *Truman*, 765.

12. Ibid., 765. Herb Block, *Washington Post* cartoonist "Herblock."

13. "McCarthyism/The Red Scare," Dwight D. Eisenhower Presidential Library and Boyhood Home, Abilene, Kansas, eisenhower.archives.gov; McCarthy abuse toward Celler, fofweb.com.

14. Celler, *You Never Leave Brooklyn*, 169.

15. Stewart Alsop, *The Center: People and Power in Political Washington* (New York: Harper & Row, 1968), 8–9. "Television Interviews, 1951–1955: A Catalog of Longines Chronoscope [CBS] Interviews in the National Archives." Emanuel Celler interviewed by William Bradford Huie and Donald I. Rogers, RE: proposal for creation of a Department of Overseas Information, headed by a cabinet officer, to coordinate US overseas information and propaganda activities, and comments on the appropriateness of propaganda for "waging peace." February 29, 1952 (200LW622). Celler interviewed by Larry Lesueur and Winston Burdett, RE: McCarran-Walter Immigration Act, immigration laws, tariff policy, and mergers in big business (200LW514).

16. Celler, *You Never Leave Brooklyn*, 170.

17. Thomas C. Reeves, *The Life and Times of Joe McCarthy: A Biography* (Lanham, MD: Madison Books, 1997), 422–23, 427.

18. Celler, *You Never Leave Brooklyn*, 171–72.

19. Celler Collection, Library of Congress, September 26, 1954, Box 21, folder No. 9.

20. Celler Collection, Library of Congress, Box 21, folder No. 6, *Brooklyn Eagle*, June 18, 1954, "His mail running 3–1 for McCarthy; Celler blasts public for 'apathy.'" The Aperion Manor rally was sponsored by Stevenson Democratic Club.

21. Lawrence Bush, "May 6: D-New York for Half a Century," *Jewish Currents: Activist Politics & Art*, May 5, 2014. RE: Joe McCarthy in 1952: "Undermining the faith of the people in their government" while dealing in "coercion and intimidation, tying the hands of citizens and officials with the fear of the smear attack."

22. Pearl S. Buck, The John Day Co. In 2004, *The Good Earth*, among *Life* magazine's 100 Outstanding Books of 1924–1944, was a comeback bestseller with Oprah Winfrey's Book Club.

23. John Day Company papers at Princeton University, August 8, 1951.

24. Ibid., August 9, 1951.

25. Ibid., September 14, 1951.

26. Ibid., October 24, 1951.

27. Ralph Hoopes, *Ralph Ingersoll: A Biography* (New York: Athenaeum, 1984), 216. *P.M.* was a liberal-leaning newspaper published in New York from 1940 to 1948.

28. Richard Severo, "Tex McCrary Dies at 92; Public Relations Man Who Helped Create Talk Show Format," *New York Times*, July 30, 2003, C12.

29. *Congressional Record*, March 3, 1953, vol. 99, no. 36; *New York Times*, March 4, 1953, 21; Celler, *You Never Leave Brooklyn*, 71.

30. Dictionary definition RE: "cant" in *New York Times Book Review* headline.

31. *New York Times Book Review*, March 15, 1953, 27.

32. *Book Review Digest*, 1953, H. W. Wilson Co., *You Never Leave Brooklyn*, $3.75, 280 pages, The John Day Co. *Booklist* review.

33. Ibid.

34. "It was a good one, and I am particularly interested that they should review a biography such as yours," R. J. Walsh said of the Harvard Law School *Record* review. Spring Rochester ad club speech. Powers hotel, May 7, 1953.

35. John Day Company papers at Princeton University.

36. Ibid., June 24, 1953, Box 3.

37. Ibid., September 14, 1953, Box 3.

CHAPTER 10: SUEZ-CIDE AND CIVIL RIGHTS, 1950S

1. "Celler Asks for Hearings in Defense of Dead Rabbis," *Washington Post*, September 23, 1953.

2. Louis Harap, "Velde Committee vs. the Jews: An Account of a McCarthyite Committee as a Destroyer of Democracy and a Danger to the Jews," *Jewish Life, a Progressive Monthly* 7, no. 10 (August 1953).

3. The NYPR Archive Collection, New York, WNYC, July 7, 1954.

4. Ibid.

5. Anthony T. Bouscaren, "Some Observations about Chip Bohlen," *Human Events* 34, no. 3 (January 19, 1974): 9.

6. *Congressional Record*, February 12, 1951, 1220. Lehman also referenced a letter to readers published in the *New York World Telegram and Sun* regarding the Hiss correspondence.

7. *Congressional Record*, June 11, 1953, 6387, and July 21, 1954, pages 9252–53.

8. Schlesinger, *Almanac of American History*, 536.

9. Arthur Herman, *Joseph McCarthy: Re-examining the Life and Legacy of America's Most Hated Senator* (New York: Free Press, 2000), 238–40, 265.

10. US senator Robert C. Hendrickson, D-New Jersey, papers, Syracuse University, Celler 1952–54, Box 9.

11. Ibid.

12. "Eisenhower Asks 10-Point Revision of Refugee Relief Act of 1953," *Jewish Telegraphic Agency*, May 31, 1955, jta.org.

13. Ibid.

14. Shanks, contributor, *Anti-Immigration in the United States*, ed. Arnold, 242.

15. Arnold, *Anti-Immigration in the United States*, 241–45.

16. Murray Marder, "Immigration Parley Turns Mostly to Golf," *Washington Post*, July 1, 1953, and "Golf vs. Immigration," *Washington Post*, July 8, 1953.

17. *Brooklyn Eagle*, Wednesday, August 18, 1954, 2.

18. "Multer Only Democrat Opposing Red Ban in Final House Vote," *Brooklyn Eagle*, August 18, 1954, 2.

19. Cose, *A Nation of Strangers*, 93.

20. Takaki, *A Different Mirror*, 391–92.

21. Ibid., 320.

22. Cose, *A Nation of Strangers*, 93.

23. David A. Nichols, *Eisenhower 1956: The President's Year of Crisis—Suez and the Brink of War* (New York: Simon & Schuster, 2011), 206, 279.

24. Ibid., 104.

25. Ibid.

26. Kefauver defeated John F. Kennedy for vice president at the 1956 Democratic National Convention.

27. Nichols, *Eisenhower 1956*, 114.

28. history.state.gov.

29. Ibid.

30. Carroll, "Emanuel Celler."

31. Nichols, *Eisenhower 1956*, 214.

32. Schlesinger, *Almanac of American History*, 547.

33. James T. Patterson, *Grand Expectations: The United States, 1945–1974* (New York: Oxford University Press, 1996), 305–8.

34. Shanks, contributor, *Anti-Immigration in the United States*," ed. Arnold, 241–45.

35. Simeon Booker, *Shocking the Conscience* (Jackson: University Press of Mississippi, 2013), 54.

36. Richard Perez-Pena, "Woman Linked to 1955 Emmett Till Murder Tells Historian Her Claims Were False," *New York Times*, January 27, 2017, A13.

37. Milton Viorst, *Fire in the Streets: America in the 1960s* (New York: Simon & Schuster, 1979), 10.

38. Celler Papers, Library of Congress, Box 454, Special Legislative File, civil rights 1956, RE: H.R. 627. Celler's 2-page statement RE: H.R. 568, the rule for consideration of H.R. 627. Manfred Berg, *The Ticket to Freedom: The NAACP and the Struggle for Black Political Independence* (Gainesville: University Press of Florida, 2005), 402.

39. Celler Papers, Library of Congress, Box 239, June 22, 1955, March 13, 1956, April 7, 1956 (Southern white man's views on integration); Dierenfield, *Keeper of the Rules*, 150.

40. Emanuel Celler Papers, Library of Congress, Box 455, Special Legislative File, H.R. 2145–85, folders 3 and 4. Includes May 5, 1956, Washington Monthly Report on status of H.R. 627, approved by the Judiciary Committee, moved to the Rules Committee, however if the committee chaired by Howard W. Smith failed to act, 218 signatures would be needed for a discharge petition. Dierenfield, *Keeper of the Rules*, 156.

41. Dierenfield, *Keeper of the Rules*, 170–71.

42. Ibid.

43. Nicholas Lemann, *Redemption: The Last Battle of the Civil War* (New York: Farrar, Straus and Giroux, 2006), 104, 167, 170–79.

44. Hofstadter and Hofstadter, *Great Issues in American History*, 52–53.

45. Ibid., 447–48.

46. Schlesinger, *Almanac of American History*, 549.

47. Emanuel Celler Papers, Library of Congress, Box 455, folder 2, civil rights hearings, rules, H.R. 6127. Box 456, folder 2, floor debate, news accounts from the *New York Times*, *New York Post*, and *New York Herald-Tribune*. Box 457, folder 1, floor debate, The American Forum [NBC], "Will Congress Pass Civil Rights Legislation?" June 9, 1957. US senator Sam J. Ervin, D-North Carolina, vs. US representative Emanuel Celler, D-New York, Stephen McCormick, moderator. Archives.gov, summer 2004, vol. 36, no. 2, Caro reference to LBJ. "HR 6127. Civil Rights Act of 1957," govtrack.us. Retrieved January 5, 2018.

48. Emanuel Celler Papers, Library of Congress, Box 455, H.R. 6127–85, folder No. 1. H.H. Bookbinder Western Union telegram, August 28, 1957. Ethel Payne letter, July 10, 1957.

49. Congresslink.org; civil rights legislation killed from 1945 to 1957.

50. Celler Papers, Library of Congress, January 3, 1957, December 26, 1956, November 16, 1956, Box 258.

51. Berg, *The Ticket to Freedom*, 157–58, 194–200.

52. Ibid.

53. William Lee Miller, *Two Americans: Truman, Eisenhower and a Dangerous World* (New York: Alfred A. Knopf, 2012), 335, 349–50, 352.

Chapter 11: Celler and the 1964 Civil Rights Act

1. Bernstein, *McCulloch of Ohio*, 96–97.

2. Ibid., 98.

3. Ibid., 100.

4. Ibid., 102–3.

5. Ibid., 104–5.

6. Ibid., 105–6.

7. Ibid., 108.

8. Celler Papers, Library of Congress, Box 462 (Twenty-Fourth Amendment eliminating poll taxes). http://history.house.gov/HistoricalHighlight/Detail/37045. Celler, principal writer of Twenty-Fifth Amendment (*Christian Science Monitor* interview).

9. "Spessard L. Holland Dies, Former Senator from Florida: Conservative Democrat Who Served 24 Years Pressed Removal of the Poll Tax," *New York Times*, November 7, 1971, 85.

10. Risen, *Bill of the Century*, 158, 169.

11. The Dirksen Congressional Center, Civil Rights: JFK's February request to Congress 05 http://www.dirksencenter.org/print_basics_histmats_civilrights64_doc1.htm dirksencenter.org.

12. Ibid.

13. Ibid.

14. Bennett, *Before the Mayflower*, 607.

15. Celler Papers, Library of Congress, Box 468.

16. Susan Breitzer, *Encyclopedia Virginia* (Charlottesville: Virginia Foundation for the Humanities, 2008).

17. "Negroes Want Fair Employment in Bill," *International Herald Tribune*, July 30, 2013, The opinion pages, 100, 75, 50 years ago (1963). http://www.nytimes.com/2013/07/30/opinion/global/100-75-50-years-ago.html?_r=0. Julius Duscha, "Celler Unit Tackles Job of Writing a Rights Bill," *Washington Post & Times Herald*, August 11, 1963, A2.

18. Letter from David Willmarth to Rep. Emanuel Celler, August 26, 1963 (National Archives), archives.gov/legislative.

19. Western Union telegram from anonymous "Southern white gentlewoman," US Archives and Record administration.

20. Brinkley, *Washington Goes to War*, 77–78.

21. Michael Fletcher, "Fifty Years after March on Washington, Economic Gap Between Blacks, Whites Persist," *Washington Post*, August 28, 2013.

22. Robert G. Kaiser, "An Overlooked Dream Now Remembered," *Washington Post*, August 23, 2013.

23. Clarence B. Jones and Stuart Connelly, *Behind the Dream: The Making of the Speech that Transformed a Nation* (New York: Palgrave MacMillan, 2011), 112.

24. March on Washington: *Encyclopedia of African American History, 1892–2008* (New York: Oxford, 2009).

25. Bernstein, *McCulloch of Ohio*, 129.

26. Ibid.

27. Ibid., 130.

28. Ibid., 129.

29. Risen, *Bill of the Century*, 123–24; Bernstein, *McCulloch of Ohio*, 132–33.

30. Risen, *Bill of the Century*, 124.

31. Michael O'Brien, *Philip Hart: The Conscience of the Senate* (East Lansing: Michigan State University Press, 1995). WGBH Open Vault media library & archives.

32. Risen, *Bill of the Century*, 125–26.

33. Rowland Evans and Robert Novak, Inside Report, "How 'Manny' Celler Was Stomped," *Washington Post*, November 5, 1963, A21.

34. Ibid.

35. Ibid.

36. Robert D. Loevy, "A Brief History of the Civil Rights Act of 1964," excerpted from *The American Presidency*, ed. David C. Kozak and Kenneth N. Ciboski, 411–19 (Chicago: Nelson Hall, 1985).

37. Celler Papers, Library of Congress, Boxes 462, 464–67. Robert D. Loevy, *The Civil Rights Act of 1964: The Passage of the Law that Ended Racial Segregation* (New York: State University of New York Press, 1997).

38. Dierenfield, *Keeper of the Rules*, 192.

39. Ibid., 194–97.

40. Poll tax constitutional amendment ratified.

41. Nick Kotz, *Judgment Days: Lyndon B. Johnson, Martin Luther King Jr. and the Laws That Changed America* (Boston: Houghton Mifflin Company, 2005), 105.

42. Taylor Branch, *Pillar of Fire: America in the King Years* (New York: Simon and Schuster, 1998), 23.

43. Ibid., 232.

44. Ibid.

45. Ibid., 233.

46. Ibid., 234.

47. Carroll, "Emanuel Celler."

48. Branch, *Pillar of Fire*, 231–33. Bruce J. Dierenfield, "The Speaker and the Rules Keeper: Sam Rayburn, Howard Smith and the Liberal Democratic Temper," Developing Dixie, WBM, JFT, LGT testaae.greenwood.com.

49. Catharine Debelle, "Georgia's HB 87: A New Generation Resists Jim Crow," *Imagine 2050—Race, Identity, Democracy*, July 3, 2011, US senator Richard Russell, D-Georgia.

50. Classic senate speeches, Everett M. Dirksen, http://www.senate.gov/artandhistory /history/common/generic/Speeches_DirksenCivilRights.htm Senate cloture and prevented filibuster by southerners. Bennett, *Before the Mayflower*, 609.

51. LBJ Presidential Library, RE: Cecil Stoughton photograph; Schlesinger, *Almanac of American History*.

52. Explanation of Title VII [employment] of the Civil Rights law by Robyn Hylton Hansen, attorney, chairman of Employment Law Practice Group, Jones, Blechman, Woltz & Kelly, P.C., May 13, 2014. Sex discrimination included barring women who were pregnant. Color discrimination could mean the employer hired African Americans but might favor light-skinned persons over darker-hued persons.

53. Lawrence Rubin, Celler Oral History memoir, William E. Wiener Oral History Library of the American Jewish Committee, June 24, 1970, 60–61.

54. Wilkerson, *The Warmth of Other Suns*, 390–93.

55. Clay Risen, *The Bill of the Century: The Epic Battle for the Civil Rights Act* (New York: Bloombury Press, 2014), 1–2.

56. Barone, *The New Americans*, 99–100.

CHAPTER 12: HART-CELLER IMMIGRATION REFORM, 1965

1. Cose, *A Nation of Strangers*, 104.

2. "Lady Liberty Refurbished," *Washington Post* editorial, August 8, 1965.

3. Cose, *Nation of Strangers*, 105.

4. Mae Ngai, *Impossible Subjects: Illegal Aliens and the Making of Modern America* (Princeton, NJ: Princeton University Press, 2004), 243.

5. Todd S. Purdum, *An Idea Whose Time Had Come: Two Presidents, Two Parties, and the Battle for the Civil Rights Act of 1964* (New York: Henry Holt and Company, 2014), 120–21.

6. Ibid.

7. Ibid.

8. Ziegler-McPherson, "Emanuel Celler," 191.

9. Ibid., 192; Hayes, *Making of Modern Immigration*.

10. Gjelten, *A Nation of Nations*, 105.

11. Ziegler-McPherson, "Emanuel Celler," 192.

12. Daniels, *Guarding the Golden Door*, 132.

13. Ibid.

14. Ibid.

15. Ibid.

16. "Celler Fails in Move to Liberalize His Subcommittee on Immigration," *Washington Post*, June 26, 1963, A21.

17. Lewis H. Weinstein Oral History, June 3, 1982, JFK Library. Ziegler-McPherson, "Emanuel Celler," 193.

18. Ziegler-McPherson, "Emanuel Celler," 194.

19. Ibid.

20. Ibid.

21. Ibid.

22. Gjelten, *A Nation of Nations*, 111–12, 116, 132.

23. Ziegler-McPherson, "Emanuel Celler," 195.

24. Ibid.

25. Ibid., 196. Johnson's bill, January 1965.

26. Gjelten, *A Nation of Nations*, 111, 129.

27. US Senate subcommittee on Immigration and Naturalization of the Committee of the Judiciary, February 10, 1965, 681–87.

28. Otis L. Graham Jr., "A Vast Social Experiment: The Immigration Act of 1965," NPG Forum, October 2005; https://npg.org/wp-content/uploads/2013/09/socialexp.pdf. Betty Koed, "The Politics of Immigration Reform" (PhD dissertation, University of California, Santa Barbara, 1995).

29. Biographical Directory of the United States Congress, US senator Hiram Leong Fong, R-Hawaii, http://history.house.gov/People/Detail/15032451315.

30. Ngai, *Impossible Subjects*, 258.

31. Ibid.

32. Ziegler-McPherson, "Emanuel Celler," 198.

33. "Affecting the Lives of Millions: The Immigration and Nationality Services Act of 1965," multi-illustrated poster that includes March 1965 Harris Poll, Richard B. Russell Jr. Collection, Richard B. Russell Library for Research and Studies, University of Georgia.

34. Gjelten, *A Nation of Nations*, 128–29.

35. Graham, "A Vast Social Experiment," see Senate Report 748, 22.

36. William McGowan, "The 1965 Immigration Reforms and the *New York Times*: Context, Coverage and Long-Term Consequences," 3, Center for Immigration Studies, August 2008.

37. McGowan, Center for Immigration Studies, 3.

38. Ngai, *Impossible Subjects*, 254.

39. Ziegler-McPherson, "Emanuel Celler," 199.

40. LBJ Library, University of Texas archives.

41. Ibid.

42. Ngai, *Impossible Subjects*, 227.

43. Daniels, *Guarding the Golden Door*, 96.

44. O'Brien, *Conscience of the Senate*.

45. Ziegler-McPherson, "Emanuel Celler," 185.

CHAPTER 13: VOTING RIGHTS ACT, 1965

1. "The Great Society Congress," The Association of Centers for the Study of Congress (ASCS), 1.

2. Lewis in 1986 was elected to Congress and at this writing has served sixteen terms as a representative from the Atlanta-area Fifth District, Georgia.

3. ACSC, 2.

4. The History Place [tm] Great Speeches Collection.

5. ACSC, 2.

6. Robert Caro, interviewed by Rachel Martin, "Leading in Crisis: Lessons from Lyndon Johnson," National Public Radio, November 12, 2012.

7. Caro, NPR, November 12, 2012.

8. ACSC, 4.

9. Ibid.

10. Ibid.

11. Ibid., 3.

12. Ibid.

13. Ibid.

14. Andrew Glass, "House Approves Voting Rights Act, Oct. 3, 1965," *Politico*, August 3, 2009.

15. Glass, "House Approves," 2.

16. "Remarks in the Capitol Rotunda at the Signing of the Voting Rights Act," August 6, 1965, *Public Papers of the Presidents, Lyndon B. Johnson* (Washington, DC: US Government Printing Office, 1966), 840–43.

17. "Voting Rights Northern Style," blackpublicmedia.org/Hampton.

18. Dawkins, *City Son*, 52, 54, 57–59.

19. Shirley Chisholm, *Unbought and Unbossed* (New York: Avon, 1970), 88. James Barron, "Shirley Chisholm, 'Unbossed' Pioneer in Congress, Is Dead at 80," *New York Times*, January 3, 2005.

20. Andrew Young, John Lewis elected in Georgia.

21. Library of Congress, US Association of Former Members of Congress, Box 2. Barbara Jordan and Shelby Hearon, *Barbara Jordan: A Self-Portrait: The Watergate Impeachment*

Hearings Had One Unpredictable Effect: They Made a Folk Hero out of a Congresswoman from Texas (New York: Doubleday, 1979).

22. Emanuel Celler Papers, Library of Congress, Box 462, H.R. 7152–88, special legislative file, civil rights administration, June 11, 1962. "Rise of Negro voters in the South," *U.S. News & World Report*, 57–58. By 1962, nearly 1.5 million blacks in the southern states were registered to vote compared to 20,000 in 1920 during extreme Jim Crowism. In 1962, blacks were 20 percent of the southern population but 10 percent of registered voters. Whites were 80 percent of the southern population and 90 percent of the adults were registered to vote.

23. Jamie Fuller, "How Has Voting Changed since Shelby County vs. Holder?" *Washington Post*, July 7, 2014.

Chapter 14: Congressional Bulldog, 1967–1971

1. Wil Haygood, *King of the Cats: The Life & Times of Adam Clayton Powell, Jr.*, (Boston: Houghton Mifflin Company, 1993), 339.

2. Thomas A. Johnson, "A Man of Many Roles," *New York Times*, April 5, 1972, 1, 30.

3. Jay Maeder, "Conduct of Defendant the Widow and the Congressman, May 1964, Chapter 326," *New York Daily News*, April 18, 2001. http://www.nydailynews.com/archives/news/conduct-defendant-widow-congressman-1964-chapter-326-article-1.902444.

4. Haygood, *King of the Cats*, 344–45.

5. Ibid., 346.

6. Ibid., 348–49.

7. Lawrence Rubin, Celler Oral History Memoir, William E. Wiener Oral History Library of The American Jewish Committee, June 24, 1970, 59–60.

8. *Adam by Adam: The Autobiography of Adam Clayton Powell Jr.*, foreword by Adam Clayton Powell III (New York: Citadel Press, 1994). Haygood, *King of the Cats*, 353, 350–51.

9. Carroll, "Emanuel Celler."

10. Haygood, *King of the Cats*, 353.

11. Carroll, "Emanuel Celler."

12. Celler Collection, Brooklyn Public Library, Box 2.18: "Congressional Bulldog," *New York Times*, February 24, 1967.

13. Haygood, *King of the Cats*, 354–55. Celler was the enemy, according to Powell.

14. Ibid., 356–57. Conyers and Pepper, Dissenting votes.

15. Haygood, *King of the Cats*, 358–59. Congress rejects Celler committee report.

16. Historical Highlights: "Representative Victor Berger of Wisconsin, the First Socialist Member of Congress," history.house.gov, http://history.house.gov/Historical-Highlights/1851–1900/Representative-Victor-Berger-of-Wisconsin,-the-first-Socialist-Member-of-Congress/.

17. Ibid.; *World Herald Tribune's* "Haunted House" editorial.

18. Haygood, *King of the Cats*, 364; 7–1 victory.

19. *Associated Press* dispatch, *Jamestown Post-Journal*, New York, Tuesday, March 22, 1966.

20. Haygood, *King of the Cats*, 372.

21. Ibid., 375.

22. Powell, *Adam by Adam*, 238.

23. Haygood, *King of the Cats*, 382, Adam Clayton Powell returns to Congress in 1969.

24. Peter Khiss, "President Here Unheralded for Mrs. Celler's Funeral," *New York Times*, March 25, 1966, 1.

26. Judith died in 1971, according to Emanuel Celler's January 1981 *Associated Press* obituary. Jane Celler Wertheimer went to Wellesley College (Class of 1938), and she lived at 303 McDonough Street, Brooklyn, according to page 50 of "The Wellesley Legenda." She married Sydney B. Wertheimer, a lawyer (who worked with Celler on the 1940 *The Draft and You* book). "Deaths, Wertheimer, Jane Celler," *New York Times*, December 14, 2006.

27. Carroll, "Emanuel Celler." The Stella Baar Celler Staff Residence of the Brookdale is a Brookdale Hospital Center twelve-story apartment building owned by Columbia University College of Physicians and Surgeons. Columbia University Libraries Info Services and CBE timeline 1981: Public Service & CBE.

28. Stephen L. Vaughn, editor, *The Encyclopedia of American Journalism* (New York: Routledge, 2008), 344–45.

29. New-York Historical Society Museum and Library, *Bill Shannon Biographical Dictionary of New York Sports*, sports.nyhistory.org.

30. Scott Sherman, "The Long Goodbye," *Vanity Fair*, November 30, 2012. Richard Kluger, *The Paper: The Life and Death of the* New York Herald Tribune (New York: Alfred A. Knopf, 1986).

Kluger, *The Paper*, 701, January 25 *Herald Tribune* series, "New York is the greatest city in the world—and everything is wrong with it;" 734, the *World Journal Tribune*: "250 workers it did not want, $2 million in added payroll it did not need. Then the pressmen's union threw a monkey wrench . . . by mid-August 1966, half of the *Tribune's* editorial staff drifted away." The *Tribune* died that month. *World Journal Tribune* daily circulation was 700,000, making it the US's fourth-largest afternoon/evening paper, but it lost $700,000 a month. There was a $39.4 million attempt to save the venerable *Herald Tribune* during the J. H. Whitney era; 742, the unions let the *New York Times* automate in 1974, making the *Times* a more attractive paper with livelier writing and cleaner typography. http://www.richardkluger.com/AboutThePaper.htm.

31. Emanuel Celler Papers, Library of Congress, Box 314.

32. Vaughn, *Encyclopedia of American Journalism*, 344–45.

33. Martin Weil, "Edna F. Kelly Dies at 91, Longtime Member of Congress," *Washington Post*, December 17, 1997, C6. Wolfgang Saxon, "Edna Kelly, Congresswoman from Brooklyn, Is Dead at 91," *New York Times*, December 17, 1997, B7.

34. Scott Sherman, "The Long Goodbye," VanityFair.com, November 30, 2012.

35. Herb Boyd, *Black Detroit* (New York: Amistad, 2017), 202–9.

36. Dawkins, *City Son*, 50–51.

37. Edna Kelly, Oral History Interview, U.S. Association of Former Members of Congress, Manuscript Room, Library of Congress, 1 (May 10–11, 1976, by Charles T. Morrisey, Part 1 of 7, 1–3).

38. Martha Griffiths, Oral History Interview, October 29, 1979, Manuscript Room, Library of Congress, 155.

39. Dawkins, *City Son*, 56.

40. Celler Collection, Brooklyn Public Library, Box 2.18: Richard Seelmeyer, "Celler at 80 . . . Still America's Legislative Giant," *Long Island Press*, May 5, 1968.

41. Celler Collection, Brooklyn Public Library, Box 2.18: Jack Leahy, "Mainly for Seniors," *New York Daily News*, June 9, 1968.

42. Emanuel Celler interview with Lehman Oral History Project, Columbia University, July 23, 1957, 231–41.

43. Charles Mathias Jr. and Marion Morris, "Fair Housing Legislation: Not an Easy Row to Hoe," *Cityscape: A Journal of Policy Development and Research* 4, no. 1 (1999).

44. Ibid.

45. Joseph A. Califano Jr., "The White House Is No Place for Wimps: The Best Presidents Stay Away from the Middle Ground," *Politico*, February 15, 2015.

46. Mathias and Morris, *Cityscape*, 23.

47. Neil MacNeil, *Dirksen: Portrait of a Public Man* (Cleveland: World Publishing Company, 1970), 322.

48. Ibid., 323.

49. Ibid., 325–26.

50. Gary Rhoades, "End of a Stormy Trip for Fair Housing Act," *Santa Monica Daily Press*, April 8, 2014.

51. Ibid.

52. Michael Lemov and Ralph Nader, *People's Warrior: John Moss and the Fight for Freedom and Consumer Rights* (Vancouver, BC: Fairleigh Dickinson University Press, 2011), 34, 32–57.

53. Celler Collection, Brooklyn Public Library, Box 2.18: Lyn Shepard, "He Does His Homework," *Christian Science Monitor*, March 1–3, 1969. During 1967 and 1968, 38.4 percent of bills and resolutions passed through House Judiciary Committee.

54. Ibid.

55. Ibid.

CHAPTER 15: OLD-WORLD LIBERAL CELLER IS UPSET, 1972–1973

1. Celler's unequivocal opposition to ERA, *Washington Post*, October 18, 1972. Bella Abzug speeches on the movement for sexual equality, now.org [Celler]. "Urges Women Doctors Acceptance in Medical Reserve Corps," letter to H. L. Stinson, *New York Times*, November 12, 1942, 27. "Gets Secretary Stinson Reply Reaffirming War Department on Commissioning Women Doctors; He [Celler] Protests, Quotes Mrs. Roosevelt and Others," *New York Times*, December 4, 1942, 29.

2. Leslie W. Gladstone, "The Long Road to Equality: What Women Won from the ERA Ratification Effort," memory.loc.gov; http://memory.loc.gov/ammem/awhhtml/awo3e/notes .html#i15.

3. Ibid.

4. "Bella Abzug on the Movement for Sexual Equality," History.com. https://www.history .com/speeches/bella-abzug-on-the-movement-for-sexual-equality.

5. Ervin and Celler's seven-year limit: http://www.now.org/issues/economic/cea/history.html.

6. Carl M. Cannon, "Youth Vote: Dems' Secret Weapon 40 Years in the Making?" Real Clear Politics, *McClatchy Newspapers*, March 25, 2011.

7. Thomas DiBacco, "The 26th Amendment's Distressing History," *Washington Times*, October 6, 2014.

8. Ibid.

9. Richard L. Lyons, "Former Rep. Emanuel Celler Dies; Civil Rights Champion," *Washington Post*, January 16, 1981, B5.

10. fofweb.com, Barnes, "Emanuel Celler."

11. Lemov and Nader, *People's Warrior*, 53.

12. Ibid., 34–36, 48–49.

13. Edward O'Neill, "Emanuel Celler Looks Back—but Ahead Too," *New York Daily News*, December 25, 1972.

14. Elizabeth Holtzman and Cynthia L. Cooper, *Who Said It Would Be Easy? One Woman's Life in the Political Arena* (New York: Little, Brown and Company, 1996), 26.

15. Foerstel, *Biographical Dictionary of Congressional Women*, 1999, 123.

16. Holtzman and Cooper, *Who Said It Would be Easy?* 27.

17. Richard L. Madden, "Celler, Now 83, to Make Race for His 26th Term in the House," *New York Times*, March 18, 1972; Phyllis Bernstein, "Old-Fashioned Campaign Wrested Brooklyn Nomination from Celler," *Washington Post* [via UPI], July 8, 1972.

18. Holtzman and Cooper, *Who Said It Would be Easy?* 28.

19. Ibid., 31.

20. Ibid., 29.

21. Lyons, "Former Rep. Emanuel Celler Dies; Civil Rights Champion."

22. Lemov and Nader, *People's Warrior*, 54–55.

23. Holtzman and Cooper, *Who Said It Would Be Easy?* 32; *New York Times* editorial scolds Celler. 381 articles about Holtzman. Linda Charlton, "Celler Defends Record as Challenger Assails It," *New York Times*, June 3, 1972, 31.

24. Elizabeth Holtzman interview June 19, 2018. She answered emailed questions. Carroll, "Emanuel Celler."

25. Holtzman and Cooper, *Who Said It Would Be Easy?* 25, *New York Times*, June 18, 1972, 32. Disorderly conduct/Break-in, roughing up at campaign HQ.

26. Holtzman and Cooper, *Who Said It Would Be Easy?* 33.

27. Ibid.

28. *New York Times*, June 22, 1972; June 21, 1972, 1.

29. "Chairman Celler Steps Aside; Does not Run as Liberal Party Candidate," editorial, *Washington Post*, October 18, 1972, A16.

30. Charles P. Pierce, "A Stunning Victory for the Tea Party and What It Means," Esquire.com, politics blog, June 11, 2014.

31. Schlesinger, *Almanac of American History*, 590–91.

32. Lemov and Nader, *People's Warrior*, 56.

33. "Understanding the 25th Amendment," constitution.laws.com.

34. Francis X. Clines, "Barbara Jordan Dies at 59; Her Voice Stirred the Nation," *New York Times*, January 18, 1996.

35. Arnold Sawislak, "Emanuel Celler—Last of the Victorians," United Press International, January 17, 1981. Edward O'Neill, "Emanuel Celler Looks Back—but Ahead Too," *New York Daily News*, December 25, 1972.

36. Ibid.

37. "Chairman Celler Steps Aside," *Washington Post & Times Herald*, October 18, 1972, A16.

38. Martin Tolcin, "Lure of Washington Proves Irresistible to ex-Congressmen," *New York Times*, March 4, 1974, 31.

39. Lawrence Feinberg, "Celler Recalls Long Career," *Washington Post & Times Herald*, December 18, 1972, C11.

40. "Depression Legislation: A Chance to Be Himself," *Washington Post*, January 11, 1973, A18.

41. Feinberg, "Celler Recalls Long Career," December 18, 1972.

CHAPTER 16: POST-CONGRESSIONAL LIFE, 1973–1981

1. Caro, *Means of Ascent*, 54.

2. Celler Collection, Brooklyn Public Library.

3. Ibid.

4. Robert Thomas Jr., "Milton G. Gould, 89, Legal Giant in a City of Lawyers, Dies," *New York Times*, March 24, 1999.

5. Tolcin, "Lure of Washington Proves Irresistible to ex-Congressmen," 31.

6. Rosalind Massow, "Life Begins at 80," *New York Daily News* magazine, August 5, 1973.

7. Celler Collection, Brooklyn Public Library, August 25, 1975, letter from Alfred Sulmonetti. Gene I. Maeroff, "Three-Year-Old Jewish College to Open Law School Here in 1974," *New York Times*, May 17, 1973, 46.

8. Tolchin, "Lure of Washington Proves Irresistible to ex-Congressmen," 31.

9. Carroll, "Emanuel Celler."

10. Lyons, "Former Rep. Emanuel Celler Dies," and Carroll, "Emanuel Celler."

11. Bernstein and Woodward, *All the President's Men*, 270–73, 367.

12. Ibid.

13. Ibid.

14. Ibid.

15. Birch Bayh statement regarding Emanuel Celler, June 18, 2018.

16. Richard V. Allen, "When Reagan Was Shot, Who Was 'in Control' at the White House," *Washington Post*, March 25, 2011, 10.

17. Christopher M. Davis, *The President Pro Tempore of the Senate: History and Authority of the Office, Congressional Research Service*, September 16, 2015.

18. Celler Papers, Brooklyn Public Library, Series 2.13: May 6, 1978.

19. Lyons, "Former Rep. Emanuel Celler Dies; Civil Rights Champion."

20. Ibid., and Carroll, "Emanuel Celler." Jane Celler Wertheimer, eighty-nine, died December 12, 2006. She was founder and president of Passkey associates, a special events firm. JCW was an opera aficionado and a Democratic Party loyalist.

21. *Congressional Record*, February 3, 1981, 1558.

22. Celler Collection, Brooklyn Public Library, Series 2.1.2.

23. Howard Kurtz, "The Private Public Prosecutor; Elizabeth Holtzman, Tough and Guarded as Brooklyn's D.A.," *Washington Post*, October 27, 1987.

24. Luca Castanga, *A Bridge across the Ocean: The United States and the Holy See between the Two World Wars* (Washington, DC: Catholic University of America Press, 2014), 161.

25. Peter Baker, "U.S. to Restore Full Relations with Cuba, Erasing a Last Trace of Cold War Hostility," *New York Times*, December 17, 2014. Karen DeYoung, "U.S. and Cuba Set to Formally Establish Diplomatic Relations," *Washington Post*, July 17, 2015.

26. Interview with Jill Rifkin, Celler's granddaughter, April 24, 2014. Broadway.com /shows/all-way/cast.

27. *All the Way*, HBO, 2016, imdb.com.

Bibliography

Adams, Willi Paul. *The German-Americans: An Ethnic Experience*. Max Kade German American Center, IUPUI, 1993.

Alsop, Stewart. *The Center: People and Power in Political Washington*. New York: Harper & Row, 1968.

Anbinder, Tyler. *City of Dreams: The 400-Year Epic History of Immigrant New York*. Boston: Houghton Mifflin Harcourt, 2016.

Arnold, Kathleen R., editor. *Anti-Immigration in the United States*. Santa Barbara, CA: Greenwood Press, 2011.

Baldoz, Richard. *The Third Asiatic Invasion: Migration and Empire in Filipino America, 1898–1946*. New York: New York University Press, 2011.

Baltzell, E. Digby. *The Protestant Establishment: Aristocracy and Caste in America*. New York: Vintage, 1964.

Barone, Michael. *The New Americans: How the Melting Pot Can Work Again*. Washington, DC: Regnery, 2001.

Bennett, Lerone, Jr. *Before the Mayflower: A History of Black America*. New York: Penguin Books, 1984.

Berman, David M. *A Bill Becomes a Law: The Civil Rights Act of 1960*. New York: MacMillan, 1962.

Bernstein, Carl, and Bob Woodward. *All the President's Men*. New York: Warner Books, 1975.

Bernstein, Mark. *McCulloch of Ohio*. New Bremen, OH: Crown Equipment Corporation, 2014.

Binder, Frederick M., and David M. Reimers. *All the Nations Under Heaven: An Ethnic and Racial History of New York City*. New York: Columbia University Press, 1995.

Bird, Kai. *The Chairman: John J. McCloy—The Making of the American Establishment*. New York: Simon & Schuster, 1992.

Booker, Simeon. *Shocking the Conscience*. Jackson: University Press of Mississippi, 2013.

Bortoli, Georges. *The Death of Stalin*. New York: Praeger Publishing, 1975. vii–viii.

Branch, Taylor. *Pillar of Fire: America in the King Years, 1963–65*. New York: Simon & Schuster, 1998.

Branch, Taylor. *Parting the Waters*. New York: Simon & Schuster, 1988.

Brinkley, David. *Washington Goes to War*. New York: Alfred A. Knopf, 1988.

Browne-Marshall, Gloria J. *The Voting Rights War: The NAACP and the Ongoing Struggle for Justice*. Lanham, MD: Rowman & Littlefield, 2016.

Buchanan, Patrick. *Suicide of a Superpower: Will America Survive to 2025?* New York: Thomas Dunne Books, 2011.

Buchanan, Patrick. *State of Emergency*. New York: Thomas Dunne Books, 2006.

Buchanan, Patrick. *The Death of the West*. New York: Thomas Dunne Books, 2002.

Caro, Robert A. *Means of Assent: The Years of Lyndon Johnson*. New York: Knopf, 1991.

Castanga, Luca. *A Bridge across the Ocean: The United States and the Holy See*. Washington, DC: Catholic University of America Press, 2014.

Celler, Emanuel. *You Never Leave Brooklyn: The Autobiography of Emanuel Celler*. New York: John Day Company, 1953.

Celler, Emanuel. *The Draft and You*. New York: Viking Press, 1940.

Chomsky, Aviva. *They Take Our Jobs! and 20 Other Myths about Immigration*. Boston: Beacon Press, 2007.

Chomsky, Aviva. *Undocumented: How Immigration Became Illegal*. Boston: Beacon Press, 2014.

Clymer, Adam. *Edward M. Kennedy: A Biography*. New York: William Morrow and Company, 1999.

Cohen, Adam. *Nothing to Fear: FDR's Inner Circle and the One Hundred Days That Created Modern America*. New York: Penguin Press, 2009.

Cohodas, Nadine. *Strom Thurmond and the Politics of Southern Change*. New York: Simon & Schuster, 1993.

Cose, Ellis. *A Nation of Strangers: Prejudice, Politics and the Populating of America*. New York: William Morrow & Company, 1992.

Dalton, Kathleen. *Theodore Roosevelt: Strenuous Life*. New York: Knopf, 2002.

Daniels, Roger. *Guarding the Golden Door: American Immigration Policy and Immigrants Since 1882*. New York: Hill and Wang, Farrar, Straus & Giroux, 2004.

Dawkins, Wayne. *City Son: Andrew W. Cooper's Impact on Modern-Day Brooklyn*. Jackson: University Press of Mississippi, 2012.

Dierenfield, Bruce J. *Keeper of the Rules: Congressman Howard W. Smith of Virginia*. Charlottesville: University of Virginia Press, 1987.

Dudziak, Mary L. *Cold War Civil Rights: Race and the Image of America Democracy*. Princeton, NJ: Princeton University Press, 2000.

Engels, Friedrich, and Leonard Krieger, editors. *The German Revolutions: The Peasant War in Germany and Germany, Revolution and Counterrevolution*. Chicago: University of Chicago Press, 1967.

Fite, Gilbert C. *Richard B. Russell Jr., Senator from Georgia*. Chapel Hill: University of North Carolina Press, 1991.

Fleming, Thomas. *The New Dealer's War: F.D.R. and the War within World War II*. New York: Basic Books, 2001.

Foner, Nancy, and George Frederick. *Not Just Black and White: Historical and Contemporary Perspectives on Immigration, Race, and Ethnicity in the United States*. Russell Sage Foundation Publications, 2005.

Foner, Nancy, and George Frederick. *New Immigrants in New York*. New York: Columbia University Press, 2001.

Franklin, John Hope. *Race and History: Selected Essays, 1938–1988*. Baton Rouge: Louisiana State University Press, 1989.

Franklin, John Hope. *Mirror to America*. New York: Farrar, Straus & Giroux, 2005.

Friedman, Thomas L. *The World Is Flat: A Brief History of the 21st Century*. New York: Farrar, Straus & Giroux, 2005.

Garrow, David J. *Bearing the Cross: Martin Luther King Jr. and the Southern Christian Leadership Conference*. New York: Morrow, 1986.

Gerstle, Gary. *American Crucible: Race and Nation in the Twentieth Century*. Princeton, NJ: Princeton University Press, 2001.

Gjelten, Tom. *A Nation of Nations: A Great American Immigration Story*. New York: Simon & Schuster, 2015.

Goebel, Julius. *A History of the School of Law, Columbia University*. New York: Columbia University Press, 1955.

Gonzalez, Juan, and Joseph Torres. *News for All the People*. London: Verso, 2011.

Gonzalez, Juan, and Joseph Torres. *Harvest of Empire: A History of Latinos in America*. New York: Penguin, 2011.

Gorman, Joseph Bruce. *Kefauver: A Political Biography*. New York: Oxford University Press, 1971.

Gottlieb, Robert. *The Next Los Angeles: The Struggle for a Livable City*. Berkeley: University of California Press, 2005.

Grant, Madison. *The Passing of the Great Race*. New York: Charles Scribner's Sons, 1916.

Griffith, Robert. *The Politics of Fear: Joseph R. McCarthy and the Senate*. Amherst: University of Massachusetts Press, 1970, rpt. 1987.

Hamilton, Charles V. *Adam Clayton Powell, Jr.: The Political Biography of an American Dilemma*. New York: Atheneum, 1991.

Hayes, Patrick J., editor. *The Making of Modern Immigration: An Encyclopedia of People and Ideas*. Santa Barbara, CA: ABC-CLIO, 2012.

Haygood, Wil. *King of the Cats: The Life and Times of Adam Clayton Powell, Jr.* Boston: Houghton Mifflin, 1993.

Herman, Arthur. *Joseph McCarthy: Re-examining the Life and Legacy of America's Most Hated Senator*. New York: Free Press, 2000.

Hersey, John. *Hiroshima*. New York: Alfred A. Knopf, 1963.

Hersh, Burton. *Edward Kennedy: An Intimate Biography*. Berkeley, CA: Counterpoint, 2010.

Hofstadter, Richard, and Beatrice K. Hofstadter. *Great Issues in American History: From Reconstruction to the Present Day, 1864–1981*. New York: Vintage, 1982.

Holtzman, Elizabeth, with Cynthia L. Cooper. *Who Said It Would Be Easy? One Woman's Life in the Political Arena*. New York: Arcade Publishers, 1996.

Jones, Clarence B., and Stuart Connelly. *Behind the Dream: The Making of the Speech That Transformed a Nation*. New York: Palgrave MacMillan, 2011.

Kazal, Russell A. *Becoming Old Stock: The Paradox of German-American Identity*. Princeton, NJ: Princeton University Press, 2004.

Kearns, Doris. *Lyndon Johnson and the American Dream*. New York: Harper & Row, 1976.

Kearns Goodwin, Doris. *No Ordinary Time: Franklin and Eleanor Roosevelt, the Home Front in World War II*. New York: Simon & Schuster, 2013.

King, Desmond. *Separate and Unequal: Black Americans and the U.S. Federal Government*. Oxford: Oxford University Press, 1995.

Kluger, Richard. *The Paper: The Life and Death of the* New York Herald Tribune. New York: Alfred A. Knopf, 1986.

Kotz, Nick. *Judgment Days: Lyndon B. Johnson, Martin Luther King Jr. and the Laws That Changed America.* Boston: Houghton Mifflin Co., 2005.

Lears, Jackson T. *Rebirth of a Nation, 1877–1920.* New York: Harper Perennial, 2009.

Lemov, Michael R., and Ralph Nader. *People's Warrior: John Moss and the Fight for Freedom and Consumer Rights.* Vancouver, BC: Fairleigh Dickinson University Press, 2011.

Lerner, Michael A. *Dry Manhattan: Prohibition in New York City.* Cambridge: MA: Harvard University Press, 2009.

Linder, Marc, and Lawrence Zacharias. *Of Cabbages and Kings County: Agriculture and the Formation of Modern Brooklyn.* Iowa City: University of Iowa Press, 1999.

Loevy, Robert D. *The Civil Rights Act of 1964: The Passage of the Law That Ended Racial Segregation.* Albany: State University of New York Press, 1997.

Lougee, Robert W. *Midcentury Revolution, 1848: Society and Revolution in France and Germany.* Lexington, MA: D. C. Heath and Company, 1972.

Lynch, Denis Tilden. *"Boss" Tweed: The Story of a Grim Generation.* New York: Boni and Liveright, 1927.

MacLean, Nancy. *Behind the Mask: The Making of the Second Ku Klux Klan.* New York: Oxford University Press, 1995.

MacNeil, Neil. *Dirksen: Portrait of a Public Man.* Cleveland, OH: World Publishing Company, 1970.

Martin, Susan Forbes. *A Nation of Immigrants.* New York: Cambridge University Press, 2011.

Mason, Alpheus Thomas. *Harlan Fiske Stone: Pillar of the Law.* New York: Viking Press, 1956.

McCartin, Joseph A., and Michael Kazin. *Americanism: New Perspectives on the History of an Ideal.* Chapel Hill: University of North Carolina Press, 2008.

McCormick, Charles. *Seeing Reds: Federal Surveillance of Radicals in the Pittsburgh Mill District.* Pittsburgh: University of Pittsburgh Press, 1997.

McCullough, David. *The Great Bridge: The Epic Story of the Building of the Brooklyn Bridge.* New York: Simon & Schuster, 1972.

McGovern, James. *To the Yalu: From the Chinese Invasion of Korea to MacArthur's Dismissal.* New York: William Morrow & Company, 1972.

Miller, William Lee. *Two Americans: Truman, Eisenhower and a Dangerous World.* New York: Alfred A. Knopf, 2012.

Moloney, Deirdre. *National Insecurities: Immigrants and U.S. Deportation Policy since 1882.* Chapel Hill: University of North Carolina Press, 2016.

Morris, Sylvia Jukes. *Price of Fame: The Honorable Clare Boothe Luce.* New York: Random House, 2014.

Ngai, Mae M. *Impossible Subjects: Illegal Aliens and the Making of Modern America.* Princeton, NJ: Princeton University Press, 2004.

Nichols, David A. *Eisenhower 1956: The President's Year of Crisis—Suez and the Brink of War.* New York: Simon & Schuster, 2011.

Oates, Stephen B. *Let the Trumpet Sound.* New York: Harper & Row, 1982.

O'Brien, Michael. *Philip Hart: Conscience of the Senate.* East Lansing: Michigan State University Press, 1995.

Patterson, James T. *Grand Expectations: The United States, 1945–1971.* New York: Oxford University Press, 1996.

Peterson, Carla L. *Black Gotham: A Family History of African Americans in Nineteenth Century New York City.* New Haven, CT: Yale University Press, 2011.

Pietrusza, David. *1948: Harry Truman's Improbable Victory.* New York, Diversion Books, 2018.

Poinsett, Alex. *Walking with Presidents: Louis Martin and the Rise of Black Political Power.* Lanham, MD: Madison Books, 1997.

Powell, Adam Clayton Jr. *Adam by Adam: The Autobiography of Adam Clayton Powell Jr.* New York: Citadel Press, 1994.

Purdum, Todd. *An Idea Whose Time Had Come: Two Presidents, Two Parties, and the Battle for the Civil Rights Act of 1964.* New York: Henry Holt and Company, 2014.

Raghavan, Anita. *The Billionaire's Apprentice: The Rise of the Indian-American Elite and the Fall of the Galleon Hedge Fund.* New York: Business Plus, 2013.

Reimers, David. *Still the Golden Door: The Third World Comes to America.* New York: Columbia University Press, 1985.

Risen, Clay. *The Bill of the Century: The Epic Battle for the Civil Rights Act.* New York: Bloomsbury Press, 2014.

Robinson, Eugene. *Disintegration: The Splintering of Black America.* New York: Doubleday, 2010.

Roediger, David R. *Working toward Whiteness: How America's Immigrants Became White.* New York: Basic Books, 2005.

Romo, Ricardo. *East Los Angeles: History of a Barrio.* Austin: University of Texas Press, 1983.

Russell, Francis. *The Shadow of Blooming Grove: Warren G. Harding in His Times.* New York: McGraw-Hill Book Company, 1968.

Schlesinger, Arthur M., Jr., editor. *The Almanac of American History.* New York: G. P. Putnam's Sons, 1983.

Schuck, Peter H. *The Judiciary Committees: A Study of the House and Senate Judiciary Committees.* New York: Grossman Publishers, 1975.

Shavit, Ari. *My Promised Land: The Triumph and Tragedy of Israel.* New York: Spiegel & Grau, 2013.

Smelser, Neil J., William Julius Wilson, and Faith Mitchell. *America Becoming: Racial Trends and Their Consequences*, Volume 1. Washington, DC: National Academy Press, 2001.

Smith, Jean Edward. *FDR.* New York: Random House, 2007.

Spiro, Jonathan Peter. *Defending the Master Race: Conservation, Eugenics and the Legacy of Madison Grant.* Burlington: University of Vermont Press, 2009.

Stone, Kurt F. *The Jews of Capitol Hill: A Compendium of Jewish Congressional Members.* Lanham, MD: Scarecrow Press, 2011.

Sundquist, James L. *Politics and Policy: The Eisenhower, Kennedy and Johnson Years.* Washington, DC: Brookings Institution Press, 1968.

Takaki, Ronald. *A Different Mirror: A History of Multicultural America.* Boston: Little, Brown, 1994.

Thomas, Lately. *When Even Angels Wept: The Senator Joseph McCarthy Affair—A Story without a Hero.* New York: William Morrow and Company, 1973.

Toyota, Tritia. *Envisioning America: New Chinese and the Politics of Belonging.* Stanford, CA: Stanford University Press, 2009.

Tugwell, Rexford G. *FDR: Architect of an Era.* New York: Macmillan Company, 1967.

Tuohy, Brian. *The Fix Is In: The Showbiz Manipulations of the NFL, MLB, NBA, NHL and NASCAR.* Port Townsend, WA: Feral House, 2010.

Urofsky, Melvin I. *Division and Discord: The Supreme Court Under Stone and Vinson, 1941–1953.* Columbia: University of South Carolina Press, 1997.

Vaughn, Stephen L., editor. *The Encyclopedia of American Journalism.* New York: Routledge, 2008.

Viorst, Milton. *Fire in the Streets: America in the 1960s.* New York: Simon & Schuster, 1979.

Wallace, Mike. *Greater Gotham: A History of New York City from 1898 to 1919.* New York: Oxford University Press, 2017.

Washburn, Patrick S. *The African American Newspaper: Voice of Freedom.* Evanston, IL: Northwestern University Press, 2006.

Wattenberg, Ben J. *Good News Is the Bad News Is Wrong.* New York: Simon & Schuster, 1984.

Weintraub, Stanley. *Final Victory: FDR's Extraordinary World War II Presidential Campaign.* Boston: DaCapo Press, 2012.

Werstein, Irving. *The Blizzard of '88.* New York: Thomas Y. Crowell Company, 1960.

White, Jonathan W. *Emancipation, The Union Army, and the Re-election of Abraham Lincoln.* Baton Rouge: Louisiana State University Press, 2014.

Wilkerson, Isabel. *The Warmth of Other Suns.* New York: Random House, 2010.

Williams, Juan. *Eyes on the Prize: America's Civil Rights Years, 1954–1965.* New York: Viking, 1987.

Wilson, Basil, and Charles Green. *The Struggle for Black Empowerment in New York.* New York: Praeger, 1989.

Wilson, John Donald. *The Chase: The Chase Manhattan Bank, N.A., 1945–1985.* Boston: Harvard Business School Press, 1986.

Winslow, Barbara. *Shirley Chisholm: Catalyst for Change.* Boulder, CO: Westview Press, 2014.

Zolberg, Aristide R. *A Nation by Design: Immigration Policy in the Fashioning of America* Cambridge, MA: Harvard University Press, 2006.

MAGAZINES AND JOURNALS

American Legion
Atlantic
Cityscape: A Journal of Policy Development and Research
Congressional Record
Jewish Life, a Progressive Monthly
Time

NEWSPAPERS

Associated Press
Brooklyn Eagle
Christian Science Monitor
Long Island Press
New York Daily News
New York Herald Tribune
New York Sun
New York Times

New York World Telegram
Virginian-Pilot, Norfolk
Wall Street Journal
Washington Post
Washington Star
Washington Times

ORAL HISTORIES, THESES, AND DISSERTATIONS

"Affecting the Lives of Millions: The Immigration and Nationality Services Act of 1965,"
    multi-illustrated poster that includes March 1965 Harris Poll, Richard B. Russell Jr. Col-
    lection, Richard B. Russell Library for Research and Studies, University of Georgia.
Emanuel Celler Collection, Brooklyn Public Library, America Jewish Committee, Oral His-
    tory Memoir.
Graham, Otis. "A Vast Social Experiment: The Immigration Act of 1965," NPG Forum,
    October 2005.
"The Great Society Congress." The Association of Centers for the Study of Congress.
Kelly, Edna. Oral History Interview, U.S. Association of Former Members of Congress,
    Manuscript Room, Library of Congress (May 10–11, 1976 by Charles T. Morrisey).
John F. Kennedy Memorial Library and Museum, Boston, Emanuel Celler Oral History.
Koed, Betty. "The Politics of Immigration Reform," PhD dissertation, University of Califor-
    nia, Santa Barbara, 1995.
Lehman Oral History Project, Columbia University, Emanuel Celler interview.
McGowan, William. "The 1965 Immigration Reforms and the *New York Times*: Context,
    Coverage and Long-Term Consequences," *Center for Immigration Studies*, August 2008.
Rubin, Lawrence. Celler Oral History Memoir, William E. Wiener Oral History Library of
    the American Jewish Committee, June 24, 1970.
Rustin, Bayard. "Interracial Primer: How You Can Help Relieve Tension Between Negroes
    and Whites." Fellowship of Reconciliation, 1944, 14. Retrieved January 2, 2018.
Speranza, Gino. "How It Feels to Be a Problem." In the Vicinity of Hull-House and the
    Maxwell Street Market: Chicago 1889–1935." *International Migration Review*, January 1,
    1972; journals.sagepub.com.
"Whom Shall We Welcome, Report." President's Commission on Immigration and Natural-
    ization, 1953, Boston Public Library.

VIDEO AND DIGITAL MEDIA

Antiquemoney.com
Archives.gov
Bklyn.newspapers.com
Digitalhistory.uh.edu
Fultonhistory.com
History.com
Historymatters.gmu.edu
Imdb.com

"Inventing L.A.: The Chandlers and Their Times," KCET-TV, 2009
Jewish Daily Bulletin
NPR.org
Nwhm.org
PBS.org
Thecrimson.com
Web.bryant.edu
Who Shall Live and Who Shall Die, Kino Lorber films, 2007
Wired.com

Index

About the Author

Credit: Michael DiBari

Wayne Dawkins is an associate professor at Morgan State University in Baltimore, Maryland. A former newspaper reporter and editor, he is the author of *Rugged Waters: Black Journalists Swim the Mainstream* and *Black Journalists: The National Association of Black Journalists Story*, as well as a contributor to *Black Voices in Commentary: The Trotter Group* and *My First Year as a Journalist*.